BBAL 2000

SCIENCE AND THE GOALS OF MAN

SCIENCE

AND THE GOALS OF MAN

A Study in Semantic Orientation

BY ANATOL RAPOPORT

Assistant Professor of Mathematical Biology
University of Chicago

Foreword by S. I. HAYAKAWA

GREENWOOD PRESS, PUBLISHERS
WESTPORT, CONNECTICUT

CONTENTS

v

FOREWORD

In August, 1943, the Society for General Semantics sent out into the world the first issue of its quarterly, *ETC.: A Review of General Semantics*. As its editor, I looked for little response from the learned world, which, along with the rest of humanity, was too much absorbed in war to be expected to notice so modest an event as the foundation of a new scholarly journal. The most I hoped for then was its survival; the times being what they were, I certainly expected little support from beyond the small circle of interested people who had started it.

It was a pleasant surprise, therefore, when in November of that year I received by military airmail from Alaska, from a writer then unknown to me, a paper for publication in *ETC.* which was so clearly a valuable contribution to semantic literature that its acceptance was a foregone conclusion before half the manuscript had been read. This paper, "Newtonian Physics and Aviation Cadets," published in *ETC.* in the Spring 1944 issue (Vol. I, pp. 154-164), dealt with the unconscious assumptions underlying the thought habits of aviation cadets to whom its author had earlier taught physics. It was an exceedingly clear analysis of the way in which primitive and even animistic notions embedded in everyday language prevent the comprehension of physical laws; as such it constituted important substantiation of some of Korzybski's theories concerning the effect of language structure upon thought and behavior. The author of this paper was Anatol Rapoport, who was at that time Captain in the U.S. Air Corps, engaged (as I was to learn later) in liaison work between the American and Russian air forces.

One good paper led to another, and still another. During our correspondence (he was transferred later from Alaska to India), I learned that in addition to being a mathematician he had earlier been a concert pianist, touring in Europe, the United States, and Mexico from 1933 to 1937; that his education in early childhood had been in revolutionary Russia, later in Chicago, and later in Vienna at the State Academy of Music. I learned, too, that he got his Ph.D. in mathematics at the University of Chicago on the eve of Pearl Harbor and had gone directly from convocation to Maxwell Field. His services to *ETC.* did not stop with his contribution of papers. In 1945, on his return to Chicago and to civilian life, I invited him to help edit *ETC.* He and I have worked on it together ever since. His chief occupation, however, is his work in mathematical biology at the University of Chicago, where he is associated with Nicolas Rashevsky.

Dr. Rapoport's basic concern in *Science and the Goals of Man* is that of many other students of general semantics as well as of many other philosophers of science. Is science "merely a tool," or can it be a way of life? According to a belief widely held among scientists no less than among humanists and men of letters, science does not, should not, and ultimately cannot determine the ends for which it is used. This view, entailing a sharp separation of science and values, Dr. Rapoport regards as a tragic fallacy. The fallacy rests, as he demonstrates, upon an imperfect insight on the part of scientists themselves into the ethical implications of their own scientific behavior.

Scientists, no less than others, instead of observing their own behavior and its implications, tend to believe what they say about themselves. Because they have been, up to now, deeply preoccupied with throwing off the prejudices of local and limited value-systems in order to clarify their vision, they have hesitated to impose their own value-system on others; they have usually talked (and many

viii

still talk) as if their scientific patterns of evaluation had no validity or application beyond the fields of their scientific activity.

Nevertheless, the scientists' "prejudice" against prejudice—that is, their preference of a general and nonpartisan point of view over a point of view colored by private or provincial obsessions—is a value necessary in all areas of life. The same is true of other value-preferences exhibited in the behavior of scientists: the preference of truth-telling over lying, which is so much a part of scientific tradition that no machinery is needed (as it is in almost all other human affairs) to enforce honesty; a preference of statements capable of verification over statements that must be taken on the authority of the speaker; a preference of logical order over the chaotic assemblage of facts.

All these preferences, Dr. Rapoport affirms, may be organized into a value-system capable of being subscribed to by all men—a value-system of which the most general directive is the preference of human agreement (and therefore co-operation) over disagreement. Like the logical positivists, Dr. Rapoport is impatient with nonsense questions and unverifiable statements, not simply because they are nonsense, but more importantly because they are among the greatest obtsacles to human agreement. Confronted with a variety of competing ideologies and value-systems, the scientist, *in order to be consistent with himself,* cannot remain neutral. As Dr. Rapoport says, "different men want to go in different directions, and some of these directions are incompatible with the direction inherent in science itself." Therefore, "the scientist must subscribe to certain values (and discard others) not because he is a 'good citizen' or a product of a [particular] culture or a member of a [particular] church, *but because he is a scientist.*"

With Korzybski, Dr. Rapoport sees in modern scientific method and orientation the foundations of individual and social sanity. Rarely have the personal, poetic meanings of the non-Aristotelian outlook—and by poetic I mean the creative and morale-giving—been stated so eloquently and feelingly as they are by Dr. Rapoport in the words he puts into the mouth of "Dr. N" in the Epilogue. Bertrand Russell's theory of types and Korzybski's concept of multiordinality are given, in Dr. Rapoport's warmly felt exposition, a human and ethical significance which, I am sure, few technical students of logic or semantics have perceived in them. The result is a philosophy of action and participation in the world, combined with critical awareness of the shortcomings of one's own abstractions. In the non-Aristotelian orientation, scepticism ceases to be the agent of paralysis that it long has been; it becomes the necessary condition of appropriate action.

Illumined by a wealth of explanatory examples and told in a direct and untechnical language that takes fully into account the problems of a reader untrained in technical logic or mathematics, *Science and the Goals of Man* provides both inspiration and provocation to everyone who has asked himself the great question which our almost universal faith in progress leaves unanswered, "Which way *is* forward?"

S. I. HAYAKAWA

PROLOGUE

In the Office of Dr. S

One winter afternoon I dropped in at the office of Dr. S and discovered him over a cup of tea with his distinguished colleague, Dr. S'. After the formalities of introduction, Dr. S evidently resumed an interrupted conversation.

"All right, S', look at it this way. For the past six years my staff and I have been working on the parapetacular properties of transgalaxium. You know the results. Hundreds of thousands of Plutonians are dead. When I was a student, dreaming of better worlds to build, I read all the excited prophecies of the discovery of transgalaxium. In those days I imagined that on the day it would finally be discovered the news would flash all over the planet and a world-wide holiday would be declared. There would be dancing in the streets of all the cities of the world, in Plutopolis and in Neptune, in X-ville and in Y-ville. The news flashed, all right, but there was no dancing. Instead of feeling the satisfaction that comes with helping solve some of the important problems confronting our species, I felt like a murderer."

Dr. S' said nothing.

"You see, S'," Dr. S continued, "all the time I was working day and night I thought I was fulfilling my appropriate function in society, the function for which I was meant, as Aristotle would have said. But now it seems to me that my function as a scientist conflicts with my function as a man."

"What function as a man?" interrupted Dr. S'. "I know what

you mean when you speak of your function as a scientist. But it is not clear to me what you mean by your function as a man. You almost sound as though you are becoming religious."

"Perhaps I am," replied Dr. S. "Science simply hasn't given me all the answers I need. And I don't see how it can."

"A scientist's job," Dr. S' retorted, "is to know that such-and-such follows so-and-so. Ehrlich didn't worry about whether syphilis was good or bad. He *studied* it. The results of his studies were incidental. And so are the results of your studies of trans-galaxium. Ethics and science do not mix."

"Perhaps you are right," said Dr. S. "But if science provides no way of choosing one's values, then something else must."

At this point I interposed.

"Do you agree, Dr. S, that science has nothing to do with choosing one's values?"

"If there is a connection, I don't see it," said Dr. S.

"I have a clipping of your testimony in the D-ville affair," I continued. "You traveled a thousand miles just to tell the jury that the ratio of the circumference of a circle to its diameter is not exactly equal to three. Why did you do it?"

"I could not stand by and see a young man punished for teaching the truth, because he violated an asinine city ordinance."[1]

"Then truth is important to you?"

"Of course. All scientists are concerned with truth. Indeed, one might say that the purpose of science is to seek truth."

"It seems then that scientific behavior is not absolutely devoid of values."

"Of course not," replied Dr. S. "For that matter, consistency and freedom of inquiry also are values implicit in science. Indeed,

---

[1] The city fathers of D-ville had passed an ordinance requiring the teachers in the public schools to take the numerical value of pi to be 3 because of the statement in the Bible that the "molten sea" in Solomon's temple had a circumference of thirty cubits and a diameter of ten cubits (I Kings 7:23).

behavior governed by these principles *defines* a scientist. But are these enough? How can concern for truth tell us what is good or bad? I rather agree with S' that the categories True and False have nothing to do with those of Good and Bad."

"And just what *do* the categories Good and Bad have to do with?" I asked.

Dr. S said nothing for a while. Then he began to speak again, haltingly but with profound feeling.

"I'm not sure I can say. You've struck the core of my problem. I can't verbalize it. And because I can't verbalize it I can't analyze it. Perhaps it is one of those things which is best left unspoken. In most cases I can tell a good action from a bad one, but I must admit I cannot tell what my criteria are. They are certainly not scientific. But they are important to me. When I am unable to make such evaluation, I find myself floundering for guidance. I have learned to stop looking to science for such guidance. It is rather disappointing."

"You are disappointed," said Dr. S', "because you are trying to do the impossible. You are trying to *choose* goals by scientific method. This is like trying to prove the postulates of geometry or that logic is logical. Ethical systems are based on postulates or on tacit assumptions. There is no unique 'true' ethical system. There are as many such systems as there are cultures.

"Why not recognize that the choice of values is arbitrary? You are a competent mathematician; yet you have not learned the great lesson of modern mathematics, the postulational method. It is instructive that mathematics began to develop much more quickly just when mathematicians discovered that there are no 'truths' in mathematics but only assumptions, rules, and valid propositions derived by rules from the assumptions."

"The mathematician does not govern his life by his postulates," replied Dr. S, "but men do govern their lives by their value systems. When groups of people with different value systems come together, it seems to the members of each group that the others are at best ignorant and usually wicked. Thus we have missionaries and Decency Leagues and crusades and wars."

"You forget," pointed out Dr. S′, "that some of the bloodiest wars were fought by people who supposedly subscribed to the same system of values, for example, Christian nations."

"No," said Dr. S. "It would not have been possible to organize people to kill each other if at least some of the values did not clash. One of the beliefs cherished by the influential Plutonians has been that Plutonia should control the world's supply of transgalaxium. The influential Neptunians, on the other hand, are equally convinced that for the benefit of humanity Neptunia should control the supply. These beliefs are rationalized into reverence rendered to one's own tribal gods, and the latter is cherished as a value."

"What would you like to do, S? Impose a single set of values or a single religion on the whole human race? It's been tried, you know, and you know what it involves. How do such ideas tally with your skeptical attitude toward missionaries and the people who object to nude statues?

"The bigots try to impose their special attitudes and prejudices on others. We must find values which would be generally acceptable."

"But are there any such values?" protested Dr. S′.

"Perhaps there are. You are a social scientist. Have you looked?"

"We have looked. We have found *needs*, which seem to be present in all human cultures. But the ways of satisfying them are widely different. These differences have given rise to different food habits, different sex habits, different status relations. Values are to cultures what co-ordinates are to co-ordinate systems. Since

xiv

you will not accept the analogy with the postulational method in mathematics, perhaps, being a physicist, you will accept the analogy with modern physics."

"I know," said Dr. S wearily. "We have talked about the social implications of the Theory of Relativity before."

"For the benefit of the young people assembled here, let us examine it again," said Dr. S'. There were now several other people in the office of Dr. S. It was their custom to gather there for a Saturday afternoon chat. Feeling that he had an attentive audience, Dr. S' continued his discussion with considerable animation. He spoke approximately as follows.

The Story of Relativity

Some time ago it occurred to physicists that since the earth is rushing through space, carrying us along with it, it would be interesting to know which way we were going and how fast. They knew, of course, the velocity of the earth around the sun, but they thought that knowledge was not sufficient. The sun itself appeared to be moving among the stars in the direction of the constellation Hercules. But suppose, wondered the physicists, it was Hercules that was moving toward us? How could we tell? So they devised an ingenious experiment which was supposed to answer the questions "Which way are we *really* moving? Which way is Forward?"

The answer was baffling at first. If the readings on the dials were interpreted in the same sense as the question was asked, they would have had to mean "We are not going anywhere." The answer was not acceptable, but there it was. It could not be ignored. The physicists were dedicated to the proposition that the readings of the dials in carefully performed experiments provided the answers to the questions that suggested the experiments.

Thus began the dramatic story of Relativity. Its fascinating chapters tell how the physicists pondered on the negative results of the Michelson-Morley experiment for a quarter of a century, how a young physicist named Einstein, instead of trying to fit the answer into the existing notions of time and space, attacked the notions themselves. It tells about his famous reformulation of the problem, about the predictions he based on this formulation, and about the way they came true; and finally the story culminates in the ominous equation $E=mc^2$, which shook the world.

An atomic explosion is spectacular, but the Theory of Relativity has produced changes even more far-reaching than the harnessing of atomic energy. It has profoundly changed ways of thinking.

It may seem strange that something so few people know anything about can have a widespread influence. Yet the Theory of Relativity was not the first scientific theory to influence great masses of people even though they did not possess the training to understand it. Few people can derive the equations that prescribe the orbits of planets; yet a great many know that Newton's Law of Universal Gravitation is "what keeps the solar system going." Few people know their way about in embryology or comparative anatomy; yet many know that Darwin's theory points to a common ancestry of men and chimpanzees. The *technical* structures of Newton's and Darwin's theories are involved and difficult, but both have implications which can be stated in ordinary words, closely linked to our everyday experiences.

The Theory of Relativity also has such implications. One of them may be stated so:

It is impossible to detect the motion of a body except relatively to another body.

If the distance between A and B is decreasing, one may say that A is standing still and B moving toward it, or that B is standing still and A moving toward it, or that both are moving. The

xvi

question "Which one is really moving?" has no sense. It all depends on one's point of view.

It may not matter whether we are moving toward Hercules or whether Hercules is moving toward us. But it is interesting to learn that a seemingly sensible question "Which way are we going through space?" is shown to have no sense, *unless a point of view is indicated.*

Such questions (which could be answered only relatively to a given point of view) were, of course, known long before the Theory of Relativity. They were mostly questions of orientation. No one ever disputed that what was "to the right" for one man was "to the left" for the man facing him. "Up" and "down" were harder to discard as absolutes; yet people had to discard them when they started going to distant places. It became clear to every European schoolboy who looked at the classroom globe that what was "up" for him was "down" for his Australian cousin. The discarding of absolutes appeared a necessary consequence of broadening horizons. One could reach the Orient by sailing west. Twenty miles per hour might have appeared a breathless speed compared with the walk of a man, but in the age of the airplane it appears slow. And matters did not stop there. Relativism, even long before Relativity, invaded moral judgments, the stronghold of absolute utterances.

"Theft is a crime," some eighteenth-century relativist might have written, "only in societies where private property is sacred. There is nothing *inherently* sacred about private property."

The thinkers of the eighteenth century challenged many other notions of sacredness.

Finally in modern anthropology the relativist attitude toward "values" became the rule. It would be rash to say that the Theory of Relativity has been a major influence in the thinking of anthropologists, but one could certainly suppose that the philosophic orientation implied by the theory gave their views powerful support. At any rate, the outlooks embodied in the new physics and the new anthropology were in tune. One could transfer some of the ways of speaking (and therefore thinking) from one to the other.

The immediate reason why most modern anthropologists discarded moralistic evaluations of the cultures they studied was that they got around too much and saw too much to take any local "morality," including their own, seriously. They saw that in some societies virginity in brides was an extremely important attribute, but in others it was practically nonexistent and not particularly desired. They saw that some tribes considered bravery in battle a supreme virtue, while others did not wage war at all, if they could help it, and had no regard for aggressiveness or bravery. They saw that in some cultures it was imperative to keep the aged in comfort even at great sacrifice, but in others it was permissible to help them depart from this world if they lived too long and became a burden.

And they saw a great deal more. They saw that in most cases contact with white men somehow disorganized the lives of the so-called "primitive" people. In many cases, they became apathetic, diseased, and neurotic. With the destruction of their "way of life" they lost a sense for living.

To the modern anthropologist, the smug arrogance of the white man, who designated three-quarters of the inhabitants of this planet as "natives," began to appear as ignorant provincialism. They coldly scrutinized the white man's claims to superiority and found them based on superstitions.

It was the business of the anthropologists to study and to compare religions. When they studied scores of them, they failed to see why one should be considered "better" than another, and in particular why it was less reasonable, inspired, or virtuous to believe in the descent from a sun-goddess than in virgin birth.

It was the business of the anthropologists to study race, another pivot of white "superiority." Their studies told them that the claims of the white "race" were either false or meaningless.

Finally, the champions of "white civilization" used to point out that theirs was a culture of rapid "progress." But to a relativistically oriented student of culture it was not evident why one particular direction of development should be considered "progressive" in preference to another; why, for example, an extremely complex technology together with a tremendous incidence of mental disease should be singled out as indications of a "higher" culture.

The anthropologists found that one could apply several different yardsticks in evaluating the degree of "advancement" of a culture. One could ask how complex was its system of religious beliefs. One could ask how complex was its social structure or its technology or its art or its mythology or its kinship relations. Incidentally, if this last yardstick were used, the most "advanced" societies would be found among the Australian aborigines.

Similarly, the anthropologists found that there were many yardsticks for measuring "values." They saw that values varied with the goals pursued, and these varied with the cultures. Thus the question of "real" or "absolute" values became as meaningless to them as the question of real or absolute motion became meaningless to the physicists.

The relativist point of view did not remain confined to anthropology. The relativist sociologists redefined antisocial behavior as simply one which showed sufficient deviation from standards accepted in a given group. Being "well-adjusted" became in the language of relativist psychologists a relation between an individual and his culture.

"Relativity of values," Dr. S′ concluded, "is as important a discovery in social science as the relativity of motion is in physical science. One cannot *seek* the 'right' values, because there are no extracultural criteria for rightness. One evaluates by means of one's values, but how can one evaluate the values themselves? Ordinarily the question does not even arise. One merely accepts the values of one's own culture as 'right.' Occasionally isolated individuals are able to develop sufficient objectivity to *compare* value systems. Presumably these people are free to choose their sets. But it is not justifiable to regard this choice (a matter of personal preference or a result of unconscious drives) as a *discovery* of what is 'right.'"

"Then social science cannot be utilized for achieving desired ends?" someone asked.

"It can," said Dr. S′, "if it is stated what the desired ends are. George A. Lundberg has made an eloquent and convincing plea for a broad utilization of social science in all human affairs.[2] But he has also stressed the inherent limitations of science: it cannot specify the desired goals. Every scientist who worries about ethical questions should memorize the Lewis Carroll quotation cited in Lundberg's book:

" 'Cheshire Puss,' she [Alice] began . . . 'would you please tell me which way I ought to go from here?'

" 'That depends a good deal on where you want to get to,' said the Cat.' "

[2] George A. Lundberg, *Can Science Save Us?*

PREFACE TO THE REPRINT EDITION

When I learned that Greenwood Press planned to reprint *Science and the Goals of Man,* I realized that it was no longer possible to avoid doing what I had perhaps unconsciously avoided, namely, seeing how my convictions of twenty years ago stood up.

When I was writing *Science and the Goals of Man* the Korean War had not yet started; nor had the hydrogen bomb yet exploded. Events in Cuba, Hungary, Suez, the Congo, Vietnam, the Dominican Republic—all these milestones of the Cold War were still to come. But most important, American science had not yet sprouted the vast service branch of the military enterprise. Of course, science had been used before in the service of war. In the past it was possible to apply science without mobilizing *scientists,* or if they were already directly attached to war research, without utilizing their thinking resources except for specific problems. Since then, the conditions of war research have radically changed. Vast research institutes were established whose main purpose was to seek more effective ways to plan and conduct war. The scientist working in such an institute can no longer (unless he is a confirmed hermit) confine his attention to his own specific problems, which heretofore could easily be detached from their lethal implications. Interacting with his colleagues in the new spirit of interdisciplinary research, today's scientist is made aware at all times that he is participating in an enterprise which may result in the extinction of civilization and even of the human race. Moreover, the disciplines and professional fields linked to war research have been enormously expanded. They now involve not only physics and chemistry and their direct war-technological applications, but also mathematics, economics, biology, psychology, and political science. The civilian strategist, serving in the capacity of advisor to policy-makers, has come to occupy an important role in the warfare states. Not infrequently, this person has genuine claim to scientific competence, not merely with respect to a narrow specialty, but also, in the broader sense, to the application of scientific criteria in evaluating evidence and in making judgments.

In view of these developments, can I still affirm the thesis developed in this book—that a viable and attractive ethical system emerges from the way of science itself and that if a man accepts the scientific ethos he thereby accepts the brotherhood of man? Frankly, I do not know. However, I do cling to my original conviction, and have tended to explain the dehumanization of science in the service of warfare by assuming that thereby mobilized scientists are dehumanized by their status as technicians. It is much more difficult to explain this conviction today than formerly, when the scientist served the war machine only as a narrow specialist. The point is, however, that "the brotherhood of man" is not a scientific concept. I thought this concept would emerge from the scientific reasoning—rejection of authority and the conventional criteria of truth and wisdom; continual, disciplined reality testing; the need for communication and cooperation; the universality of scientifically tested beliefs, and so forth. The fact that "the brotherhood of man" is an irrelevant idea to so many men who do possess scientifically oriented habits of thought, throws a shadow of doubt on the idea that a humane ethos emerges naturally from the specific ethos of science. In short, I have been forced to re-examine my fundamental assumptions; namely, that perversion and evil in human behavior stem primarily from error originating in superstition, prejudice, or semantic confusion. The fundamental and terrible fact of our age is that unspeakable crimes can be committed by collectives of men, not one of whom is either evil or deluded. These collectives, organized into the monstrous war machines of our day, seem to have purposes, wills, and compulsions of their own which emerge from the way the men who compose them perform their professional duties, not from the way these men view the world.

I believe, therefore, that something else is needed if the ethos to be derived from science is to come to life. The nature of this "something else" warrants a discussion in its own right. Therefore, should the reader feel that something important has remained unsaid in this book, I hasten to assure him that now I feel this also.

A. R.

Ann Arbor, Michigan
May 13, 1970

PREFACE

There was a great deal said on those Saturday afternoons in the office of Dr. S. I suppose similar conversations were carried on at various times in Athens and in Paris and wherever conditions permitted fearless inquiry and free exchange of ideas. I thought those conversations were quite important, and so I have recorded some of them almost verbatim in the last chapters of this book.

I was particularly concerned by the roles played by Dr. S and Dr. S' in human affairs. Dr. S is a physical scientist. Others like him set out three hundred years ago to understand how the world works. Their progress has been spectacularly successful. They have come to understand more and more what it means to understand the world. They have learned to ask more and more meaningful questions. They have developed a language which in principle enables them to settle *with satisfaction to both sides* any controversy that may arise about the way events happen. In matters pertaining to their studies, they are undisputed authorities. When material environment has to be manipulated, both democratic and totalitarian leaders turn to engineers and technicians, and they, in turn, derive their skills from the work of the physical scientists.

Dr. S' is a social scientist. People like him have comparatively recently begun to study relations between human beings without assuming any supernatural interference. For this purpose they have organized research into the disciplines of anthropology, sociology, economics, and some branches of psychology. They too have succeeded to a considerable degree in formulating broad principles from which the events they study can be deduced in an organized way. One would expect, therefore, that when relations between human beings need to be controlled or improved, the people to whom such matters are entrusted (statesmen, religious leaders, etc.) would turn to the social scientists for information and advice. But this seldom happens. Largely this is because in political, economic, and ethical affairs we are still guided by individuals who have little use for the scientific approach to problems.

Yet sometimes the social scientist *is* called upon to help bring order into our affairs. Such an exceptional event occurred in 1947 when anthropologists were asked to help frame the World Bill of Rights.[1] They seemed uneasy about that task. Their declaration emphasized the findings of anthropology about the "relativity of values" and was in fact little more than a warning against attempting to impose a single set of values on the entire human race.

However, for some anthropologists, even *this* opinion appeared too directive. Even the plea for cultural tolerance was considered unworthy of a social scientist, who, according to the extreme relativists, should only observe and study humanity and never, never, under the risk of losing his prestige as a scientist, *advise* humanity.[2]

In other words, when a social scientist was finally asked how the world could be made better, he should have replied (so say the extreme relativists), "I don't know."

To be sure, not all social scientists take this point of view. Some like Dr. Lundberg point out that social science *could* be as useful to humanity as physical science has been if only the people who steer the course of history asked the right sort of questions: "How can we achieve this?" or "How can we achieve that?" and "What are the costs and consequences of this or that course?"

In fact, these are precisely the questions asked of the physical scientists. A leader may ask "How can we give electric power to

[1] Cf. "Statement on Human Rights," *American Anthropologist*, Vol. 49, No. 4.
[2] H. G. Barnett, "On Science and Human Rights," *American Anthropologist*, Vol. 50, No. 2.

five million people?" The answer is provided. Or he may ask, "How can we kill five million people?" Again there is a prompt, practical answer. As for "costs and consequences," as far as the physical scientist is concerned, they are confined to calculations of expenditures in money, energy, or labor power. That is just what Dr. S was so worried about.

I suspect a great many people are worrying about it. They are frightened by the aloof impartiality of Science. All too often, science is thought of as a kind of inexhaustible reservoir of blessings and scourges, of miraculous drugs and poisonous gases. The scientist appears in popular imagination as both a benevolent magician and a practitioner of human sacrifice.

In view of what is happening, these views are not unjustified. Yet other things are happening too. An ever-increasing number of physical scientists are awakening to their social responsibilities. They not only worry about the uses to which the new formidable technology may be put; they *warn* the leaders of the impending catastrophe in store for *all* if the gifts of knowledge are turned into weapons of violence.

Not all social scientists are in accord with Dr. S'. While recognizing that a great many values held "sacred" in different cultures are only different ways of evaluating the world, they still believe that men could be helped to evaluate *better*; and they even agree on what it means to evaluate better. So there is a great deal of concern with questions of "good and bad" among scientists, and not all of them are as confused as Dr. S.

Dr. S is uneasy because he separates his "function as a man" from his "function as a scientist." He participates in the social awakening of the scientist and speaks over national hookups on the advisability of using science for good rather than for evil. But if one were to ask him why he does this, he would say that he "feels" it to be right. So naturally he loses his arguments with Dr. S'. When he says he wants a sane world, Dr. S', sitting across the Round Table, tells the millions of listeners that what is sane for Dr. S is not sane for the Hottentots. When Dr. S talks about a world of justice and equality, Dr. S' says he understands how Dr. S feels. Equality is a notion Dr. S picked up in his culture, and it is to be expected that Dr. S, a product of his culture, should think that equality is a goal desirable in itself. Nevertheless, Dr. S' points out, one should not imagine that all of mankind would consider that goal desirable. Dr. S' can name many cultures where people want no part of equality. They want a well-defined hierarchy, where every man knows his place, etc.

On the subject of the scientist's social responsibilities Dr. S' says that they are no different from any man's social responsibilities. A scientist should vote. He should freely air his opinions. He should support causes he believes in. But he should not put the authority of science behind those causes, because there could be nothing scientific about opinions on "right" and "wrong."

"The morality of an act," Dr. S' keeps saying, "can be judged only in relation to the values of a given culture."

This book is an attempt to show that the scientist, in order to be consistent, must subscribe to certain values (and discard others) not because he is a "good citizen" or a product of Neptunian culture, or a member of the X-ist church, but because he is a scientist.

This point of view implies the existence of a common denominator of values, not conditioned by any of the existing cultures. The common denominator in turn implies an *extracultural* standard of evaluating cultures. Thus a possibility is pointed out for consciously *cultivating* cultures which may replace the present "wild" types, which, in the words of Kluckhohn, "just grew."[3]

The book is about the scientific outlook, in particular as it

---

[3] C. Kluckhohn, *Mirror for Man.*

affects three aspects of being human. The first of these is *communication*. To study it, we shall use a tool called semantics. The second is *orientation*, which will be considered the subject matter of metaphysics. Metaphysics is an old and somewhat discredited word (especially disliked in scientific circles) but Philipp Frank has recently dusted it off and given it new meaning and respectability (cf. Chapter 11). The third aspect is *values*, traditionally the concern of ethics.

Perhaps a good way to start discussing communication is by seeing what happens when people disagree. Often one can discern in these cases a breakdown of communication, which may result in conflict. It will be useful to examine some typical conflicts.

Conflicts have often been described from several points of view. Historians have given lengthy and more or less accurate accounts of migrations and wars, revolutions and persecutions. Sociologists have tried to study conditions under which conflicting population groups come into being. Psychiatrists have postulated drives which either directly or indirectly (through being frustrated) result in aggression and conflict. There is no dearth of theories of the origin of conflicts, ranging from the thesis of the inherent wickedness of man to economic determinism.

Some, all, or none of those theories may account for some of the events they try to explain. But in all of them one step in the process leading to conflict is tacitly assumed. It is taken for granted that under certain conditions an individual will *evaluate* a situation as calling for conflict. This evaluation may be as simple as a dog's baring his teeth; or it may be extremely complex, involving "ideologies," "loyalties," "identifications," etc.

Therefore a study of conflicts leads to a study of these *evaluative processes*.

First we shall examine actual familiar cases of verbalizations where controversies develop. We will find that it is instructive to examine a great variety of them, both where so-called "value judgments" are obviously involved and where they do not appear to be involved. This will lead us to the study of what happens when experiences are translated into words.

Next we shall inquire into the nature of the abstracting process, the making of the individual's "map of the world," his metaphysics. This will be described as a built-in framework, through which all the experiences of the individual are filtered. Thus the genesis of an integrated world outlook will, it is hoped, become apparent. We will then compare two such outlooks, the prevailing "Aristotelian" one with a more sophisticated "non-Aristotelian" outlook, and will try to show why the latter is to be preferred.

In these studies we shall hope to get some insight not only into disagreements ranging from taste in caviar to modern warfare but also a partial understanding of a more general nature, of how we react to the world around us. We shall raise questions more general than the question of controversy. In proceeding this way we shall be following the venerable traditions of intellectual inquiry and of geographic exploration. The alchemists, seeking synthetic gold, were forced to ask so many questions (which in turn necessitated the formulation of other questions) that something vastly more valuable than gold evolved from their work, namely, modern chemistry. Columbus, setting out to find a new route to the Indian spices, made discoveries that eventually forced Europe out of its barbaric state. The advice "Seek, and ye shall find" can surely be put into even more promising terms: "Seek, and ye may find something better than that which ye have been seeking."

The reader is invited upon this search. Questions will be raised on the way, and they will rarely be answered "completely." Rather, attempts to answer them will give rise to more questions. If at the end the reader is confronted with more unanswered questions than he has now, I will feel rewarded for this attempt. I feel that a completely answered question is rather an occasion for regret, like a death. And just as death is somehow compensated by the birth of ever-fresh progeny, so answered questions should be replaced by a host of new ones. *We will measure the value of an orientation not by the number of answered questions it contains but by the abundance, variety, and meaningfulness of the unanswered questions it gives rise to.*

The reader will find a certain unevenness in the degree of readability. Perhaps some chapters will appear almost trivial, others too involved. Some of this is due to the fact that for the purpose of this inquiry a broad range of subject matter has to be drawn upon. It is necessary to point out that when a toddler asks what holds the moon up and the philosopher worries about the "freedom of the will" basically similar processes are involved. But it is a more difficult task to reorient a philosopher than a toddler. Therefore the discussions have to range from the simple to the complex. It was hoped that it would be possible to arrange the chapters in the order of difficulty so that the reader could stop whenever he felt that a further expenditure of effort on his part was not worth while. This can sometimes be done in textbooks on specialized subjects, but unfortunately the scheme can be only partially applied here. The continuity of the argument has to take precedence.

My thanks are due to a number of people who have helped me in the writing of this book. Most of them I have never met. A great many have been dead for centuries. To these ideological ancestors acknowledgments are made in Chapter 16. But there were others too, intimate friends who gave me personal encouragement and valuable assistance. First of all, S. I. Hayakawa, with whom I have spent many soul-searching hours, both happy and painful, in conversations of the kind that leave a lifelong stamp. During the past several months Hayakawa was working on his own book, *Language in Thought and Action*. Nevertheless, he took the time to read several successive drafts of this book and to offer many helpful suggestions. For critical readings of the manuscript and further suggestions I am likewise indebted to Wendell Johnson and Russell Meyers of the University of Iowa, to Irving J. Lee of Northwestern University, to my friend and coworker, Alfonso Shimbel and to Connie Shimbel of the University of Chicago, to my wife, Gwen Goodrich, of the University of Wisconsin, and to my old friend, Sara Goldberg, who in addition undertook the tedious task of typing the manuscript.

Finally, it should be pointed out that this book is not a report of new discoveries. Both learned volumes and popular works are already written on the same subject. Nevertheless, we are going to imagine that we are about to enter unexplored territory. The reader will forgive this little game if he has ever felt the thrill of pretending to look at the world for the first time.

A. R.

Chicago, Illinois
June 1, 1949.

SCIENCE AND
THE GOALS
OF MAN

CHAPTER 1

What Happens When People Disagree?

> Whereupon the Emperor . . . published an edict, commanding all his subjects, upon great penalties, to break the smaller end of their eggs. The people so highly resented this law, that . . . there have been six rebellions raised on that account . . . It is computed that eleven thousand persons have, at several times, suffered death, rather than submit to break their eggs at the smaller end.
>
> Jonathan Swift, *Gulliver's Travels*

Case 1. Here are two children quarreling over a toy. One of them says, "It is mine," and the other, "No, it is not yours; it is mine." They fight.

Case 2. Here are two statesmen. One says:

"We desire Peace. But our neighbors, the Plutonians, are intent on War. See how they are arming."

The other statesman says:

"It is we, the Plutonians, who desire Peace. The Neptunians are the warmongers. See how *they* are arming."

To prove their peaceful intentions, the Plutonians and the Neptunians continue to arm themselves. The generals of each nation declare that all they desire is to be better armed than the others in order to be able to maintain the Peace. It seems if only a state of affairs could be reached where *each* of the nations were better armed than the other, both would be satisfied. But for some obscure reason, this never comes about. Either the one or the other is not sufficiently well armed, and the race goes on. It then becomes obvious to the general staffs that the only way to maintain Peace is to make War.

Case 3. Here is a couple quarreling because of what each says about a hat.

Case 4. Here are two men quarreling because of what each says about "what this country needs."

Case 5. Here is a man tried for heresy. He is saying, "The earth revolves around the sun." To an outsider (perhaps the proverbial intelligent Martian) observing only overt behavior—behavior that shows—it seems that the Inquisitor is making the same sounds except that the words "sun" and "earth" are interchanged. It seems to this observer that if only the heretic pronounced the words the same way as the inquisitor, he would be set free. But for some reason the heretic persists in saying the words as he does. He says he is willing to die for the Truth.

In all these cases the parties to the controversy failed to agree.

But here are some other cases.

Case 6.

A: Look at this quiz question. What is the capital of Turkey?

B: Constantinople.

A: No, it's Istanbul.

B: I say Constantinople.

A: Here is the latest almanac. Why, we are both wrong. It's Ankara, and, by the way, Istanbul is the same city as Constantinople!

B: Well, what do you know?

Case 7.

A: No sense boiling that water any longer. You'll never get it any hotter than its boiling point at the same pressure.

B: Why not? The longer I heat it, the hotter it gets, doesn't it? That's Common Sense.

A: Here is a thermometer. Try it and see.

2

B: You are right. It doesn't go over 212° no matter how long I boil it.

Case 8.

A: If you keep moving toward something, you will eventually get there.

B: Not necessarily.

A: Well, *either* you get there *or* you stop short of your goal.

B: Not necessarily.

A: Now wait. How can you both fail to get there and not stop short of there? If you don't stop short, you've *got* to get there. That's logic.

B: Not necessarily.

A: This you've got to prove to me.

B: If I show you a single case where a point keeps approaching another point without ever reaching it and without ever stopping short of it, will you accept this as a proof that you don't always *either* get there *or* stop short?

A: Fair enough.

B: Is it possible for a body to move with a certain speed and *without stopping* change its speed?

A: Sure, I do it every time I step on the brakes.

B: Then suppose two points two miles apart. One is moving toward the other at a mile a minute. But when it gets within a mile, it changes its speed to half a mile a minute. During the second minute, it will travel only a half mile. Next it halves its speed again, so that during the third minute it will travel only a quarter of a mile. Continue this way, and you will see that, although the moving point will always be approaching the other, it will never quite reach it.

A: Let's see. At the end of three minutes it will still be a quarter of a mile away. At the end of four minutes, it will be an eighth of a mile away . . . Yes, I guess you are right. But what is the practical value of this sort of talk anyway?

B: What sort of talk?

A: Talk about points moving toward each other. I admit you have given a theoretical example disproving what I said. But what about Real Life? I know that if I get into my car and start going somewhere, either I make it or I don't, and if I don't, that means I've stopped short. I've never seen anyone or anything behave like your point, cutting its speed in half all the time just to prove a freak exception to the rule.

B: If people didn't think and talk about moving points and things like that, you wouldn't have a car to get into.

A: You mean mathematics?

B: Yes.

A: And logic, I suppose?

B: And logic. There isn't much difference. Some people say mathematics is a branch of logic; others say that logic is a branch of mathematics.

A: Who is right and who is wrong?

B: Both may be right.

A: Now wait a minute. How can both be right? One is saying one thing, and the other the opposite.

B: Before you argue whether mathematics is a branch of logic or vice versa, you have to define both. Some people define them in such a way that mathematics includes logic. Others define them in such a way that logic includes mathematics.

A: But which is the correct definition?

B: See that bright star? Folks call it the Evening Star. Astronomers call it Venus. The Romans called it Hesperus. Which do you think is the correct name?

Case 9.

A: That gas station is on the right side of the road.

B: No, it's on the left side.

A: No, I remember distinctly . . . Wait. How do you approach it? I come from A-ville; so I approach it from the south.

B: I forgot to say that I come from B-ville, from the north. No wonder. Anyway, we agree that it's on the *east* side of the road.

A: That's right.

Case 10.

A: Caviar is a wonderful delicacy.

B: I think it tastes awful.

A: You mean you don't like it.

B: No, I don't.

A: Well, I do.

B: All right, you can order some, and I won't.

A: Good idea.

An obvious difference between these cases and the first five is that in the last ones the controversies are resolved, and in the first ones they are not. It is instructive to look at some probable consequences of the unresolved and the resolved controversies.

Case 1, "Who owns the doll?" usually results in a bloody nose.

Case 2, "Who wants to make war?" usually leads to:

    1. The destruction of cities.

    2. The premature death of people.

    3. The invention of more efficient methods for doing the same thing again.

    4. Other results, which will become apparent only years later.

    5. A conclusive "proof" for the Neptunians that the Plutonians *really* had warlike intentions and an equally conclusive proof for the Plutonians that the Neptunians intended to destroy *them*.

Case 3, "How do you like my hat?" may lead to a sleepless night spent pondering on the unanswerable question "How can he be such a brute?"

Case 4, "What is good for this country?" usually leads to a better opinion of himself and a worse opinion of the other on the part of each opponent.

Case 5, "What revolves around what?" has in many instances led to the burning of a man alive and to a feeling of a task well done in those responsible for the burning, for having saved the heretic's immortal soul.

On the other hand,

Case 6, "What is the capital of Turkey?" leads to increased information on the subject.

Case 7, "How hot can water get?" leads to increased information on the subject.

Case 8, "How effective is Common Sense?" leads to some interesting discoveries.

Cases 9 and 10, "Where is that gas station?" and "How good is caviar?" turn out to be no disagreements at all.

In the "happy" cases, A and B begin by disagreeing and end by agreeing. True, agreeing to disagree about the taste of caviar is different from coming to an agreement by consulting the almanac, and coming to the same conclusion by looking at a thermometer is different from arriving at agreement by mathematical analysis. Yet there is a method by which A and B come to agreement about all these different things, a method which could with profit be applied elsewhere.

The unhappy cases also are different from each other. Two children quarreling over a toy or a husband and wife over a hat is one thing; two nations sick with fear and letting this fear govern their actions is another. Yet fundamentally different as they seem, these cases are similar in some respects, as we shall see.

Controversies among people are usually accompanied by "assertions," where one party maintains that something is "so," while the other maintains that it is not so.

What Happens When People Disagree?

The assertions usually lead to other assertions or to overt acts.

When "overt acts" (such as blows, shooting, or executions) replace assertions, the chances for coming to an agreement considerably diminish. One might think, therefore, that so long as "discussions" go on there may be a chance for agreement.

In fact, some controversies are resolved (disappear) in the discussion that accompanies them, as we have seen. But it is equally true that others do not. The remarks of the two children about the rightful owner of the doll, of the two statesmen about their respective intentions, of the inquisitor and the heretic about astronomy are soon reduced to the " 'tis-'tain't" level, and when this happens the discussion serves only as a stimulus to overt violence.

Can we say anything about how controversies based on assertions might be resolved? Perhaps we could if we learned something about assertions.

CHAPTER 2

What Are Assertions Made About?

When you say "I am thirsty" you seem to be talking about yourself, but when you say "Grass is green" you are presumably talking about grass.

The word "grass" is the subject of the sentence, "Grass is green." We are taught in grammar school that the subject of the sentence is the thing talked about; so it seems proper for us to infer that a man talks about the subject of his sentence. Let us see how reliable that inference is. Suppose, instead of saying "Grass is green," the man said, "I think that grass is green." If you remain faithful to what your grammar school teacher taught you, you will say that *now* he is talking about himself, because "I" is the subject. Very well. But now suppose he says "Grass seems green to me." Again "grass" is the subject; so again he seems to be talking about grass. Now examine all three sentences,

1. Grass is green.
2. I think that grass is green.
3. Grass seems green to me.

The meaning of the third sentence is closer to that of the second than to that of the first. Both the second and third sentences express the man's *opinion* about the color of grass, while the first seems to be stating a "fact." Yet if meaning is taken from sentence structure (syntax), the first and third sentences are alike and differ from the second, because the former seem to be talking about grass and the latter about the speaker, that is, about something that goes on *inside* the speaker.

These examples are meant to show that one cannot always tell by the syntax (subject-predicate relations) of an assertion whether its meaning is supposed to convey something about the inside of the speaker or something about the outside world.

In order even to begin to evaluate an assertion, it is important to know what it asserts. If it asserts something about things, there are certain ways of checking it; but if it asserts something about the inside of the speaker, it is, in general, difficult to check it. In most cases, one simply has to take the word of the speaker. Most difficult to evaluate are those assertions which seem (by their syntax) to say something about the outside world but do not do so by their meaning.

An important class of such assertions are called value judgments. These assertions seem to maintain that something is good or evil, beautiful or ugly, moral, decent, proper, or immoral, indecent, improper. For example, if A asserts that the practice of caprocity is evil, he seems to be saying something about caprocity, but really all he tells us is that *he* does not like it or that most of the people he knows do not like it. He is talking about himself and the people he knows, not about caprocity.

How might controversies based on assertions be resolved?

First, it is necessary to know what the controversy is about; in other words, what the assertions assert. As we have seen, this is not easy, because assertions often seem to say one thing and mean another.

Second, there must be a desire to resolve the controversy. This desire must be stronger than the desire to win the controversy.

Third, there must be some area of agreement from which to start.

Usually if people who disagree wish to agree, they will say:

"Let us do so-and-so. If such-and-such happens, then we shall say you are right, and if thus-and-so happens, then you are wrong."

Essentially, this is what A and B did in each of the "happy" cases. First they established communication. That in itself was an agreement, namely, an agreement that specified just what they disagreed about. Then they agreed on a *procedure,* to decide who was right. But in some cases that was not necessary: the very search for the point of disagreement showed that there was no such point! But let us take the cases one by one.

In Case 6 (capital of Turkey) they agreed to compare their assertions with another assertion made in the almanac. Both A and B accepted the authority of the almanac on capitals as final.

In Case 7 (boiling water) they agreed to look at a column of mercury in a glass tube with the tacit understanding that if the column stopped at a certain mark, A would be right, and if it kept climbing, B would be right.

In Case 8 (motion) B appealed to A's imagination, and A responded. He began to imagine events suggested by B. After imagining a certain sequence of such events, A declared that B was right. It is important that A agreed to imagine what B suggested, to follow his line of reasoning to *whatever conclusion it took him.*

In Case 9 (gas station) A and B restated their assertions in other words and found that their disagreement suddenly vanished.

In Case 10 (caviar) they again restated their assertions. Instead of saying "Caviar tastes foul" or "Caviar tastes fine," which seem like contradictory assertions, they said, in effect, "A likes caviar" and "B does not like caviar," which are not at all contradictory, since both may be true. They discovered that they had been talking about themselves, not about caviar.

As a matter of fact, in every one of those cases a restatement of the problem was involved. Instead of saying "Istanbul is the capital of Turkey" (a categorical assertion), B agreed to restate his belief as a *conditional prediction*, namely, "If you look in the almanac, you will find that it says so-and-so." In another example, instead of asserting that the properties of boiling water *are* such and such, they said in effect, "If you look at the thermometer, you will find that it behaves so-and-so." Instead of staying on a " 'tis-'tain't" level, they suggested *operations* which would lead to the resolution of their controversy.

So in all cases the conditions for resolving the controversies were fulfilled. Whenever necessary, A and B restated their assertions to make clear what they were talking about. They had a desire to agree, because it seemed more important to them to arrive at a correct judgment than to win the argument; and there was in each case an area of agreement: they agreed on the operations that would settle the controversy.

Now let us turn to the "unhappy" cases.

"The doll is mine," yells Little A.

"Mine," screams Little B.

What are the assertions about? The syntax tells us that Little A and Little B are discussing the doll. But syntax is not always to be trusted. The children are really discussing themselves. The meaning of Little A's remark is something of this sort:

"*I, I, I* want that doll!"

The subject of that sentence is "I" and rightly so.

Somewhere there may be property rights to the doll in question and a way of ascertaining them, but that is *not* what the controversy is about. If it were, it might possibly be resolved provided there were agreement on how to determine the rights and their extent.

"The Plutonians threaten us," shout the Neptunian generals,

11

journalists, and public officials. The Neptunians seem to be talking about the Plutonians, but if what they are saying is to have any meaning, most of it should be said about themselves:

"We interpret the actions of the Plutonians as threats."

Somewhere there may be agreements as to what constitutes "threat." Somewhere psychiatrists discover that persons acting under the stress of constant fear are likely to commit acts of violence. Some sociologists suspect that certain principles of psychology are applicable to mass behavior. But there are no psychiatrists, no institutions for the treatment of nations crazed with fear. They are at large, growling at each other. The growls have syntax which makes them appear to be assertions about things existing in the world, "democracy," "peace," "free enterprise," "imperialism," "national honor." But there are no attempts to agree on the subject of disagreement; no desire to decide upon a procedure to resolve the controversies. If meaning is to be attached to the growls, it is simply this:

"I am afraid of you, and I hate you," an assertion about the speaker, not about the world.

In any disagreement, the desire to agree can usually be formulated in a readiness to ask the question: "How did we come to disagree?" It reveals the belief that somewhere there is common ground, and somehow, after having traveled together along the same road, the opponents became separated. It reveals a readiness *to go back to the fork in the road,* to the area where there was still agreement, and to try again. Going back to the fork means stating those assumptions which *both* parties consider "true" and "right" and then trying to arrive at other assertions through reasoning and/or experiment.

Are there no such areas of agreement? There are. The men in the state departments and in the foreign offices who cannot agree on how to promote peace will all agree that the world is round

12

and continuous and keeps shrinking in terms of the time necessary for communication and travel. They will agree that if people have insufficient food, they get sick and die. They agree that it is possible with modern weapons to kill most of the inhabitants of a large city in a few seconds. These are "facts" (assertions about things).

But they will agree to more than just "facts." They will even agree in evaluating many things as desirable or undesirable. For example, hardly any statesman, diplomat, politician, captain of industry, or general will publicly maintain that starvation or disease of mass populations is desirable. A great majority of them will even agree (at least in their public pronouncements) that peace is preferable to war. These are value judgments. So there is no lack of areas of agreement. There are many forks in the road to which they could go to start over.

Why, then, do they continue to disagree? Is it because they are "illogical," will not follow "correct" rules of deriving true assertions from other true assertions as A and B did in Case 8? Is it because they don't know all the "facts"? Is it because they are "dishonest," that is, they conceal some of the facts or make assertions knowingly contrary to fact? Is it, perhaps, because they interpret the "same" facts in different ways? If so, how does this come about?

Or perhaps they do not intend to come to agreement in the first place? Can it be that all the solemn pronouncements of the statesmen concerning "peaceful intentions," the "rights of nations," etc., although syntactically more complicated, are semantically equivalent to "*I, I, I* want that doll"?[1]

What prevents the statesmen from putting controversial issues

---

[1] A somewhat more precise translation may be "*We, We, We* want those transgalaxium mines."

13

into terms which suggest solutions, as A and B did in their controversies?

It is sometimes argued that men in power become stubborn and wicked or else that they represent groups of people who are interested only in extending their possessions and influence, people who derive benefits from the *process* of armed conflict (which makes them rich).

It is often added in such arguments that the causes of armed conflict are to be sought in economic dynamics, in the contradictions brought about by certain modes of production and distribution and that, therefore, to study the genesis of conflict by analyzing the meanings of assertions is misleading and even plays into the hands of those who wish purposely to confuse the issues. Yet it is difficult to see how studying the problem from an additional point of view necessarily obscures the issue.

Obviously the verbalizations of the Neptunian and the Plutonian statesmen are not *in themselves* important. They are important only inasmuch as they are symptomatic of or instrumental in aggravating already existing tensions which finally unleash torrents of destruction upon them.

So if we raise the broader question about how cataclysmic conflicts among men are precipitated, we can hardly dodge the semantic issue. It is idle to say that the Neptunians and the Plutonians are fighting for transgalaxium, because few of the Neptunians and the Plutonians will possess any transgalaxium mines no matter what the outcome of the struggle will be. In fact, it is safe to say that the vast majority of the people of both nations will be worse off for having fought, no matter whose "victory" it is.

To maintain that ordinary people are *forced* to fight merely postpones analysis. *How* are they forced? Are they rounded up with bayonets? Perhaps such methods were used at times, but that is not what happens today. It is only necessary for certain ink marks to appear in the newspapers and certain noises to come over the radio, and millions of people begin to behave according to a well-organized pattern: they abandon their normal occupations, aggregate in predesignated places, go through certain motions, embark on ships, and shoot at each other. How does all this come about?

Suppose, as Carl Sandburg's little girl once said, "they gave a war, and nobody came"? But somehow it never happens. Every time "they give a war," people flock to the colors as to the World Series. Why do they?

To obtain reasonable answers to such questions, it is necessary to study the way organisms with nervous systems respond to stimuli in their environment. For most organisms, such stimuli are largely energy changes—pressures, rises and falls of temperature, impacts of sound and light waves, etc. But man responds in a special way to another class of stimuli—symbols. These special stimuli call forth responses in a way fundamentally different from the non-symbolic stimuli.

Two things make it difficult to settle controversies.

1. Mistaking assertions about the speaker for assertions about things.

2. Desire to be "right," which is stronger than the desire to come to an agreement.

Leaders discussing "peace policies" and "doctrines" resemble children quarreling over a toy in that they mistake assertions about themselves for assertions about things, and in that "victory" seems terribly important to each.

Quarrels of statesmen and other leaders differ from quarrels of children in that they often serve as sparks for world-wide explosions of violence.

The study of people's reactions to symbols is important for analyzing the bases of verbal controversies and of the way verbal controversies can be transformed into physical conflict.

15

CHAPTER 3

More Obstacles to Agreement

Suppose, when people talked about things, they knew how to tell a "true" assertion from a "false" one, and suppose they agreed that it is always better to make true assertions than false ones. Then there would never need be any controversy about what is "true."

Unfortunately it is not simple to achieve this state of affairs. There are many reasons for this.

1. *People often wish to "win arguments" more than they desire to come to agreement about what is true.*

2. *People often think they are talking about things in the outside world when they are talking about themselves.*

These difficulties were discussed in the preceding chapters. There are many other formidable obstacles to agreement.

3. *People often have their private notions of how to tell "true" from "false" or else they simply subscribe to some current notion of what is true.*

Fifty years ago people in this country believed that "love apples" (tomatoes) were poisonous, because everybody believed that love apples were poisonous. This superstition, like many others, died a natural death without causing any serious hardship. But when potatoes were first introduced in Russia, the peasants would not plant or eat them, because, they said, they were "devil's apples." The rulers realized that the potato could become an important factor in agricultural economy; so they tried to overcome the

16

peasants' reluctance by *forcing* them to eat potatoes. The question how to verify the assertion "potatoes are devil's apples" never arose. The peasants said it was "true," and the officials said it was "false." This controversy caused a great deal of unhappiness.

4. *It is not even universally agreed that "true" statements are to be always preferred to false ones.*

In the belief that they are "shielding their children from filth," many parents give fantastic answers to the questions children ask about some natural processes. Since children in their early years learn largely by imitating parents, a deep-seated preference for true assertions fails to take root. Truth is not today a universal value.

Here is an even more striking example of contempt for truth.

Throughout the Christian centuries it was accepted fact that the natural sciences afforded man no edification. Lactantius, who was chosen by Constantine the Great to tutor his son, put the position very clearly when he asked in so many words what heavenly bliss he could attain by knowing the sources of the Nile, or the twaddle of the physicists anent the heavenly bodies . . . Let me assure you that mankind is about to find its way back to this point of view. Mankind will soon perceive that it is not the task of true science to run after godless understanding; but to reject utterly all that is harmful, yes, even all that ideally speaking is without significance, in favor of instinct, measure, choice. It is childish to accuse the Church of having defended darkness rather than light. She did well, and thrice well, to chastise as unlawful all unconditioned striving after the "pure" knowledge of things, such striving, that is, as is without reference to the spiritual, without bearing on man's salvation; for it is this unconditioned, this a-philosophical natural science that always has led and ever will lead men into darkness.[1]

5. *People sometimes treat assertions about things as if they were matters of opinion.*

---

[1] Naphtha's diatribe against scientific humanism from Thomas Mann's *The Magic Mountain.*

17

Many will recall having heard conversations like this one.

P: . . . So I says to him, Why don't you finish the job? And he says, It's five o'clock, Mr. P, I don't work after five o'clock. Too darn lazy, those Gaminos. That's why they never get anywhere.

Q: I know a Gamino who works in a law office downtown. Lots of times I've gone by that building as late as eleven, and as often as not there's a light shining in that office. Once I saw him coming out with a brief case. Told me the fuse blew out, so he was going home to do some more work. *That* Gamino ain't lazy.

P: Sure, there are exceptions. I'm talking about most of them.

Q: Now be honest, P. There are ten thousand Gaminos in this city, and you know you don't know most of them.

P: Do you have to know most rattlesnakes to know what they're like? Gaminos are Gaminos, and most of them *act* like Gaminos.

Q: What do you mean, "act like Gaminos"?

P: Just what I said. They're lazy, and that's that.

Q: If I knew as many rattlesnakes that didn't act like people say they do, as I know Gaminos that don't act like you say they do, I'd change my mind about rattlesnakes.

P: You don't have to tell me how you feel about Gaminos, Q. I've known it all along. But I'm tolerant, see? You are entitled to your opinion, and I'm entitled to mine. Just don't go around telling me what *I* should think.

Note that "Gaminos are lazy" is *not* a value judgment, because it can be verified at least to some extent by examining facts, such as the average number of hours Gaminos work, the efficiency of their work under conditions similar to those in which non-Gaminos work, etc. To the extent that this assertion is verifiable, it is *not* a matter of opinion any more than the population of A-ville is a matter of opinion. Mr. P, however, prefers to pass this assertion off as his opinion. Mr. P has a great many other opinions, for example on "evolution," on the causes of juvenile delinquency, on the reliability of women drivers, etc. Evidence in these matters is irrelevant for him, because he firmly believes that he is entitled to his opinions.

6. *Few people know how to test whether or not a statement they make contradicts other statements they have made. For that matter, few people feel the need of making such tests* (they have not had enough practice in the use of logic).

Besides the Gaminos, Mr. P objects also to the Nujos, of whom he says, "They always stick together and never accept any outsiders as friends." Mr. P has also signed an agreement with some of his neighbors to prevent any Nujo from owning property in his neighborhood. If one were to ask him why he objected to the Nujos, Mr. P would say, "They are always trying to horn in where they are not wanted. Why don't they stay with their own kind?"

7. *Some people* (though not many) *have had too much practice in logic.*

This obstacle to agreement will be discussed in Chapter 12.

We have seen that value judgments are not assertions about things. Therefore, criteria for "good" and "bad" are probably not the same as those for "true" and "false." Yet if people could agree on some few fundamentals concerning what was "good" and what "bad," it might be possible to refer other judgments to these fundamentals. It is obvious that the *fewer* fundamentals are chosen for this purpose the *easier* it becomes to get almost everyone to agree to them. We see, however, that often the following is a major obstacle to agreement.

8. *Instead of choosing a few consistent principles of right and wrong to believe in, people often believe in a great many such principles, most of which are peculiar to the environment in which they live.*

In New Orleans it is considered shocking by most people to see

19

a Negro and a white person dining together, but few people object to taverns and other places of amusement being open on Sundays. In New England people may, in general, dine with whom they please, but in many localities it is considered a breach of something or other to amuse oneself in certain ways on Sunday.

Again, most people in the United States consider it shocking if two persons with different skin colors marry, but it is not considered immoral to buy something as cheaply as possible in order to sell it as dearly as possible. In the U.S.S.R. people may choose mates regardless of skin color without fear of public disapproval, but commercial speculation is severely punished.

9. *Things people believe in contradict not only things other people believe in but often contradict one another.*

It is imperative to "love one's enemy" and also to "rush to the defense of one's country"; it is possible to believe in Co-operation (with a capital C) and at the same time to oppose consumer co-operatives, because they are "socialistic." Many people deplore the spread of venereal diseases and oppose effective measures for their eradication.

Now, perhaps, we are beginning to see the outlines of the prodigious task before us. To make the resolution of controversies possible, we should throw away our beliefs in many "principles" of local, provincial character, and instead agree on a few fundamental ones, acceptable to a vast majority. Moreover, we should carefully check these principles so that they don't contradict one another. We should agree on how to tell a "true" assertion from a "false" one and, moreover, a preference for true assertions should be included in the fundamental principles. We should be well versed in logic, so that we do not make self-contradictory assertions; and yet there is some danger in trusting logic too much.

How can we learn all these things? One must begin somewhere, and we are going to begin with the notion of truth. Although we have pointed out that truth is by no means a universal value, yet a great many people take this value seriously. In many cases a party to a controversy in defending his point of view will solemnly state that he is defending the truth. The frequency with which leaders of nations hurl the epithet "liar" or its equivalent at each other at international conferences also testifies to the fact that lying is considered despicable by great numbers of people. Even Mr. P, while modestly representing the assertion "Gaminos are lazy" as his "private opinion," would, if pressed, insist that he believes the assertion to be true, thus intimating that truth is a guide in his *choice* of "private opinions."

Fundamental, therefore, to any controversy are the notions that the parties to the controversy entertain about truth.

What are some of these notions?

CHAPTER 4

Concern With Truth

"Every one that is of the truth heareth my voice."
Pilate saith unto him,
"What is truth?"

John 18:37-38

Some three and a half centuries ago, as the reader probably knows, there lived in Italy a great man by the name of Galileo Galilei. His greatness was in the profound influence he has had on people's thinking about the world. He steered the thinking of those who understood his teachings *away* from fear. Perhaps this sort of evaluation of a man's contribution to mankind will be more common in the future. Perhaps to determine a man's greatness it will be more pertinent to ask "How many people has he made less afraid?" than "How many people were afraid of him?"

Anyhow, Galileo taught a theory advanced for his time, namely, the *heliocentric* theory, which maintained that our earth was just another planet, not essentially different from the five then known, and that all of them revolved around the sun. The prevailing opinion was that this earth of ours was a very special place (or else the Saviour wouldn't have bothered to come here), occupying the center of the universe and having the sun, the moon, and the five planets, and the "firmament" of fixed stars to boot, revolving around *it*.

22

In Galileo's time it was dangerous to teach any theory so radically departing from accepted views. The Church played a prominent part in human affairs, and its authorities declared in no uncertain terms how one was supposed to think about the universe. In due time, Galileo's ideas were called to the attention of the Inquisition (a sort of Committee for Investigating Un-Pious Activities), and after some conversations with the inquisitors, Galileo recanted and proclaimed that he was mistaken.

Now, most people's sympathies (that is, the sympathies of those who have heard of him at all) are with Galileo. If one were to ask why they sympathize with him, many people would say that Galileo proclaimed the truth, that the inquisitors were bigoted, narrow-minded men, whose object was to keep the truth from the people for fear that the truth would jeopardize the influence they wielded.

This is unlikely. More convincing than a picture of a sinister schemer is the portrait drawn of the inquisitor by George Bernard Shaw in his play *Saint Joan*. There you see a scrupulously honest[1] and selfless[2] man, deeply concerned with Joan's immortal soul and convinced that it is his duty to mankind and to God to wage a merciless war against "heresy" (any teaching contrary to the current teaching of the Church). In fact, there is reason to believe that many (though not, of course, all) of the functionaries of the Church were really convinced that "heresy" was not only "wicked" but actually "false," above all, "contrary to common sense," "illogical."

The Russian Flier and the Moslem Scholar

In the last war I made the acquaintance of a Russian flier, a quiet, cultured young man, fond of Puccini's music and tomato

---

[1] Believing what he says.

[2] Believing that he gets no personal gain from his efforts.

juice, and admirably adjusted to the business of risking his life every other day, as a matter of routine. We talked about social problems, that is, those facing the United States, because he could not recognize any serious social problems facing the U.S.S.R. To his way of thinking, the only problems the Russians had left to deal with were problems of technology.

"We have solved our social problems," he said. "We have yet a long way to go to achieve your standard of living and to make the sort of world we want, but we are on the right road, and we know it. All we need to do is keep increasing our production through improved technique. This will give us more leisure. As the people get more leisure, their intelligence and cultural level will rise. To be sure, we must always be on the alert against deviationists and saboteurs who would block our progress. Some of the measures we take against our enemies may seem harsh to you outsiders. We don't like them any more than you do. But don't you see that is the only way? We must get to our goal."

"I wish," I said, "I could say for my country that we have solved our social problems."

"Then why don't you solve them? The solution is available. It's no secret. There are no patent rights on social inventions. Anyone can make use of them. On the shelves of every library, even your libraries, as you have told me, stand the works of Marx, Engels, Lenin, and Stalin, men who have devoted their lives to the solution of just such problems. They have pointed out how a just social order can be constructed and have proved by iron logic the inevitability of the social revolution and of the dictatorship of the proletariat. But I suppose the bourgeois outlook of your intellectuals prevents them from seeing the Truth. One thing I will tell you: nothing is dearer to me than Truth. I will die for it if necessary."

I believed him.

24

On another occasion I met a Moslem scholar, a young man with shining black eyes and a neat, downy beard, who spoke fluent English, Arabic, Persian, Bengali, Urdu, Greek, and French.

"The devotion of the ignorant to the Koran as the greatest source of knowledge," he told me, "is purely emotional. Many of them, being illiterate, have not even read the Koran. What they know of it is by hearsay, quite inaccurate and therefore worthless information. I too am convinced that the Koran is the greatest and the most reliable source of knowledge. But my conviction is based on *fact*."

"How so?"

"You see, our scholars study the Koran in a different way from the way your scholars study the sources of your knowledge. We make a much more thorough study of it, learning great portions by heart. It is learned with painstaking accuracy. Not only every word of the text but every punctuation mark is significant. In this way, when copies of the Koran are made, they are *absolutely* accurate. Not only every word, every dot is exactly as in the original. What I am saying is true, believe me. If you could read Arabic, I would show you what I mean. Sometimes an entire edition is discarded because of a misplaced phonetic mark."

I believed him.

"And you will not deny," he continued, "that no such pains are taken in perpetuating your sources of knowledge."

I did not deny.

"I have heard that some of your holiest scripts have become completely perverted as a result of accumulated errors in successive copies."

The evangelist John attributes to Pontius Pilate the remark, "What is truth?" It is not clear from John's narrative whether he considers Pilate the villain of his story—the story is told in pretty much a matter-of-fact way. But most people today, who take the story to heart, consider Pilate's question the height of cynicism. Yet it is hard to see why the question should be considered cynical.

Perhaps I can tempt *you* to ask it.

Do you believe in duckbills? Perhaps you have seen one in a zoo. Does that settle the question for you? Will you say, "I have seen a duckbill; therefore I know it exists." But do you take the man seriously who says that it is possible to saw a girl in half and put her together again with no appreciable damage, because he has seen it done in vaudeville?

What is so ridiculous about the farmer who said "There ain't no such animal" when he saw a giraffe?

Again, do you believe the world is round? Does it *look* round? Do you believe that the "sun is standing still" even though it seems to go around the earth every day? Which criteria do you use when you assert that something is true? Are they always the same criteria? Are you sure your criteria are always valid?

Of all animals, only man is concerned with something he calls "truth." The answers to Pilate's question have been many and varied. In most discussions about truth, "that which we perceive by our senses" is generally conceded to be a substantial part of "reality" or truth (although in many judgments the "perceptions of the senses" are somehow discounted). But whether the "senses" are taken as the final authority or altogether discredited, they are almost always *mentioned* in any discussion of truth. Let us therefore see what we will mean by the "senses."

THE SENSES

Physiologists now say that the old classification of the senses into the Five is too crude and of little use in studying the way organisms react to the world about them. Many more senses besides the Five are now described.

To begin with, there are various aspects, "modalities," or "dimensions" of each of the old senses. The "sense of sight" includes the ability to distinguish shapes, distances, and color independently of each other. The "sense of touch" includes different mechanisms for distinguishing heat and cold, pressure and pain. The so-called "proprioceptive sense," previously roughly included in "touch," does not seem to have anything to do with any of the Five Senses.

Secondly, instead of sharply dividing the environment into internal and external, modern physiologists tend to look at environment as a whole. For example, is the feeling of disturbed balance due to the "outside" (force of gravity) or the "inside" (position of the semicircular canals in the inner ear, which tells us about our position in space)? In the last analysis, the "inside" always participates in our knowledge of the external world. If we had no retina, the light "outside" would never affect us the way it does, and if we had no cochlea, air vibrations would be air vibrations, not sounds.

The senses used to be described as receiving only the "outside" stimuli. Once the distinction between the "outside" and the "inside" stimuli becomes vague, a great many reactions to environment, internal or external, may claim to be included in the senses: hunger and thirst, sexual desire and inner "aches." Even the so-called "emotions" inasmuch as they can be described as reactions to environment (internal or external) can be included in the "senses."

Animals differ widely in the senses they possess. Many are color blind, but some can distinguish colors. Many are sensitive to pitch, but the range of the frequencies they can hear varies. Dogs can hear higher frequencies than men and bats still higher. Some have special senses. Homing pigeons are suspected to react to the earth's magnetic field, so that they may literally come home "on the beam" by means of a built-in device like those used by our fliers. They may have an "electromagnetic sense."

We said a while ago that of all animals man is the only one concerned with something called "truth." This "something" has to do with the fact that of all animals man is the only one seriously preoccupied with symbols. He may be said to possess a "symbolic sense." It should be kept in mind that we are defining a "sense" more broadly than it is usually defined in physiology, where the existence of a sense presupposes the existence of special receptors for it. We mean by a sense simply a way of reacting to some special class of events, external or internal. The symbolic sense is, accordingly, a certain way of reacting to symbols.

A symbol, roughly speaking, is something that stands for something else.[3] The cross, the swastika, the hammer and sickle, and the star-spangled banner are all symbols. So is the picture of the Smith Brothers, the three intersecting circles on ale advertisements, the wooden Indian that used to stand in front of cigar stores, and the star on a policeman's uniform. The ink marks you are now looking at are symbols. They stand for words, which themselves stand for something else, which is not words, and are therefore also symbols. So are musical notations, blueprints of machinery, and road maps.

We are surrounded and react to symbols all through our lives. Nothing is a symbol unless it is reacted to in a way which is independent of the symbol's direct impact. A word in a language we don't understand is not a symbol for us. We may react to its sound, but we do not react to the thing it is supposed to stand for. If we react to a camel as we would to a camel, it is not a symbol, but if we reach for our cigarette case, it is.

So ingrained are our reactions to symbols that the advertisers of

[3] In Chapter 9 a narrower definition will be given.

28

a carbonated water for a long time pictured a situation where a young but obviously mature girl walked about hotel lobbies and restaurants bare breasted, while the gentlemen she approached seemed to be interested only in the carbonated water she was supposed to represent. Whether the advertisers were aware of it or not, they were making a significant comment on our symbolic way of life.

The physiology of the symbolic sense has not yet been worked out to any degree of thoroughness. However, we can talk about it and learn something about it from the way it operates. Two characteristics of the symbolic sense are of utmost importance in understanding behavior.

1. *The response to a symbolic stimulus is, in general, independent of the intensity of the stimulus.*

We said stimuli were energy changes in the environment of the organism. A primitive organism will generally respond to these changes depending on their intensity. For example, a frog whose leg has been dipped in hot water will withdraw the foot the more rapidly the hotter the water.

But a symbolic stimulus works in a different way. Its "intensity" has no significant effect on the response. If someone whispered into your ear, "There is a rattlesnake right behind you," you would take as drastic measures as if it were shouted.[4]

Even better examples of violent reactions to symbolic stimuli (whose actual intensity in terms of energies involved is quite low) are seen in the rising of a man's blood pressure as he reads something in the paper or a hay fever patient's sneezing at the sight of *artificial* flowers.

The effect of a direct stimulus may be compared to that of a

---

[4] Sometimes responses to loud warnings are more prompt or intense, but that is probably because loud noises are themselves nonsymbolic (direct) stimuli and may elicit responses depending on their intensity.

29

stretched bowstring; the effect of a symbolic stimulus to that of a released trigger. The arrow will fly the farther the more you stretch the string; but it does not matter how hard the trigger is pressed: it is not the trigger that sends the bullet on its way; it is the powder charge *inside the gun*. Similarly, the action of a symbolic stimulus is not in itself but in the reactions it sets off *inside the recipient*.

This important property of symbolic stimuli will be taken up again in a later chapter. For the present we are more interested in the second characteristic.

2. *Response to symbols makes possible comparison of experiences out of which the notion of truth arises.*

To be concerned with truth is to compare experiences.

Without the symbolic sense, language of any kind would be impossible. Without language, concern with truth is meaningless, because concern with truth involves comparison either of

(1) language with other language (one symbolic experience with another) or of

(2) language with direct experience (information supplied by the symbolic sense with that supplied by other senses).

In our concern with truth, we may, of course, compare non-symbolic experiences with each other. But the motivation for such comparison lies in symbolic experience.

Suppose we are looking at one of those invisible show windows. We think, "Maybe there is no glass there." It is this *assertion* (verbalization of experience) that we set out to test when we stretch out our hand to convince ourselves that the glass is there. Our sense of sight gave us a false report, and we sent our sense of touch to correct the impression. On the other hand, suppose we cross our index and middle fingers and touch the tip of our nose so that it comes between the fingers. We may think, "My, two noses!" This time our sense of touch gave us a false report, and we look in the mirror to reassure ourselves.

The skeptical farmer confronted with a giraffe was, of course, also comparing experiences—the sight of the giraffe and the totality of his previous experiences with "animals," from which he derived a notion of what an "animal" is like.

As far as we know, animals other than humans (that is, those which do not possess a symbolic sense) do not engage in such critical investigations of what their senses tell them. *Concern with truth necessarily involves language and therefore the symbolic sense.*

Usually conflicts between sense reports are easy to resolve. In the case of invisible glass, our verdict will go to the sense of touch, perhaps because we know that our sight is handicapped by the transparency of the glass and by the elimination of the difference between the angles of refraction of air and glass (or simply because we have touched invisible things before, such as air currents). In the case of the double nose, we realize that our sense of touch is handicapped by the unusual position of the fingers (or simply because we review our past experiences with our own nose); so we give the verdict to the sense of sight.

The greatest difficulties in man's concern with "reality" involve the reports he gets from his symbolic sense, biologically the newest of his senses, whose implications and limitations have begun to become known only in recent times. A simple symbolic experience will illustrate how our concern with truth involves the comparison of such an experience with a nonsymbolic one.

We hear someone make a set of noises, "Grass is green." "Grass" is a word. So is "green." So is "is." Words are symbols, and we react to them through mechanisms which constitute our symbolic sense. We react something like this. When we hear "grass" we start having experiences which are somewhat similar to the many experiences we had with actual grass, except that they are more vague and seem to come entirely from the "inside."

31

The same happens with "green." All the experiences we have had with leaves, traffic lights, and paper money somehow merge together into one vague "inner" sensation. The "is" tells us that we are to fuse the two sets of experiences (the grass experiences and the green ones) together. We do this. Now, in our concern with the "truth" of the noises "grass is green," we compare the resulting "picture in our mind" with an actual experience of grass and see if the two experiences are similar. Grass does not have to be around for us to do that. We can recall an actual grass experience and compare our symbolic picture with our recollection picture. We have compared a symbolic experience with a non-symbolic one, that is, language with fact.

Now let us take another set of noises, "The world is round." Our experiences with the symbol "round" have to do with oranges, basketballs, and soap bubbles. How about our experiences with "the world"? Do we think of a landscape? A city sky line? The United Nations? A map? Are any of these experiences "round"? Perhaps we are thinking of a globe? Very likely we are when we are thinking of the world in the context of the assertion "The world is round." But is the globe actually the world? Or is it just another symbol, which was made to conform with the assertion "The world is round"? Or perhaps we do not even think of the globe but of the words we once read in a geography book or the words the teacher said.

It does not matter. What is important is that the truth of the assertion "The world is round" cannot be inferred from a comparison of symbolic experiences with direct experiences alone. Such an inference necessarily involves the comparison of the symbolic experience "The world is round" with *other symbolic experiences,* such as

(1) a similar set of noises made by someone else,

32

(2) a set of ink marks interpreted in the same way as the set of noises,

(3) identification of the world with a round object supposed to represent it, or

(4) a set of comparisons of assertions called *proof*.

One circumstance that seems to hold some promise for the resolution of controversies is the fact that people do become concerned with something they call "truth." The promise is implied by the necessity to *check* one's beliefs. Such concern is peculiar to human beings and may be attributed to a "symbolic sense," which only human beings possess and which makes language possible. Thus both the origin of verbalized controversies and the possibility of their resolution are rooted in language.

The Russian flyer and the Moslem scholar are both concerned with truth and compare experiences. Many of their convictions may appear bizarre to us if we do not share the tacit assumptions that they make about the absolute standard of comparison, the works of Marx, Engels, etc., for one and the Koran for the other.

Comparisons may be either

(1) direct comparisons of symbolic experiences (reaction to someone's assertion) with nonsymbolic ones (involving one's own nonsymbolic senses) or

(2) comparisons of symbolic experiences with each other, such as comparisons of assertions, authorities, etc.

Since direct checks of assertions are rarely possible, we are forced to rely on checking what we are told against things we have been told before. If discrepancies are discovered, we must, in general, discard one set of beliefs in favor of another. How can we decide which set of beliefs is to be kept and which set discarded? *What is a reliable authority?*

CHAPTER 5

Whom Do You Believe? What Do You Believe?

When we want to get to the railroad station in a strange town, we generally take the word of the first person we see in the street. It does not matter whether we ask "Is this the way to the station?" or "Which is the way to the station?" We are confident that the man, whom we have never seen before and whom we probably will never see again, will not "deceive" us.

In some Oriental countries you are supposed to know how to ask that question if you want the right answer. According to the guidebooks our soldiers used for communicating with the inhabitants of those countries, it was not a good idea to ask "Is this the way to the station?" If you happened to be wrong, you might not be corrected, because the inhabitant might consider it impolite to tell you that you are wrong. He might say "Yes" just to make you feel good. If you asked, "*Which* is the way to the station?" you would get the right answer without the inhabitant's risking to "offend" you. If you think that custom foolish, consider the question "How do you like my new hat (or my new husband)?" as it is treated in our own society.

If a man behind the counter in a reliable jewelry store tells us that the stone we are buying is a genuine ruby, we will generally believe him. But we will not, as a rule, believe such a statement if it is made by a stranger approaching us in the street.

In matters of spelling, we will believe the dictionary more than ourselves; in matters of growing nasturtiums, we will believe our neighbor, who has grown them for years, more than the president of the state university, if he is just intending to grow them; in matters of rearing children, we will probably prefer our own ideas to those of everyone else.

How can we tell whether we are told the truth?

WHY DOES HE TELL ME THIS, AND HOW DOES HE KNOW?

Two things are important to consider when we are being told something.

1. What are my informant's motives?
2. How does he know that what he is saying is true?

If the object of every communication were only to inform, we should not have to worry about motives. Fortunately there *are* regions in human affairs where the only object of communication is to inform. They are the areas of scientific inquiry, *where information can be constantly checked*. It is in the best interest of the scientist who has discovered a new element to give its atomic weight, chemical properties, etc., to the best of his knowledge, because the very nature of scientific inquiry is such that other scientists will immediately start checking up on him. No amount of prestige makes the findings of any scientist immune to criticism and to checkup. A false report cannot stand up long.

Areas of scientific inquiry are *by definition* those where assertions are constantly checked against experience, for example, astronomy, physics, chemistry, anatomy, geography, etc. Many people have recently learned to trust the motives of the scientist when he makes scientific assertions. That is why assertions having little or nothing to do with science, but calculated to gain the confidence of the public, are often made in a language which *simulates* the language of science. Such assertions can usually be recognized by the vagueness of the references to the methods pursued in the inquiry and by the emphasis placed on the urgency

35

of certain actions. A mystic cult, for example, will describe in esoteric terms the "vibrations" and "forces" discovered in the "mind"; but usually such discussions end with an offer of a book, a talisman, or a course in "concentration" for sale. Political parties and "lobbies" often publish pamphlets full of statistics and charts, but the main functions of these organizations are not the collection and dissemination of verifiable information.

Science is one area of communication where the motivation to deceive can be said to be practically eliminated, not necessarily because scientists are extraordinarily virtuous people, but because the nature of scientific activity is such that deception can be easily detected by other scientists. Therefore, we can at least trust the scientists' sincerity whenever they tell us something about the results of their studies.

Let us now turn to the other criterion, "How does he know?" This is a more difficult question to answer. Ask yourself how you know what you know, and you will be appalled at the amount of information that is at least secondhand. Trace it to its source, and again it turns out to be secondhand. Keep tracing it, and soon the sources become obscure, and you are left with a piece of information of undisclosed ancestry.

In asking "How do we know what we know?" we are asking for a definition of knowledge. Definitions, however, are rather arbitrary. There is no *a priori* reason why a word should be defined one way rather than another. The important thing is to be consistent in the meaning of a word once we have defined it; or, if the meaning of the word *has* to change in a different context (this is often inevitable), to keep track of the changes. However, there is a practical consideration for choosing one definition for a word rather than another, and that is existing usage. To give an example, there is no *logical* reason why I cannot choose to call cats dogs, and dogs cats, provided I notify everyone with whom I wish to communicate on this subject that I am reversing the usual meanings of those words. But such a change would introduce unnecessary inconvenience. To avoid confusion, it is advisable to choose definitions which are already implied in the way words are used by a great many people.

Knowledge, too, can be defined in a variety of ways. Depending on the definition, the sources of knowledge will be taken to be different. We shall assume that the most practical definition of knowledge is one which connects this word with experience. A great many people in a great many different cultures use the word "to know" in this way (although they use it in many other ways, these other ways differ considerably among themselves). Let us take, therefore, the *greatest common denominator* of what people mean by knowledge. We "know" that the moon is full, if we look and see that it is full; we "know" that cherries are sweet, if we taste them and find that they are sweet.

To be sure, the senses often deceive us. Direct experience cannot always be trusted. But what makes us distrust some direct experiences is, in the last analysis, other experience (direct or symbolic), and again we are faced with the problem of tracing "knowledge." The only step at which this process can be terminated, the only thing that need not be traced further (unless we have reason to distrust our senses) is direct experience itself.

Thus, to answer the question "How do I know?" is to establish a chain of comparisons between assertions, and the *last link of that chain must be something that is not an assertion; it must be direct experience.*

One need not go all the way back to the direct experience each time. Once we have established knowledge by direct experience, we can "preserve" it by putting it into the form of an assertion. Then we can be satisfied with the source of some other knowledge if it can be traced to this assertion, which represents "canned knowledge." In fact, proofs are constructed in this way. In a valid proof of an assertion about things, a chain of connections is established between assertions (if P is true, Q is true; if Q is true, R is true, etc.), which, if traced far enough back, leads to someone's direct experience.

I work by the light of a single lamp, and suddenly it goes out.

I wish to "know" what I ought to do to restore light; so I set up a chain of assertions.

1. *Either the lamp has burned out or the fuse has blown.*

This is based on reports I have heard to the effect that the most frequent causes of bulb failure are blown fuses and burned filaments. These reports may be based on other reports, but they can be traced to someone's experience.

I turn on some other bulb in the house and find that it lights up. I have another link in my chain.

2. *The fuse has not blown.*

This also is based on a chain of reports that a fuse affects all the lamps in the circuit and that generally the whole house is on one circuit. Again these reports may be *n*th-hand knowledge, but originally someone's experience backs their reliability.

I draw my conclusion:

3. *Therefore the bulb has burned out.*

I draw further conclusions from further considerations.

4. *This bulb will not burn again.*

5. *Bulbs recently bought are generally serviceable.*

6. *If I wish to restore light, I ought to replace the burned-out bulb with a fresh one.*

This conclusion represents "knowledge" of what I ought to do in order to restore light. It is based on the proof of certain assertions.

Some arguments sound or look like proofs but really are not, because the chains of assertions do not lead to someone's direct experience. A common example of such a chain is the so-called "chain of circular reasoning."

Whom Do You Believe?

"Our Book of Knowledge, Virtue, and Etiquette contains only true statements and all the true statements worth knowing."

"How do you know?"

"Because it was written by the great prophet Kokoko, and he would not write anything not true, nor would he omit anything worth knowing."

"How do you know?"

"Because Kokoko was inspired by the great spirit Tututu, who knows everything."

"How do you know?"

"It says so in the Book of Knowledge, Virtue, and Etiquette, and this book contains only true statements."

Other chains of reasoning end in a blind alley, that is, an assertion which has never been verified by experience because it is a "self-evident truth." Philosophy has known a great many of these "self-evident truths," which we shall treat in their proper place.

DEMOCRATIZATION OF KNOWLEDGE

Francis Bacon (1561-1626) said this of knowledge:

"Man . . . can do and understand so much, and so much only, as he has observed in fact . . . of the course of nature; beyond this he neither knows anything nor can do anything."

"First of all we must prepare a *natural and experimental* history sufficient and good; and this is the foundation of all."[1]

"All depends on keeping the eye steadily fixed upon the facts of nature, and so receiving their images simply as they are . . ."[2]

Were these assertions of Bacon about the source of knowledge assertions about things? They were taken to be such by many philosophers and probably by Bacon himself. Long, tedious, and

[1] *Novum Organum*, ii, 10.
[2] *Ibid.*, i, 68, 124.

bitter disputes followed on whether experience, as Bacon maintained, was really the only source of knowledge or whether other sources existed. But can one make assertions about something without first defining the something? Bacon does not define knowledge formally in his discussion. Rather, his assertions about knowledge must themselves be taken as definitions. What he is saying in fact is,

"When I speak about knowledge, I speak of those assertions which can be linked with experience."

There is no arguing with a definition. The man is using a word, and he tells you what that word refers to.

It is in this sense that we are going to use the word "knowledge." There is no question of our logical right to do so. But there is also a practical reason for using the word in this way. As has been pointed out above, the word "knowledge" is already used as something connected with experience by a vast majority of all people, except that they do not always realize it. People "prove" a great deal of what they know by appealing to an "authority." The implication (though not often stated) is that the "authority" must have sources of knowledge (experiences) inaccessible to ordinary people. "Knowledge" of the will of the gods is disseminated by the priests (authority), but the priests are also credited with the ability to communicate with the gods directly and thus to ascertain their will by experience.

Galileo's contemporaries based their notions in physics on the teachings of Aristotle, because Aristotle was an "authority." Presumably, then, Aristotle had sources of knowledge which were unimpeachable. The contemporaries of Galileo must have depended on direct experiences a great deal in their daily lives. They could not have discarded them completely and survived. But they simply discounted direct experience when it contradicted "authority." When Galileo showed them the satellites of Jupiter through his telescope (the first in Italy), they could not believe

40

their eyes and said it was a trick, because Aristotle had failed to mention those satellites. They simply thought Aristotle's "experience," whatever it was, superior to their own.

Bacon denied that one man's experience can in principle be superior to another's. He would have admitted that one man can make more accurate observations or more far-reaching deductions than another, but he would have insisted that, given *equal means of making observations*, no man's experience is to be preferred to another's. Nor would there be any reason to do so, because if sufficiently accurate observations were made, essentially the *same* observations would be made.

Bacon's definition of knowledge thus implied a *democratization* of knowledge. It took the privilege of knowing away from "authorities" and placed it at the disposal of anyone who would take the trouble to seek knowledge.

This approach to knowledge (and therefore to truth) is an important step forward toward the resolution of controversies. At least it points to a method which makes it possible to agree on assertions about things. Knowledge must be linked with experience. But is this the whole story of how knowledge is acquired?

If each of us had to accumulate his own store of knowledge by immediate experience, we would know extremely little. We have already seen that a vast bulk of our knowledge is secondhand. We have also seen that we can expect to depend on secondhand knowledge provided the chains of assertions that support it have roots in someone's experience. We know there must be a connection between *language* and experience for language to be of value in transmitting knowledge. But now some perplexing questions arise:

How is this connection made?

How is experience translated into language?

How is language translated into knowledge?

CHAPTER 6

Language

No knowledge is more important than a correct appreciation of language . . .
Verbal discourse contains defects which have escaped detection.

Alexander Bryan Johnson, *A Treatise on Language*

Experience is the source of knowledge. We are interested not only in the source of knowledge but in the way knowledge is transmitted from person to person, from generation to generation. One thing is apparent. Experience cannot be transmitted as *experience*: it must first be translated into something else. It is that something else which is transmitted. When it is "received," it is translated back into something that *resembles* experience. We will illustrate this by an example from technology.

In the old primitive telegraph, the operator at one end beat out a rhythmic pattern with the key. Each time the key was pressed, an electric circuit was closed. Thus the same rhythmic pattern of current spurts was established in the circuit. *It is these current spurts* which were transmitted over the wires, *not the movements of the key*. The current spurts were a *mapping* of the key movements. At the other end, the current spurts activated an electromagnet, which attracted and released an iron disk. The movements of the iron disk were then a mapping of the current spurts and therefore of the original key movements. Thus the key movements

42

were mapped on the currents; the currents were mapped on the disk movements.

An analogous process takes place in the telephone. We speak into the receiver; the sound waves are mapped on the vibrations of a disk; these are mapped on electric current patterns; these are transmitted over the wires and are mapped on the vibrations of another disk, which duplicates the vibrations of the first disk and hence those made by our voice.

The radio works by the same principle, except that the electromagnetic waves are carried through the "ether" instead of over wires.

The phonograph record is, of course, also a mapping. The pattern of the grooves in the record is a mapping of the vibrations of the recording needle, which in turn is a mapping of the vibrations of a crystal, etc. Thus Chaliapin, who has been dead for years, can "sing" for us: his voice has been mapped and preserved.

Now, every communication engineer knows what is meant by fidelity. In fact, when we go to buy a radio, we too are concerned about fidelity. We would like the sounds that come out of our loud-speaker to resemble as closely as possible those that come out of Toscanini's orchestra in the studio. We want no static. We want no distortion. We want the full range from the double basses to the piccolos. Radio engineers understand these wants and are doing their best to satisfy them. On the whole, they are doing an excellent job.

The transmission of experience by means of language is also primarily a communication problem. It too involves mappings. Experience itself is not words. It is completely inside us and cannot be transmitted as such. To be transmitted, experience must be *mapped* on language.[1] It is this language, then, which is transmitted.

[1] We are really using "language" here in its broadest possible sense as any system of signals that can transmit experience. To the extent that music, for example, can serve as such a carrier it too is a "language" in this sense.

But to complete the analogy with the telegraph, etc., language must be retranslated into experience on the receiving end. Here the analogy with technical communication breaks down. Language is not translated into *direct* experience at the receiving end, no matter how vivid it may be. It is translated into something *resembling* direct experience. Let us see how this happens.

We have an experience. Certain spots of light affect the cells in the retina of our eye. A complex series of mappings occurs. Nerve impulses travel from the retinal cells along the optic nerve to the occipital lobe of our brain and the patterns of excitation are mapped upon it. From there other series of nerve impulses are initiated and travel to our association areas, where our past experiences of similar nature are stored. Other impulses travel to the speech area and still others to the muscles of our mouth, to our tongue, lips, and vocal cords, and we form the sounds "I see a dog."

An altogether different sequence of events happens inside our neighbor who hears this remark. The sounds are mapped on his eardrum. The vibrations of the drum are mapped on the vibrations of the ossicles in the middle ear, then on the fluid in the inner ear as waves, then on impulses of the auditory nerve to an area in the parietal lobe of the brain, also to the speech association areas and to other association areas where all *his* experiences with dogs are stored. It is those experiences of *his* that he draws on to form a "mental image" which resembles somehow the experience of seeing a dog.

Think how complicated the process is and how many different things can go wrong with it. Think also how imperfect this sort of communication is compared with the electromagnetic transmission of sounds. The noises "I see a dog" do not even approach our actual experience of seeing a dog. The dog may be a St. Bernard or a Chihuahua; he might be sleeping, running, or walking on his hind legs. "I see a dog" tells nothing of that. True, one can say a great deal more, *but one can never tell all one sees.* Now consider what happens to our neighbor. The images he invokes in response to the information we give him depend not only on the information we give him, but also on the way he translates it *in terms of his own past experiences.* If he has never seen a dog, even the best description will not make him see a reasonable facsimile of a dog in his mind's eye when he hears our remarks.

I am not trying to point out the ineffectiveness of language as a means of communication. On the contrary, it seems marvelous that, inaccurate and incomplete as the mappings involved in language communication are, we nevertheless do succeed to a certain extent in communicating with each other. We pass the salt at the table. We tell the events of the day. Somehow Dickens succeeds in making us have vicarious experiences of child labor conditions in an English canning factory in the 1840's. Shakespeare can almost make us feel as if we had murdered somebody; and after reading Dostoevski we think we know how it feels to converse with the devil, even though we may be convinced that there is no such person.

Then there is science. The Japanese biologist communicates to his French colleague the innermost secrets of heredity. He tells him that he has isolated a "gene locus" in the second chromosome of a fruit fly responsible for a certain mutation, and the Frenchman verifies and extends his results. Newton has concentrated his description of the universe into four sentences. These four sentences and a few observations enable the astronomers to come to perfect agreement on when the eclipses are going to occur during the next several centuries. Not only do the astronomers agree with one another, but their predictions agree with observation.

Of course, men use language also in another way.

American newspapers insist that the United States is a democracy and that the Soviet Union is a tyranny. The Soviet jurist Vyshinsky in his book on Soviet law declares that the Soviet Union is a "million times more democratic" than the most democratic of the "bourgeois" countries. Who is right? Who is wrong? Instead of asking such a question, let us see this verbal fight in terms of a communication process. Are the Americans and the Russians communicating when they call their respective countries "democracies" and their neighbors' countries "tyrannies"?

How does the conviction "United States is a democracy" arise? To begin with, this conviction is implied in the Constitution, where it is stated that the power of government of the United States resides in the elected representatives of the people. The Russians too have a constitution, where it is stated that the power of government resides in the elected representatives of the people. Democracy is implied in many other aspects of American life, frequent election, unrestricted criticism of government officials and of the party in power, free education, frequent examples of "successful" careers, etc., etc. The Russian also has many of these things to show. Elections are also frequent. Government officials are not only criticized but often actually "purged," educational opportunities are widespread, and so are "successful" careers (from lathe worker to factory director, from peasant to party functionary, etc.).

"But," says the American newspaper editor, "this is only sham. You may have elections, but there is only one list of candidates to choose from. Your successful careers depend not only on ability but also to a great extent on conformity to the party line, etc., etc."

"On the contrary," says the Russian journalist, "it is your democracy that is a sham. You have two parties, but they both represent the capitalists. You disfranchise many of your people because of the color of their skin. Your successful careers are often the rewards not of public service but of unscrupulous methods and profiteering at the expense of other people's misery, etc., etc."

Let us consider this argument about democracy as a discussion in good faith, not as a camouflage for "I am afraid of you and I hate you." Why do such arguments fail to effect agreement? Inasmuch as they contain no value judgments, they seem to be built on assertions about things. The controversy is not about which country is "better" or more "moral" (such a controversy would be about the speakers, not about the countries), but about which is the more "democratic." Such an argument is an attempt to reduce a controversy about values into a more objective discussion, presumably about "facts." We have seen cases where resolution of controversies becomes easy once the argument is reduced to questions of fact and facts are produced (see Chapter 1). Here the opponents apparently agree on basic "values" (democracy is good). They try to be objective. They try to cite only facts. Still they get nowhere. The discussion invariably degenerates into a certain pattern:

"We have achieved universal literacy."

"Ah, but you are told what to read. Now, *we* have freedom of expression."

"Ah, but most of your press is controlled by monopoly interests. *We* have *n*-tupled our production."

"By using forced labor. We still have the world's highest standard of living."

"And lynchings."

Like any other mechanism, communication fails if its workings are poorly understood. Language is perhaps the oldest of human inventions. Actually it is quaint to call it an invention. In doing so, we follow the picturesque usage of some biologists who sometimes call such things as sexual reproduction and binocular vision "inventions." These inventions were never planned, designed, or patented. They just grew. Their users usually have not the slightest idea of how they work. Language too is such an "invention." It is peculiar to our species. For thousands of years we have used it just as we have used our digestive tract, all but unaware of its existence.

Just as to understand the malfunctioning of the digestive tract we must understand its structure and functioning, so in order to understand the failure of language as a means of communication we should study its structure and working. This is not an easy task. It is more difficult than to understand the structure and working of the most complex piece of machinery ever designed by man.

And it is probably much more important.

Semantics, a comparatively new science, is devoted, among other things, to the study of the functions and malfunctions of language.

Why It Is Important to Study Semantics

We have seen examples of language at its best: great literature, which enables people of different cultures and eras to "relive" the experiences described by authors; and the language of science, which enables people of even wider cultural differences to come to perfect agreement concerning the workings of the world. We have also seen examples of language at its worst: debased growls, masquerading as assertions about things, largely prevalent in the accusations that proponents of rival political doctrines hurl at each other.

Bad use of language usually leads to unresolved controversies.

Unresolved controversies are always a waste of time and often lead to destructive conflicts.

To resolve controversies, there must be a desire to agree.

A desire to agree arises if we become concerned with truth.

Language

The concern with truth involves "symbolic experience," hence language.

It also involves the question of the source of knowledge.

Agreement might be effected if it were understood that experience is the only ultimate source of knowledge.

But experience is not transmissible as such. It is transmissible only through the medium of language, that is, through communication.

Malfunctioning of language often results from our ignorance concerning its structure and function.

Semantics is concerned with the effective function of language and, incidentally, with its structure, since the latter sheds light on the former.

If experience is to be transmitted by language, then language must be the carrier of *something* significant.

To that something we give the name "meaning."

CHAPTER 7

What Do You Mean?

Student: Yet in the word must some idea be.
Mephistopheles: Of course! But only shun too oversharp a tension,
For just where fails the comprehension,
A word steps promptly in as deputy.

Goethe, *Faust*

Let us return to our two patriots arguing about the respective merits of their countries. We are dealing with Jones and Ivanov, discussing U.S.A. and U.S.S.R., as many Joneses and many Ivanovs actually did in Teheran, Berlin, Fairbanks, Poltava, wherever they met and whenever an interpreter turned up.

As long as they are saying, "My country is a better place to live in than yours," they are making value judgments, talking about themselves. They can, of course, agree to disagree by recognizing the fact that they are not talking about their countries at all. But although it is easy to agree to disagree about caviar and remain friends, it is not so easy to disagree about a "way of life" and remain friends. "Ways of life" have a way of spreading and their spreading invites resistance. Thus, each of our friends wishes to make the other "see the light."

"My country is a democracy," says Jones, "and yours is a dictatorship."

"On the contrary," counters Ivanov.

What Do You Mean?

As they are saying it, the discussion seems to be on the hopeless 'tis-'tain't level. Yet, as we have seen in the preceding chapter, there *is* an area of agreement. Both Ivanov and Jones believe that "democracy" makes a country good to live in and its ideals worth while to defend.

If it were possible for each of them to "prove" to the other that his country has some aspects of "democracy," they would have to agree that there are at least some good things in the ways of life of both. But the potentialities for agreement are not realized, because "proofs" are rejected *in toto* by each opponent.

"Ours is the *real* democracy; yours is a sham one," each of them says.

They are not communicating, because the experiences that have led to the word "democracy" for Jones are not similar to the experiences that have led to that word for Ivanov. The words are the same, but their meanings are different. The agreement on the principle "Democracy makes a country good to live in" is only a *verbal* agreement. For Jones "democracy" means the two-party system, Fourth of July speeches, stories of newsboys becoming millionaires, Town Hall meetings, informality, hot dogs, trailer camps, soapboxes, the Inquiring Reporter. For Ivanov "democracy" means the one-party system, full employment, social security, stories of peasant boys becoming engineers, aviators, and concert violinists, shop meetings, May Day parades, quick action by the state against individuals who become rich by illegitimate means (by means illegitimate for Ivanov but legitimate for Jones), and the line of people in Red Square waiting to see the embalmed body of Lenin.

Even without studying semantics, Jones and Ivanov may still take another step toward agreement. Each may ask the other to *define* democracy. But here other pitfalls await them. They may think they agree on a definition "Democracy is a form of gov-

51

ernment where the people rule." But again this agreement is only verbal. The experiences that Jones summarizes in the expression "the people rule," are different from those which Ivanov summarizes by the same words.

For thousands of years philosophers have inquired into the "real" meanings of words, with no agreement to show for their efforts. From the semantic point of view, to inquire into the *real* meaning of any word, whether democracy or tyranny, friendship or virtue, taxation or education, is senseless.

Take the word "rot." To a German it means "red," to a Russian "mouth," and to us you know what. How good a philosopher do you have to be to discover the "real" meaning of "rot"?

One may object to this example, since there is nothing remarkable in the fact that a similar sound may have different meanings in different languages.

Take, then, the word "rod," and consider what it means to a land surveyor and what it means to a gangster, both presumably speaking English. Words do have a variety of sometimes unrelated meanings, and these are not inherent in the words themselves but in their *usage*. Usage depends on the experiences associated with the *use* of words. The various meanings of a word may overlap in spots. But it is no less important to know that other areas of their meanings may be far apart.

There is a mistaken belief that the etymology (ancestry) of a word is somehow a key to its "real" meaning.

Some time ago the Ukrainian delegate to the United Nations charged the government of Greece with "antidemocratic" motives in wanting to demilitarize the Bulgarian border. The Greek undersecretary of foreign affairs replied:

"Democracy is a Greek word, and Greece knows better than anyone else how to interpret it."

Sigmund Freud once pointed out in a lecture on hysteria that men as well as women were often subject to its symptoms. A distinguished Viennese professor upon hearing this walked angrily out of the hall.

"Never have I heard such nonsense," he fussed. "Men subject to hysteria! Why the very word 'hysteria' is derived from the Greek word for *womb!*"

Both the Greek diplomat and the Viennese professor were making the same common mistake: they were confusing words with the things to which words are supposed to refer.

Words are invented by human beings, and their meanings are attributed to them by persons. These meanings arise out of experience. Different sets of experiences may map on the same word.

Definitions of Definitions

How, then, can the meaning of a word be made clear? Obviously by indicating the experiences associated with it. But how do we communicate experiences? By words. Are we in a vicious circle? It looks serious, but there may be a way out.

The question "What do you mean?" asks for the meaning of some words or expressions you are using. Meaning is associated with experience. So actually the question "What do you mean?" is a request to share the experiences associated with the words you are using. In answer to such a request, a definition is usually made.

We shall examine several types of definitions and gauge their usefulness from the standpoint of sharing experience.

1. *Defining a word by giving a synonym.*

Pocket dictionaries are full of such definitions. Asked to define "man" a pocket dictionary will often tell you that a "man" is a "human being."

2. *Making a definition by classification.*

Such definitions haunt the classroom. Pupils who can rattle off "Autocracy is a form of government in which power is con-

53

centrated in the hands of one man" and "Capitalism is an economic system based on competition and free enterprise" are most likely to get an A in civics. In the days of Aristotle (about 350 B.C.), "man" was often defined as a "rational animal," also a definition by classification. Such definitions tell first what sort of thing the word you are defining refers to (capitalism is a sort of economic system; man is a sort of animal); then it tells how to distinguish the *special* thing the word refers to (not *any* kind of economic system, but one based on competition and free enterprise; not *any* kind of animal, but a rational animal).

3. *Defining a word by enumerating words to which it refers collectively* (definition by enumeration).

Spices are cinnamon, cloves, paprika, ginger, and such.

The kings of the house of Stuart were James I, Charles I, Charles II, and James II.

4. *Defining by exhibiting an example.*

That is the way Robinson Crusoe taught English to Friday. He would point to a hairy animal and say "goat," to the strange object he carried and say "umbrella," etc. Friday learned fast. Children also learn to speak this way.

5. *The Operational Definition.*

Such definitions are commonly used in modern science. A physicist asked to define, say, the "Joule-Thompson effect" will *usually describe the experiments*, in which this effect can be *observed*. A more homely example of an operational definition can be found in the *recipe*.

An operational definition tells *what to do* in order to experience or to recognize the thing to which the word defined refers.

Now let us see how the different kinds of definition serve their purpose. We recall that a definition is used to answer the question "What do you mean?"—a request to *share experience*.

What Do You Mean?

Definition by synonym is useful only if the synonym is closer to our experiences than the word defined. Sometimes this is the case. People for whom "abdomen" is just a noise, may know very well what "belly" stands for. But the opposite situation is rare.

If you have used pocket dictionaries a great deal, where words are defined by synonyms, you must have experienced the disappointment of finding a synonym that means no more to you than the word you have looked up. The disappointment may grow into a minor frustration if you look up the synonym only to find it defined by the original "sticker."

Definitions by classification are more often useful than definitions by synonym. Their usefulness depends on the familiarity of the person who asks for the definition with the *class* of things into which the word defined is placed. For instance, Jones can explain the grapefruit to Ivanov, who may never have seen one, by such a definition.

"A grapefruit is a citrus fruit, more sour than an orange and less sour than a lemon, larger than both, and canary yellow."

Ivanov has eaten both lemons and oranges. He can form at least some idea of what a grapefruit is like. The shortcomings of a definition by classification is that it does not *necessarily* bring the word defined closer to experience.

A Jabberwock can be defined by "classifying" it.

"A Jabberwock is an animal with 'jaws that bite and claws that snatch.'" But the definition does not bring us any closer to an actual experience with a Jabberwock.

Similarly, one can define anything one pleases by stringing words together in such a way as to make it appear that one is clarifying meaning. Here are a few examples. It is easy to invent them.

"An irresistible force is a causative agency, able to overcome all obstacles."

"The First Cause is that event which was preceded by no other."

"The Good is what all things aim at."

"The devil is a being who is responsible for the existence of evil."

"Love is that affection which, being compounded of animal desire, esteem, and benevolence, becomes the bond of attachment and union between individuals of the different sexes, and makes them enjoy in the society of each other a species of happiness which they experience nowhere else."

Definitions which by their sentence structure seem to be clarifying something, but actually are not, resemble useless patent medicines. The harm of patent medicines is often not in themselves but in that the addicts keep hoping they will be helped and delay seeking competent advice and effective measures. Similarly, the addicts of definitions by classification (Aristotelian definitions) are often pedantic in "defining their terms" without realizing the futility of such definitions.

Definitions by enumeration are useful in defining classes of things if the names of the members of the class defined are closer to experience than the class itself. A person may not know to what the Pentateuch refers, but he may be familiar with Genesis, Exodus, Leviticus, Numbers, and Deuteronomy. He may have seen frogs, newts, and salamanders, but he may not know that biologists refer to all of them collectively as amphibia.

As a rule, definitions by enumeration do carry words closer to experience, because terms referring to collections of events are less directly connected with experience than the events themselves. We have used this sort of definition above when we defined Jones's democracy by Town Hall meetings, etc., and Ivanov's democracy by May Day parades, etc.

The weak spot in this sort of definition is that some words seem to refer not to classes, as, for example, the sun, and some classes are too large to enumerate. If I wanted to define "man" by enumeration, I would have to put down some two billion names, a fourth of them Chinese, a difficult and rather useless task. Fortunately, in some cases only a few examples are needed to make the meaning of the class clear. An "etc." placed at the end of such a partial list is a reminder that the class has not been exhausted.

A great advantage in making definitions by *exhibiting an example* is that one cannot define fictions that way. Just try to define Jabberwock or the First Cause by pointing to something and see how sticking to definition by exhibiting an example protects you from believing in ghosts. However, this advantage becomes a disadvantage when one wishes to define something which is not immediately at hand or something more abstract than objects to which one can point. Jonathan Swift made great fun of definition by example. He describes in his satire, *Gulliver's Travels*, how the academicians of Lagado decided to do away with spoken language altogether, arguing that

. . . since the words are only names for things, it would be convenient for all men to carry about them such things as were necessary to express the particular business they are to discourse on . . .

Accordingly, says Swift, the learned men of Lagado

adhere to the new scheme of expressing themselves by things, which hath only this inconvenience attending it, that if a man's business be very great, and of various kinds, he must be obliged in proportion to carry a greater bundle of things upon his back, unless he can afford one or two strong servants to attend him.

The great value of making a definition by exhibiting an example is that it does bridge the gap between words and experience. This, in fact, is the only purpose of definition. Definition by synonym and definition by classification may indirectly bridge this

57

gap if the words used in the definition are closer to experience than the words defined. But this is not necessarily so. In the case of definition by example it is *necessarily* so, because what you exhibit is *not* a word. Still a difficulty remains, quite aside from Swift's objections, to this kind of definition. Many words refer to real things, and these may not be at hand to point to, or one may not point to them at all. Here are a few examples:

electric current	hydrogen
standard deviation	habeas corpus
the French language	mumps
acrophobia	sonata
chiaroscuro	taxes

The *operational definition* succeeds most effectively in connecting such *abstract* words with experience.

In discussing operational definitions of abstract physical concepts, Philipp Frank says:

These sentences [operational definitions] contain the abstract words of the physical principles like "current" . . . also the words of the everyday English language. Obviously, they contain words like "wire" and other words which describe the apparatus by which the intensity of a current is actually measured.[1]

Note how the operational definition works. One cannot point to an ampere of electric current (the most one could point at would be the wire that carries it). But one does not dodge the issue by defining a word with other words without bothering to determine whether they are any closer to experience. One gives a set of *directions*, in words, to be sure, but words almost certainly closer to experience than the word defined (wire, magnet, etc.). If one follows these directions, one has the experience summarized by the words "one ampere of electric current."

[1] Philipp Frank, "Science Teaching and the Humanities."

58

What Do You Mean?

Sometimes a definition that sounds like an Aristotelian one performs the job of an operational definition. If I say "Acrophobia is a mental disturbance characterized by a fear of high places" I seem to be making an Aristotelian definition. But it can easily be translated into an operational one: "Question a great many people on how they feel about high places, and you will find that a certain percentage of them will declare that they are 'afraid' of high places. Furthermore, if such a person happens to be on a roof or a mountaintop, he usually exhibits a quickening of heart beat and expresses a desire to get down. Such people are said to suffer from acrophobia."

Let us see what happens when we apply an operational definition to a fiction. A vampire, for example, can be defined by a good Aristotelian definition: "A vampire is a person who habitually sucks other people's blood." If we attempted to translate this definition into an operational one, we would have to say something like this: "Have a great many persons watched at night, and you will find that some go abroad and suck blood out of sleeping people, usually from a small lesion in the neck. Such people are called vampires." This operational definition is formally as good as the one of acrophobia except for one thing: you will probably not find any people with blood-sucking habits.

So it appears from the operations prescribed by the operational definition that if any "meaning" is to be attached to the word "vampire," it cannot refer to a person (since no such persons are observed). The operations have revealed that the Aristotelian definition of a "vampire," although formally flawless, is meaningless.

Practically all operational definitions say in fact "Do so-and-so, and you will find . . ." They *predict* an experience. They may also be called definitions by prediction.

In modern semantic literature, definitions by synonym and by classification are often called "intensional definitions," while those by enumeration, example, and operation are called "extensional definitions." From the standpoint of bridging the gap between words and experiences, extensional definitions are to be preferred. As a matter of fact, if that gap is bridged at all, somewhere ·a definition by example or an operational definition is involved.

The definition by example need not involve language at all. The syntactic structure of an operational definition involves an imperative form of a verb (do so-an-so) and a predictive assertion, (you will find . . .). This structure is sometimes clumsy and may be discarded for the elegant structure of the Aristotelian definition (a so-an-so is a such-and-such which is characterized by a this-and-that); but if a definition is to serve its purpose (sharing experience), an indication of experience must be involved.

"The stockyards are an area where animals are processed into meat" is a short, elegant definition of the stockyards. But the *reality* of the stockyards is implied in another, clumsier definition, which I would give to a visitor in Chicago if I wanted to bring the stockyards within the range of his experience.

"Take the Halsted Street car to 39th St., etc. . . ."

"Hell is the place where the wicked go when they die" also looks like a definition. But when you try to translate it into operational terms you will immediately get into difficulties. You will be at a loss to indicate a proper procedure in order to experience hell.

Just as assertions about things must be traced to the experiences that gave rise to them, the meanings of words must also be traced in this way.

Words which fail to show an ancestry of experience may nevertheless be well "defined" by intensional definitions, that is, by other words. But they usually cannot be defined by extensional definitions, especially by exhibiting an example and by the operational definition, because these, by their very nature, imply connection with experience.

Extensional definitions, therefore, especially the operational ones, are more generally valuable for the purpose for which definitions are intended—to bridge the gap between words and experience.

An operational definition can do everything all the others can do and often more. In some cases only an operational definition can bridge the gap between words and experience. Its drawback is that grammatically it is not very elegant. Therefore, if one is concerned with literary style, one might avoid the operational definition; but if one is concerned with communicating meaning, one should use it at the slightest indication that the meaning is otherwise not clear.

Granted that a way can be found to map experience on language, how can the infinite variety of experience to which we are subject be mapped on a language of only a few thousand words, to which the vocabulary of most people is limited?

CHAPTER 8

Abstracting

M and N, two friends of mine, currently employed as subjects in the Century Psychophysical Laboratories, often met at the Simian Club and talked shop. As they smoked their cigars and swung leisurely on two adjacent ropes (M and N are chimpanzees), they discussed mainly the personnel—the keepers, the professors, the assistants, etc.

"Is it stupidity or mischief," wondered M, "that inspires those inane games?"

N pondered the question awhile, punctuating his thoughts with puffs of smoke.

"The absence of a serious purpose in life," he said, "may well be responsible for foolish or mischievous behavior. The keeper does not play those silly games. The keeper has important functions to perform. He brings the food, cleans the cages, rigs up the swings. Even the assistants sometimes pitch in and do some useful work. But the professor is superfluous. Let him vanish tomorrow, and life in these laboratories will go on as it has been going on ever since I remember myself. No one will miss him. He probably wishes to assert himself in some way, prove his importance. So he makes a bid for attention by inventing games to play with us."

"It is pathetic and touching in a way," said M. "I can't say I am not rather fond of the little man. He is so much less ugly than the others. At times he looks almost simian. I humor him."

Abstracting

"So do I. The latest game seems to be to hide my food in one of several boxes. First I thought the idea was to tease me, make me go through several boxes before I found the food. So I pretended to be perplexed and looked for it as long as possible, although it was quite evident which box contained the food. But then I found that he was even more pleased when I got to the food quickly, so I started going directly to the right box. He seems delighted. He evidently attributes my successes to my superior intelligence. If he only knew how simple it is to guess where the food is hidden! I have discovered a fundamental law of nature—"

"Yes, yes," M interrupted excitedly, "I too have discovered this law. You know the professor plays the identical game with me. I made some bad guesses a few times. But then the Truth of that great Law suddenly flashed on me. From then on it was so easy. The box with the food always has the Right Marking on it. The empty ones have the Wrong Markings. One has only to go to the box with the Right Marking, and there is the food!"

"Of course," N said.

At this moment the keeper came in with two boxes and announced lunch. One box was marked with a yellow triangle, and the other with a green circle. M jumped for the box with the triangle, and N for the one with the circle. Then they stopped abruptly and looked at each other in silent surprise.

"What are you doing?" M finally said. "There is no food there. The food is in *this* box."

"Now, M, you yourself told me that you discovered the Law of Nature. Boxes containing food are marked with a *circle*."

"What are you talking about? What's a circle?"

"Don't you know what a circle is? Look, those swinging rings are circles. The professor's eyeglasses are circles. And this mark on the box is a circle. It is a Law of Nature that boxes marked with circles contain food. Look at the mark on the other box. That's a triangle. I know all about those things. Not only does it mean an empty box, but, I remember now, one can get a shock by tampering with boxes marked with triangles. No, *sir*! You won't get me to touch *that* thing."

"Triangles, circles!" M scoffed. "That is not what I see. I see that your box is marked *green*. It's the boxes marked with green that give you shocks. Look at my mark. It's yellow. This means food. Boxes with yellow on them always contain food. It is a Law of Nature that I myself have discovered."

While they are deciding the question, let us leave them for a while and consider the problem in a more general context.

N was right within the limit of his experience, and M was right within the limit of hers. They were both wrong, of course, in believing that they had discovered natural laws. But perhaps in view of their long association with professors, we shall forgive them this mistake. Let us see how M and N came by their opinions about boxes and their markings.

Both were "conditioned" by the professor. It is supposed that the processes in the various nervous systems have some common pattern. The pattern of the processes in M and N's nervous systems may be simpler but not too different in principle from certain analogous patterns in the professor's nervous system. So the professor believed he might find out something about such patterns by observing behavior thought to be the result of processes called *abstracting*.

In order to do so, he invented a "game" that he played with N. He would present him with several boxes, one of which contained N's lunch. The boxes were marked in different ways, but always the "right" one was marked with a circle. It might have been a large one or a small one, red, green, yellow, or purple, but always a circle. On the other hand, boxes marked with triangles (no matter of what color or size or in what position) gave N electric shocks whenever he touched them. Soon N learned to avoid any box with a triangle on it and to open boldly any box marked with a circle. To him circle on the box meant food, triangle meant shock, while the colors on the markings meant *nothing at all.* N learned to *abstract*, that is, to perceive *only those properties which were of interest to him.* M also learned to abstract. But she was so conditioned that shapes did not mean anything to her, but color meant the difference between an electric shock and a lunch.

When M saw the yellow triangle on one of the boxes, she saw *yellow*, not a triangle; when she saw a green circle, she saw *green* not the circle, and she drew her "conclusions" on the basis of what part these colors played in her past experience. N, when he saw the yellow triangle, saw the *triangle*, not that it was yellow, and in the green circle he saw a *circle*, not that it was green. Being in different experimental groups, M and N learned to abstract different properties from the markings on the boxes. If they had not met to compare notes, each would have gone on thinking that he or she had discovered a "fundamental law of nature." If they were human, each would consider the behavior of the other "irrational," unless they were acquainted with the nature of abstracting. But, being simian, they could not concentrate very long on an intellectual discussion. They soon got tired and opened both boxes, saying "Hang the theories."

But the professor pondered deeply on the results of his experiments and published his findings in a learned journal.

"Different monkeys," he concluded, "may abstract in different ways."

The practice of amateur psychology requires no license. Here is an experiment you can easily perform on unsuspecting friends.

They must be really unsuspecting, otherwise the experiment will not succeed.

Show the subject four playing cards at a time, two of which are red pictures and two black nonpictures. Each time tell him you have one of the two pairs in mind and let him try to guess which. Each time tell him whether his guess is right or wrong. Continue until he *catches on* that you are consistently choosing the red pictures. Do not tell him this; just correct his guesses and let him draw his own conclusions. It is important that the experiment be carried out in silence as far as possible. Don't let the subject verbalize his guesses; just let him point. After he has made several correct guesses in a row (you will see that he catches on quickly), present him with two *red nonpictures* and two *black pictures*. See how he guesses. Does he guess the red nonpictures because they are *red* or the black pictures because they are *pictures?*

If you like this sort of amusement, try the experiment on as many of your friends as will submit to it and tabulate your results. How many are "picture conscious"? How many are "color conscious"? Try the experiment with objects other than playing cards; for example, with colored pieces of paper cut in different shapes. If you have noted a great predominance of picture consciousness over color consciousness in the playing card experiments, see if you get a greater percentage of color consciousness when pieces of colored paper are used instead of playing cards.

Abstracting as a Selecting Process

At the end of the preceding chapter, we asked how it was possible to communicate by only a few thousand words the endless variety of experience to which we are subjected. Abstracting is the mechanism that makes this possible.

Abstracting is a *selecting process*. Each time you see a dog, the experience is different. No two dogs are the same. Moreover, no dog is the same at two different times. But your nervous system selects certain characteristics which are mapped on the word "dog." You can see the importance of being able to abstract if you substitute "tiger" for "dog." For the primitive man in the jungle it was probably of little importance how one tiger differed from another. When one man saw a tiger, it was necessary to communicate just that and to communicate it quickly.

For our purposes it is important to know that in different circumstances different people will abstract different things. Hence the same word never means quite the same thing to two different people. The meaning of a word (the totality of experience mapped upon it) is in the person who uses it (either in transmitting or in receiving experience), not in the word itself. This is the reason Jones and Ivanov, even if they sincerely desire it, find it so difficult to agree on the "meaning" of "democracy" (see Chapter 7).

Animals can communicate with each other to a certain extent. Their "languages" are much simpler than ours; consequently, they cannot do as much with them, nor can as many things go wrong with their languages. Many birds can say "danger," and their cry is sufficient to raise the whole flock into the air. But no bird can say "The end of the world will come in thirty days" and have the flock neglect its normal occupations waiting for this to happen. Lacking a language, the beavers cannot invent engines to build their dams more efficiently, but neither can they fight a war among themselves over the successor to the throne of Spain, over the "freedom of the seas," or over the allegiance to the Pope.

The great advantage of human (symbol) languages over other animal (signal) languages is that our symbols are able to evoke images of the things they stand for even in the absence of those things.[1] Moreover, the images can be *manipulated*. This manipula-

---

[1] A seemingly genuine case of symbol comprehension in a dog has been reported by Gustav Eckstein in *Science*, May 13, 1949. Topper, an English setter, gave proof of understanding the abstraction "table" in the following way: He

tion makes possible the communication of *conditional* assertions, which no other animal can make.

"If you do this, that will happen."

Such an assertion can give you the result of "this" *even if you are not doing this.* Thus it is possible to transmit experience long after it has been completed. But it is also possible to give out as experience something that has never occurred or to predict experience that will never occur. No animal except man can lie.[2]

Lying taken in its broadest sense does not necessarily involve an intent to deceive. Men lie unwittingly when they transmit information which at some stage was not born legitimately of experience. And even the "truest" sort of assertion is a dilute solution of certain constant characteristics from a complex variety of experience and therefore never tells "all about it." No one can tell the whole truth.

Abstracting is a mechanism by which an infinite variety of experience can be mapped on short noises (words). The mapping is accomplished by selecting only a few characteristics of the experience.

Different persons will select different things in their experience of the same event.

---

had been taught to react to the words "Table, Topper" by carrying the bone he was gnawing under the kitchen table. This in itself is no proof of symbol comprehension, since "table" might be only a signal to crawl under a *particular* table. However, Topper demonstrated his ability to *generalize* the notion "table" by obeying the command when in the presence of *other* tables. Then one day at a picnic his mistress said "Table, Topper" *when there was no table in sight.* Yet Topper *sought out* an old picnic table some distance away (which he might have seen before and remembered) and carried his bone there. Topper is probably a canine genius, and his case should not be considered typical.

[2] We use "lying" in such a way as to exonerate the opossum's playing dead. The opossum is not really communicating with his enemy; therefore, he is not "lying." If a bird gave a warning cry when it was *not* frightened, this would be lying. As far as we know, this does not occur.

Abstracting

Thus we cannot be sure that two different persons will "verbalize" the same event in the same way.

Nor can we be sure that two different persons will interpret the same verbalization in the same way, because the retranslation of words into (past) experience depends on that experience.

Science is an attempt to systematize abstracting of experience. Where science has been most successful in systematizing abstracting from experience, there has been the greatest agreement between scientists. In the most successful areas of science (physics, for example) a tremendous amount of past experience can be described and an almost equally tremendous amount of *future* experience predicted by just a few symbols, the mathematical descriptions of physical laws.

We should now inquire how we can systematize abstracting, keeping in mind that an efficient way of abstracting (as in science) goes together with the greatest amount of agreement.

CHAPTER 9

Classification, Learning, Symbolization

CLASSIFYING

Because we can abstract we can classify. To classify means to recognize that certain things belong "together." They are "alike" in some respects and can be referred to collectively.

One of the laws of classification as taught in formal logic is that the larger the class of objects one is talking about the less one can say about *all* its members.

Let us start with a large collection, say all the people in the world (over two thousand million people). There is not much we can say about every person in the world. We can say some things, for example, "Every person in this world has one head." Now, if we add to the number of things we say about people, we decrease the number of people we can say it about. If, for example, we choose to say "Every person in our collection has one head and lives in the United States," we have cut down our collection to only about one hundred forty millions. If we add "and is a female," we again cut the number to about seventy millions. If we add "blonde," we reduce it still further, etc. We can keep adding characteristics until only one person in the world will satisfy them, or we can give so many characteristics that no person will satisfy them all.

It is doubtful that any qualified applicant will respond to an advertisement such as this:

"Wanted: young man between the ages of 23 and 24, who can

speak Bengali, plays the xylophone, has twin maiden aunts, and whose birthday falls on February 29."

We have *overdefined* our class.

The general rule is that the more things we specify about a collection the less members it has, and vice versa. The more we say the less we are talking about.

We will again refer to this rule of classification in Chapter 10. But what interests the semanticist (as distinguished from the logician) is primarily not such rules, but the mechanics and the implications of classification. *How* do we classify? We have seen that different people abstract different characteristics. How does this affect experience and communication?

Human beings are able to classify their experiences quickly on the basis of verbalizations they make about them. They can also *change* the basis of classification, but this usually involves a change in a language habit. So we find variations of flexibility in people's classification habits. As usual, in science, where words are constantly put to a test against experience, these classification habits are flexible; in those areas of human activity where language habits are frozen, where words are treated as things, these classification habits are rigid. In those rigid areas controversies are seldom resolved and often lead to conflict.

It is true that all animals and even inanimate objects can "classify," but such classifications are more or less fixed, determined by comparatively rigid systems. We will begin our study of classification by describing a number of abstracting machines.

We will perform what the Germans are fond of calling a *gedankenexperiment*, that is, an imaginary experiment. This will save us the trouble of rigging up the apparatus. What is the good of such an experiment if the results are also imaginary? In general, we actually want to see the results of an experiment. For example, if we wish to know whether or not a bell will sound in a vacuum, it will not do just to imagine that we have placed a bell under a jar and pumped the air from under it. If we don't know the answer, we will not be any wiser by imagining such an experiment. But the purpose of a *gedankenexperiment* is not to discover new facts but to try to get some general idea from facts already known.

We already know that magnets attract iron and do not attract copper. We already know that metals sink in water and wood floats, and that in a centrifuge heavier particles are segregated, etc. We are going to perform this imaginary experiment not for the purpose of verifying these well-known facts, but to illustrate a relation between them, a relation which will yield a notion not included in any of the isolated phenomena. We are going to see a sort of abstracting in action. The abstractions will not be in the "minds" of scientists or chimpanzees but in inanimate objects, parts of our imaginary apparatus.

The objects will be a large collection of spheres and cubes of many kinds. Some will be wooden, some iron, some brass, some gold, some cork, some glass. Some will be one centimeter in diameter, some two centimeters, and so on to the largest ones, five centimeters in diameter. Some will be painted white, some black.

Now, in the first experiment we will imagine all our spheres and cubes in a basket mixed up at random. We introduce a large, powerful horseshoe magnet into our basket and see what we can catch. One can guess, of course, that all the iron ones will cling to the magnet and only the iron ones. Size and shape will not matter. If the magnet is powerful enough, it will lift even the heaviest iron cubes. Can we say that the magnet has abstracted the "property of ironness" from all the other properties of our cubes and spheres? Perhaps we can, but let us go on.

We now fill a bathtub and throw our cubes and spheres into the water. The gold ones, the iron ones, the brass ones, and the glass ones will sink to the bottom, but the wooden ones and the cork ones will all float. Size will not matter; color will not matter; even weight will not matter, since some of those which float (the large wooden ones) will weigh more than some of those which sink (the smaller glass ones). Only those will sink whose *specific gravity* is greater than that of water. Has the water in the tub abstracted specific gravity?

Now let us throw our cubes and spheres into a basket full of round holes, such that the spheres and cubes smaller than a certain size can fall through. Material will not matter; specific gravity won't; color won't. Size alone will matter and to some extent shape, since some cubes will not get through where the spheres of the same diameter will. Has the basket abstracted size and discriminated between shapes?

Now let us use a centrifuge. Only weight will matter. All the heavy ones, regardless of size, shape or color, will be separated from the light ones. Has the centrifuge abstracted weight?

Next let us put all our spheres and cubes on a smooth board and tilt it a trifle. All the spheres will start rolling, but the cubes will hold on a while longer. Has the inclined plane abstracted shape?

Put them all on a black cloth and dim the lights. You will see only the white ones. Put them on snow and stand some distance away; you will see only the black ones. Have your eyes abstracted color? Or was it the cloth and the snow that did the abstracting?

Actual abstracting, the kind done by our abstracting machines (brains), is a complex process, so complex that it is not too useful to call the simple selections illustrated in our experiment abstractions. However, it is often instructive to examine the simple in attempting to understand the complex.

We have seen how simple machines can, by abstracting certain characteristics of objects, *classify* them. This ability to classify is, of course, not an exclusive property of magnets, bathtubs, and

73

inclined planes. Living things classify the objects in the world about them in a way which helps keep them alive. Even such "simple" organisms as one-celled animals do it. By some mechanism as yet (1949) poorly understood, these animals without the aid of eyes, smell receptors, or nervous system, for that matter, can distinguish food particles from the countless similar bodies that they constantly encounter. Many species of these little animals can "tell" one strain of the species from many others as indicated by their mating processes.

If one examines more and more complicated organisms, one finds that their ability to classify becomes more and more extensive.

LEARNING TO CLASSIFY

Although the ability to classify seems to transcend the somewhat "fuzzy" boundary between the living and the nonliving, other properties of organisms which seem closely associated with this ability can be more accurately attributed exclusively to the living. This property is the ability to learn. As everyone knows, this ability is possessed by different animals in varying degrees. To be sure, some of the "lower" animals are believed to lack completely any learning ability.

A moment's reflection brings to light the great importance to the survival of the organism of these two abilities, the ability to classify and the ability to learn. Food must be distinguished from nonfood, water from dry land and air, enemies from mates. For an animal unable to abstract certain aspects of its environment (i.e., unable to classify) all the things surrounding it would be in the same class, the "outside"! Such an animal would have no basis for different kinds of behavior.

The ability to classify is of fundamental importance in making it possible for an organism to have some set of reactions necessary for the business of living in an environment. Therefore, this ability came first in the evolutionary development of organisms. Many classes of animals have remained at this stage of development. They classify, but they do not learn. *They have an innate repertoire of reactions.* As long as the environment does not present them with "surprising" situations, they "know" what to do. Any radical new change in their environment, however, finds them with no appropriate behavior in their set to cope with the changed situation. Some animals have gone further. They have not only acquired a complex set of behavior patterns appropriate to the particular environment in which they live, but have also developed the important ability to *change* this set. If changes in the environment make it necessary, they add new forms of behavior to their set or subtract old ones, if these forms of behavior become useless or harmful in the new situation. These animals have acquired the ability to *learn.*

Even simple animals can learn. An experiment shows rather neatly the extent of learning of which the earthworm is capable. The apparatus consists of a tube in the shape of a T, through which the worm can crawl so that at the top end of the stem he can choose to turn either to the left or to the right. A small electric battery is adjusted so as to give the worm a small shock at the end of one of the arms of the T-tube. A warm, moist chamber, as a reward for taking the correct turn, is provided at the end of the other arm. The worm has a choice: if he goes to the right, he gets a shock; if he goes to the left, he is comfortable. At first his movements are arbitrary. Sometimes he goes the wrong way and gets the punishment; at other times he goes the right way and gets the reward. But bye and bye he learns.

The trips to the right become less frequent, until the worm *always* turns to the left. Now the moist chamber and the battery are reversed. What was the correct turn becomes the wrong turn.

75

Slowly, painfully, after several hundreds of mistakes, the worm *relearns*. Now he always takes the right turn.[1]

We say the worm has "learned." What does it mean? We say the child has learned his multiplication table if he says "fifty-six" when someone asks "How much is seven times eight?" We say a dog has learned a trick when he lies down at the command "lie down." What have all these phenomena in common, if anything? Interesting as this question is, we cannot go into it at length because it would take us astray. We will have to leave the fascinating study of the mechanics of learning to the physiologists, psychologists, mathematical biophysicists, and other scientists who study the dynamics of the nervous system. We will merely observe the following fact that seems to underlie all learning: somehow an organism begins to react not directly to an event affecting it but to *some other event* associated with the main event *preceding* it. Thus our worm, even without training, would react negatively to an electric shock (shrink away from it) and positively to moist warm places (seek them). But after training he reacts to an entirely different situation, namely, the turn in the tube, to which he had been previously indifferent (as shown by his random turns). After conditioning he avoids the right turn (associated with the shock) and accepts the left turn (associated with the moist chamber).

Now perhaps we see the connection between the ability to learn and the number of things in the environment that the organism is able to classify. Previous to his "training" our worm could tell moist from dry, shock from nonshock. He was born with that "knowledge." But after graduating from a T-tube he knows more: he knows right from left. Right and left have acquired "meaning."

You can teach your dog to "understand" you. You will say "Fido, sit!" and Fido will sit. You can associate any signal with almost any act of a dog by a process called "conditioning." When

[1] This experiment was first performed by R. M. Yerkes in 1912.

the dog has learned to respond to a signal in the new way, he is exhibiting a "conditioned reflex." The classical experiments in this field were performed in Russia at the turn of the century by the great physiologist Ivan Pavlov and his students. Psychologists have been basing their work on the conclusions of those experiments ever since.

For us, the phenomenon of the conditioned reflex indicates what in all probability lies at the root of "meaning." Meaning in its most basic form is the association of one experience with another. One of the experiences may be a *noise*. Thus noises may become associated with experiences, specific noises with specific kinds of experience. We may be standing on the threshold of language.

LEARNING AND LANGUAGE

Now let us see what qualifications an animal must have in order to be able to learn to use a language (where language is defined as a way of transmitting experiences by the mapping process described in Chapter 6).

First, the animal must be able to make and distinguish a great many different kinds of noises (he must be able to articulate). It will not do to map *all* experiences on "arf!"

Second, the animal must possess an efficient learning apparatus. His "conditioning paths" must be numerous and must not interfere with one another.

Third, and most important, he must be able to associate not only words with experiences but words with *each other*. He must be able to understand words *in context*. The words must be not merely *signals* to him but symbols.

To illustrate the difference between signals and symbols,[2] we will again examine Fido's learning capacity. You can teach Fido to

[2] This is the more precise definition of "symbol" that was promised in Chapter 4.

77

recognize the name of a friend of yours. With many people in the room, you can say, "Fido, go to B," and Fido will go to B. Even in B's absence, you may get a rise out of Fido by mentioning B's name. You have no way of knowing whether Fido is actually "thinking" of B, but he behaves as if he might be. Now you can also teach Fido the "meaning" of "thief." Not your meaning, of course, in the sense that a thief is a person who violates the rights of private property, but Fido's meaning, in the sense that a thief is a person who should be barked at and chased. If you don't mind making a public nuisance of yourself and of ruining the reputation of your dog, you can demonstrate Fido's understanding of language by pointing to people on the street and calling them "thief." Fido will chase them.

But here is something you cannot teach Fido to do. *In B's absence*, you cannot convince Fido that "B is a thief," to the extent that Fido will chase B next time he sees him. Not that Fido has an unshakable faith in B's honesty. The trouble with Fido's understanding is that to him words are signals, not symbols. B is always B and elicits always the same responses: in his presence, he is to be approached when his name is mentioned; in his absence, a bark is in order. A thief also elicits a definite response: when master points at a man and says "thief," *that* man is to be chased. These "meanings" are fixed, independent, and constant. They cannot be combined in a new context, "B is a thief." Fido is *pre-Aristotelian*.

Some animals other than men have developed signal languages. But to our knowledge (1949) no animal except man has ever developed a symbol language. A nonhuman, if it communicates with another, can "talk" only about what is *here* and *now* and *actually taking place*. Humans can talk about events thousands of miles and thousands of years removed, and about things that are or are not true, or only potentially true. A nonhuman can say

78

"Danger!" But we can say "It is dangerous to drive from A-ville to B-ville over fifty miles per hour in wet weather, because the pavement is usually slippery then, unless it has been recently repaved." A nonhuman can say "Food!" But we can say "If you don't work today, you shan't eat tomorrow." A nonhuman can say, perhaps, "I love you." But we can say "If it were not for the fact that you and I are married to different people or if the folks in this town were not so gossip-loving, I would make love to you."

Not only can we talk about faraway things and of past, future, and conditional matters, but we can talk *to* people removed in both space and time. We still talk about what Aristotle said about ethics. And we leave things for the people of the forty-fifth century to worry about.

Just as learning increases the number of things an organism can classify, so symbolic language increases to a huge extent the number and the complexity of things an organism can learn.

An obvious function of language in accelerating the learning process is that it makes learning possible *without* direct experience. This is done by the communicative function of language. When you buy a gadget, you need not find out for yourself how it works. You read the directions.

But language performs another important function besides that of communicating experience. It is of immense help in solving problems where mental activity is involved. A series of experiments provides dramatic evidence of this function. The ability of rats and men to learn mazes has been compared. A maze is a twisting corridor with a number of choices of turns. If the rat takes the correct sequence of turns, it reaches a reward in the form of food. The number of runs a rat takes under various conditions to learn to make the correct turns without a mistake indicates its ability to learn the maze. Now, this maze-learning ability of rats has been compared to that of men (running pencils over maze puzzles), and the results were not flattering to our species. We did not do much better than the rats.

The big point in these experiments is that maze learning does not involve symbolization. We learn a maze by establishing a set of habits, and we are probably no better in establishing habits than rats. But we score much higher than all other animals where "figuring out" is required. That is where our language proves to be such a powerful tool. It is the same situation as in the case of a man with an ordinary hammer and a man with a steam hammer. The steam hammer has no advantage over the ordinary one in driving a nail into a beam, but it does have in driving the beam into the ground.

Not only do we tell each other through language about the world around us, but we also *tell ourselves* what we experience.[3]

We make a map of our experiences and then study the map. Sometimes we become so preoccupied with the map that we forget its symbolic nature and take it for the experiences themselves. We shall see the unfortunate consequences of this mistake in the succeeding chapters.

All organisms can classify.

Some organisms can *learn* to classify and thus learn to behave in new ways. They can cope better with changes in the environment. They can increase their repertoire of reactions.

Learning is accomplished by associating one experience with another. Certain experiences then become signals to react in a certain way that has been learned.

---

[3] "Communication reduces to the event, both commonplace and awesome of Mr. A. talking to Mr. B. And most commonplace and strange of all—possibly the most distinctively *human* occurrence to be found or imagined—is the case in which Mr. A. and Mr. B. are one and the same person: A man talking to himself." Wendell Johnson, "Speech and Personality," published in *Communication of Ideas*, Lyman Bryson, Editor.

Classification, Learning, Symbolization

For nonhumans, signals remain signals, always eliciting the same responses and effective only immediately and on the spot.

Humans have learned to manipulate the signals, making them symbols. Symbols acquire different meanings through their relations with other symbols: they acquire meaning in a *context*. Symbols can represent not only things and actions but also *relations*.

Such a system of symbols representing things, actions, and relations (a language) becomes a mechanism for mapping experience.

Such a mapping can be used to transmit experience (as in communication) or it can be *examined* as a substitute for direct experience (as in problem solving).

The effectiveness of transmitting experience and of solving problems (the "communicative" and "heuristic" functions of language), then, depends on how faithful a picture of the world our mapping gives us.

How good are our maps?

CHAPTER 10

Maps and Frameworks

In many libraries and museums you can see some curious maps: North Americas without any Canada, grotesquely distorted Europes, with the Volga River shown connecting the Caspian Sea with the Arctic Ocean, countries that don't look like themselves at all.

Turn to an ancient history book, and you may find maps of the world as Herodotus and other Greek scholars thought of it. Greece is shown in the center, big and fairly accurate. There is a strange-looking Italy, bits of Africa, Asia Minor, perhaps fairly good outlines of the Black Sea, and that is all; no Britain, no Scandinavia, no Far East, no New World. Around the disk representing a territory of some two thousand miles in diameter flows a narrow river labeled Oceanus. Beyond is the end of the world.

A few years ago someone jokingly published "The New Yorker's Map of the U.S." On this map Manhattan Island stretches along the east coast down to the Carolinas, with its streets and parks plainly shown. The West Coast is immediately west of Chicago. California is a town in the state of Hollywood. Most people laughed when they saw that map. Many people smile when they see the maps of the ancient scholars and the charts used by the sixteenth-century explorers. But they take the maps published in the *National Geographic* magazine seriously. Somehow they feel that those maps "look" right. On them "Cuba looks like Cuba, and Iceland looks like Iceland,"[1] and Ohio looks like Ohio. Yet how do people know what Ohio looks like?

A moment's reflection will reveal that it is not a matter of "looks." People have confidence in modern maps because they are convinced that modern mapmakers "know their business." If pressed further, they will say that modern maps "represent the territory more accurately, because they were made by accurate measurements."

What does it mean to "represent the territory accurately"? It means, I suppose, that the places shown on the map will be found on the territory, and the relations between them will somehow correspond to the relations between their images on the map. The relations we are particularly interested in are directions and distances. If A-ville is due east of B-ville, it will be directly to the right of B-ville on a good Mercator projection. If the distance between A-ville and B-ville is twice that between B-ville and C-ville, the map will show just that.

Ancient maps were not so good as the modern maps because the methods of measurement and surveying used in the old days were cruder than ours. But this is not all. Not only were the measurements that served as the basis for ancient maps crudely made; sometimes they were not made *at all*. The Volga River is shown connecting the Caspian Sea with the Arctic Ocean, not because the mapmaker had sailed up the river and reached the Arctic Ocean, but because he thought he *might*. The flat earth of the ancient Greek scholars is shown to have edges, not because someone had traveled "to the end of the earth" and had seen those edges, but because the scholars reasoned that all things must end somewhere, and so the earth too must have an end. Many of the ancient maps or parts of them showed not what their makers saw of the world

---

[1] Quoted from William F. Osgood's *Advanced Calculus*.

but what they *thought* about it. And usually it was not clear where experience ended and imagination began.

The American Automobile Association informs me that they keep a staff of men in all parts of the country constantly checking road maps against the territory they are supposed to represent. If the mileage between two towns says 17 miles on the map, they drive the distance to see whether it does amount to 17 miles. If they discover a detour, they report it. If they discover danger of landslides, they report it. If a new road is being built, they report it so that it can be included in a later issue. The A.A.A. people are proud of their skepticism in their own maps. Far from telling the members to have blind faith in those maps, because they were so carefully made, they tell people not to take the maps too seriously, but to come into their offices often and get the latest information on *how the maps lie*. It is this skepticism that makes the A.A.A. map service valuable for motorists.

Many maps used for serious purposes (navigation, weather predicting, etc.) get quickly out of date. For example, a navigator's chart shows so-called magnetic deviations which tell the navigator how much his magnetic compass is deceiving him. The compass needle hardly ever points directly north but usually several degrees off according to the idiosyncrasies of the earth's magnetic field. If the pilot knows how much the compass is wrong, he can make the necessary correction and be right. But the earth's magnetic field *won't stay put*. It keeps changing, so that the navigation chart is obsolete a few years after it is made. If you want to navigate accurately, there is nothing you can do with an old map except throw it away and get a new one. A weather map, showing the disposition of barometric pressures, is an even more striking example. It is obsolete a few *hours* after it is made, and is then useless. Even the physical maps, which show the outlines of continents, courses of rivers, and altitudes of elevations, become obsolete eventually (though it takes thousands of years).

Maps and Frameworks

No map contains all the information about the territory it represents. The road map we get at the gasoline station may show all the roads in the state, but it will not as a rule show latitude and longitude. A physical map goes into details about the topography of a country but is indifferent to political boundaries.

Furthermore, the scale of the map makes a big difference. The smaller the scale the less features will be shown. The map of our state may show every town of the state, but the map of the United States on the same-sized sheet of paper can show only the larger cities, and a map of the world may not show any.

We have noted four characteristics of maps.

1. *The accuracy of a map depends on the accuracy of the measurements that have gone into its making.*

2. *Even the best maps become obsolete sooner or later.*

3. *Different maps show different features.*

4. *The more territory a map covers the less it can say about it.*

Characteristics 3 and 4 remind us of the characteristics of abstracting which we discussed in Chapters 8 and 9, namely,

1. *Different people abstract different things.*

2. *In abstracting the characteristics of larger and larger classes less and less can be said about all the members of the class.*

In fact, maps are excellent examples of abstraction. Maps are also symbol systems, because the features of the map stand for something, and the relations between the symbols also are part of the map. Up stands for north, blue stands for water, so many inches for so many miles, etc.

Being meaningful symbols, maps can be used in communication, just like language. The reason the characters in *Treasure Island* fought over the possession of a certain map was because the map could be translated into a valuable communication from a pirate who had died long ago. Indeed maps are often more effective in communication than ordinary language. Think whether you would prefer to travel from Portland, Maine, to Portland, Oregon, on the basis of information given to you orally at the starting point or having in your possession an accurate map.

We are concerned with effectiveness of communication. Good maps bring about effective communication. Perhaps we might try to learn the principles of effective communication from the principles of sound mapmaking. Or perhaps we might learn something about the difficulties of communication from the difficulties of cartography.

Let us see in somewhat greater detail how modern maps are made. Of great value in modern mapping is aerial photography. A plane with a camera protruding from its belly takes several pictures of the locality to be mapped. In a way, the pictures themselves are already maps. They are distorted maps, however, because of the foreshortenings in them caused by the angles at which the shots are made. All that is taken care of by the mapmakers, who know just how much each picture was distorted.

Suppose, however, that the mapmakers did not know how much distortion had occurred. Suppose, further, that the distortions were due not only to the "point of view" from which the pictures were taken but also to some peculiarities of the lens unknown to the mapmakers. Suppose, moreover, that the chemicals of the plates were not evenly distributed and were not of even sensitivity, all this also unknown to the cartographers. Suppose now that the map, such as it was, was finally made. How much information could be obtained from it if the reader were not only ignorant of all the irregularities that went into its making but did not even know the scale?

When we "perceive" reality, we are, so to say, "mapping" it on something, which we, for the time being, will designate by the old and, in some quarters, disreputable term "consciousness." Some of this mapping is much like photography. The eye, for example, is constructed almost exactly like the camera. It has an automatically adjustable lens which can focus on near and faraway objects in a fraction of a second. Its coating can be used over and over again throughout one's lifetime. The effect of the chemical lasts only while light is acting on it and is sensitive to colors. No permanent record is left. Truly a wonderful apparatus. But where are those awful distortions which we have hinted at? Let us inquire further into our "perception of reality."

Suppose we are at a party. We are talking to a charming young girl sixty-four inches high and sixteen inches broad at the shoulders. She stands a foot away from us. Her twin sister is standing eight feet away, that is, hardly any distance at all. If you whispered her name, she would hear it; if you took three steps toward her, you could touch her. Close your eyes and picture the situation. Would you say that the two girls are of the same size? That is not what our "supercamera" eye reports to us, if we should take its report literally.

The image in our field of vision that forms on our retina (the photo-sensitive area inside the eyeball) is a mapping. If we take a single scale for this map, then, if we estimate our companion to be sixty-four inches high, her twin sister appears as a creature eight inches high and two inches broad! If you made a "logical" deduction about the weight of the girl eight feet away, then, estimating the weight of our neighbor at 128 pounds, we would have to guess the weight of her sister to be four ounces!

"Is this," the Intelligent Reader might ask at this point, "what you mean by the built-in distortions in our visual perception?"

"Yes, one of many," I would reply.

"But," the I.R. might continue, "I fail to see that our idea of the world is *distorted* by it. On the contrary, if a literary interpretation of the relative sizes of the images on our retinas gives us a monstrously distorted picture of the real world, wouldn't you call the arrangement that does not allow such interpretation as a *corrective* device rather than distortive? If the girls were weighed, their weights would be found to be approximately equal. And as a result of our visual estimate we conclude them to be of about equal weight. Of what significance is, then, this 'literary interpretation' of the image? We ought to be glad we *don't* take it literally. If we did, it would seem to us that an eight-inch high creature suddenly increased in bulk 512 times by just taking three steps in our direction!"

Quite so. But let us examine the meaning of a corrective device. A correction is a reinterpretation of data "known" to be "false." You will see the reason for the quotation marks in a moment. If you know your watch is fifteen minutes slow, you will add fifteen minutes to its reading and have the right time. If someone, unknown to you, sets your watch right, and you continue to add fifteen minutes to its reading, you will have the wrong time. Since you first began to use your eyes, you have learned that what appears on your retina as a rapidly growing image means only that an object is approaching. An introspective psychologist will say that you ascribe this "meaning" to the growing image. The Gestalt psychologist will say that this "interpretation" is an inherent part of the perceptive process. This argument need not concern us.

Now suppose someone wants to deceive you. We will take quite an innocent deception at first. For example, Walt Disney in one of his animated cartoons wants to show you the face of a fierce gorilla approaching with breath-taking rapidity from a distance into your immediate vicinity. All he has to do is to photograph a series of such faces of successively larger areas. When you see this series of photographs, you are deceived twice. First, you interpret the several photographs to be a single photograph of the gorilla face that is rapidly growing. Second, you interpret the growing as *approaching*. This approaching gorilla has nothing to do with "reality." "Reality" in this case is only a white screen with colored lights projected on it. Yet how "real" it seems can be seen from the nightmares some children have after viewing animated cartoons. For that matter, cases have been reported where persons in the audiences of picture theaters shout advice at the shadows on the screen or even start shooting at them.

As another illustration of this type, consider the figure on this page. If you think you see a cube, you have been "deceived," because it is nothing but nine line segments drawn at various angles, none of which are right angles.

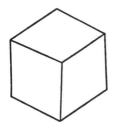

As a final illustration, we offer the following set of ink marks.

If you see the word "semantics" you see considerably more than meets the eye. You have supplied the missing parts.

You see not so much what you see but what you think you *ought* to see.

In other instances you see what you wish to see. In still others what you are afraid to see. Even if we think we are in direct contact with "reality" we cannot be sure that we get undistorted information. We receive the world through a filter of our past experiences, and there is no human alive whose experiences are limited to direct observations. All of us think in terms of language.

Our language habits crystallize into a framework inside of us, and it is through this framework, through all its distortions, exaggerations, and deletions, that we see the world.

Ichabod Crane was scared out of his wits not by what he saw but by the image of the Headless Horseman *inside of him*.

Paphnutius muttered a prayer at the sight of a sphinx, and to him a bat which happened to fly out of the sphinx's ear was an evil spirit driven out by his prayer.

To the child in Goethe's poem, the rustling of the leaves was the whispering of the Erlking's daughters. He had been *told* about them.

According to the way some of our senators talk, the civil rights program means the raping of all white women in the South by the Negroes.

A certain organization interested in the mechanism of race prejudice once performed the following experiment:[2] In a well-lighted room, a picture was placed depicting a policeman threatening a cowering Negro with a straight razor. Individuals were brought into the room and left there for a few minutes. Then they were led into another room, where several persons were seated. None of these latter persons knew about the picture. The person who saw the picture was told to whisper what he had seen to one of the persons in the room. This person then whispered it to another; this one to a third, etc., until the whispered description of the picture went around the room. The last person to hear it was then asked to repeat what he had heard. The result was instructive. In the last telling it was the Negro threatening the policeman with the razor or actually hacking away at him.

What happened?

A quantity of liquid has no shape of its own. But poured into a

[2] Reported by Bruce Bliven in the *New Republic*, Dec. 22, 1947.

spherical vessel it assumes a spherical shape and poured into a cylindrical vessel it assumes a cylindrical shape. The shape is in the vessel, not in the liquid. If we suppose that certain frameworks already exist within the nervous systems of people, within which the information they receive from the outside world is interpreted, we would expect just such distortions to take place.

The relation "Negro threatens policeman with razor" is already in the framework of people whose knowledge of Negroes is confined to the stereotypes by which they are depicted. Given the words "Negro," "razor," policeman," *no matter in what context*, even in the relation directly opposed to the one demanded by the stereotype framework, the stereotype relation will nevertheless prevail. The relation directly perceived will be disregarded. A "correction" will be effected, and the preconceived notions will determine the interpretation.

The experiment above was performed on people of limited education. Educated people, engaged in scientific activity, also may be confined within their frameworks when interpreting evidence.

When the first people who looked through the microscope turned the lens on a specimen of human sperm, many of them "saw" a "homunculus," a tiny, perfect human being, crouching within the spermatozoon. There is no such homunculus. The spermatozoon is a single cell which together with the egg forms the "zygote" from which the organism develops by complicated processes of cell division and differentiation. But those people *expected* to see a homunculus, because the philosophers had reasoned that such a being was within the sperm, ready to "grow" into an adult.

More recently, an anthropologist found "proof" of the mental inferiority of Negroes in the differences he thought he discovered between the skulls of Negroes and those of whites. However, when he was examining the skulls, he knew which were the skulls of Negroes. When confronted with a number of skulls without being told which were which, he could not distinguish them. The anthropologist probably did not "fake" his findings. He could have been scrupulously honest. But he had certain preconceived notions about mentalities of races. He set out to prove something which he already "knew." He found the evidence he was looking for.

The extreme case of finding the evidence looked for is manifested in a type of psychosis called paranoia. A paranoiac may be convinced that people about him, even perfect strangers, passers-by, etc., are constantly conspiring to do him harm. Paranoiacs often construct elaborate and quite "logical" proofs that their suspicions are justified. In fact, their reasoning appears so calm, analytic, and consistent that it often seems to someone who does not understand the nature of their disease that it would be possible to "reason" with the patient, to "prove" to him that he is mistaken. The patient often willingly enters into a "rational" discussion and actually "wins" the argument. That is to say, he acquires an uncanny ability for *fitting into his chain of proof* the most trivial observations.

Boundaries between normality and abnormality, health and disease, sanity and insanity are not sharp. People who are not sick enough to be institutionalized may have paranoiac tendencies. It is common to observe people who are habitually "suspicious." They will attribute the most trivial actions of their friends to "hostility" directed against them; they will interpret friendliness as hypocrisy or "masked" hostility. It is possible that such attitudes are symptoms of some sort of a "rigid framework" within the abstracting mechanism of their nervous systems, an aberration, which if sufficiently pronounced may be the basis of paranoia. Depending upon the seriousness of their condition, such people are, of course, more or less dangerous. In positions of responsibility they can do a great deal of damage.

An example of such an attitude in a person occupying a responsible government position may be seen in the memorandum to the War Department submitted by General J. L. De Witt, February 14, 1942. Until that date there had been no evidence of sabotage by persons of Japanese descent either in Hawaii or on the West Coast. Precisely this *absence* of sabotage was judged by General De Witt as a "disturbing and confirming indication that such action will be taken."[3] It was on the basis of this "confirming indication" that the general urged the removal of all persons labeled "of Japanese descent" from West Coast areas.

Other examples are found in history among the wielders of absolute power, whose main preoccupation consisted of devising ways and means of safeguarding their power from scheming rivals. Those people spent a great deal of time developing elaborate spy systems, uncovering plots, and poisoning persons suspected of undue ambitions.

Between the first mapping of "reality" on the senses of the individual and his verbalizations about "reality" a whole series of abstractions and distortions takes place.

These distortions occur in the framework of interpretation already established within the individual's receptor machinery, associative processes, and linguistic habits. The evaluation of each new experience is an additional deposition on the existing framework.

This framework may be considered, figuratively speaking, as the individual's *map* of the world. Since we get a vast amount of our information about the world symbolically (through language), we learn to rely on that framework more than we do on direct

[3] Quoted from Carey McWilliams's *Prejudice.*

93

experience. We often exclude the information conveyed to us directly by our senses and turn our attention to symbols instead. These act like triggers, setting off reactions *within us*. It is these reactions which we often mistake for "reality."

What determines what will go into one's map?

CHAPTER 11

What Metaphysics Do You Use?

Now a more explicit meaning can be given to "concern with truth." We said "concern with truth" was important for establishing a basis for agreement. Obviously we meant by "concern with truth" something other than a readiness to spring to the defense of one's convictions. Rather we meant a readiness to *re-examine* one's convictions, to put them to a test in the light of new evidence, to revise one's map when it appears inadequate.

When we are in a strange town, we will do well not to trust our own "map" of the town which we may be carrying around in our head. We will do better to trust the published maps or the maps the inhabitants are carrying in their heads. Our concern with truth in this case will express itself not in a persistence of our own notions but in our willingness to compare our map with other maps.

We make our way through the town by asking questions. The answers we get will depend on the questions we ask. Our evaluation of the answers will go into the making of our map. And our map (or the blanks on it) will determine future questions. Both concern with truth and people's maps of the world are intimately bound up with the *asking of questions*.

What questions do we ask? I don't mean questions like "What time is it?" or "How do I get to Prairie Avenue?" I mean general questions about the world. We asked a great many before we could read. Let us recall some.

Here is little A aged two. He has learned to say "What's this?" It is a sign of curiosity and intelligence, and his parents are delighted. Every time he asks "What's this?" he is told the name of an object. He may really want to know the names, but perhaps he does not realize what he wants to "know." It is a nice game anyway. By saying "What's this?" he gets smiles and attention from the people around him. If he imitates the noises that people make after he says his "What's this?" he gets even more smiles and attention, and everybody is happy.

Little A is now three. He has learned to say "Why?" "Why?" gets even more attention from people than "What's this?" But "Why?" can be overdone. Sometimes instead of approval it gets nothing but "Oh, be quiet."

Depending on early circumstances, encouragement, discouragement, kinds of answers given, the question-asking pattern of the young human is formed. It becomes a framework within which the total scope of his knowledge about the world will be enclosed. It determines his metaphysics.

Here is little Ilyusha in the novel *Oblomov* by Goncharov. He notices the light and dark patches moving over the fields. As the clouds pass, it becomes in turn lighter and darker where he is playing.

"Why is it, Nurse," he asks, "it's dark over there and light over yonder? Now it gets dark, now light again?"

"That's because the Sun moves to meet the Moon. When it doesn't see the Moon, it gets gloomy; and when it sees it, it is glad again and bright."

For little Ilyusha the sun becomes a young girl, probably resembling the princess in a fairy tale, the moon a young man. Now it becomes meaningful for him to ask questions about the color of the moon's hair, etc.

"What's this?" and "Why?" are probably the most often repeated questions of the young child. It is likely that he begins to say these things even before he is aware of the meaning of a "question." Depending on the answers he gets, attitudes are established to "What's this?" and to "Why?" Usually it is discovered that the first is to be asked about unfamiliar objects. The expected and fully satisfactory reply is a name. The context in which "Why?" is to be asked is less clear, and the answers are likely to be more vague, and usually it is hard to decide whether "Why?" may or may not be asked again about the answer. But always there is a limit to "Why?" determined by the metaphysics of the person asked and by his patience.

The child often acquires the habit of asking "Why?" just to be talked to or just as a protest against prohibitions. But let us take the child (or the adult, for that matter) who asks "Why?" because he wants to know. *What* does he want to know? What is the meaning of "Why?" for him?

We said language performs its communicative function if it transmits experience. There are several modes of speaking: the indicative mode, which by its very form seeks to inform; the interrogative mode, which questions; the imperative mode, which requests and commands. But clearly all these modes of speaking serve to carry information. For example, the imperative mode informs of the desires of the speaker and can be translated into the indicative mode. "Give me food" (imperative) is equivalent in meaning to "I want you to give me food" (indicative). Similarly, the interrogative mode is translatable into the imperative and therefore into the indicative. "Why does the moon change its shape?" (interrogative) is equivalent to "Tell me why the moon changes its shape" (imperative) and to "I want you to tell me why, etc." (indicative).

We see that every question carries information about a *need* (or want) of the speaker. Language performs a useful social function if needs communicated by it are alleviated. But in order to alleviate a need one must know of what the need consists. If we have bread, it is easy enough to satisfy a man's hunger. If we have atabrine, it is easy to give him relief from malaria. What can one do to satisfy the needs communicated in questions? Obviously some "answer" is wanted. We can suppose that some tension induces the asking of the question, and an answer will relieve that tension. But what sort of answer will do that?

Somewhere a child asks why the moon changes shape. He is told that an old woman slices a little piece off every night, using the scraps for stars, and hangs a new moon up every month, which grows into a full moon. The child is happy. His need to *connect* new experiences with old, familiar ones has been satisfied. It never occurs to him that by such connections he is constructing a false map. It does not occur to him that he may have to navigate by that map and that navigating by a false map may lead to disaster.

It is not well to construct worthless maps for the child. It would be better to give him an orange and make him go around a light with it, so that he may see why the moon changes shape. But suppose he asks why the earth-moon system revolves around the sun. Shall we tell him that it does so to obey "eternal laws of nature" or to realize the "harmony of creation" or shall we go on to Newton's formula, $F = km_1m_2/r^2$?

And if we ask ourselves why Newton's laws hold, what sort of answer do *we* want?

The sort of answers to questions about the world that seem satisfactory (relieve the tension accompanying the questions) determine one's metaphysics. The metaphysics in turn determines the sort of questions one will ask about the world.

Philipp Frank has described the principal systems of metaphysics that governed European thought from the times of Athen-

98

ian learning to the present day. He speaks about the so-called organismic metaphysics formulated by Aristotle and prevalent throughout the Middle Ages and of the mechanistic metaphysics that replaced it at least in the realm of physics and remained current in that field until the end of the nineteenth century. Professor Frank gives the following vivid example to illustrate the method of "organismic science."[1]

When we see a man dashing off in a particular direction, it appears strange at first, but when we learn that in that direction gold coins are being distributed gratis, his action becomes understandable . . . When a hare rushes off in a hurry, we understand this action, if we know that there is a dog after it. The purpose of any motion is to reach a point that is somehow better adapted than the point from which it set out.

Just as different kinds of behavior are exhibited by various organisms depending on their "nature," so "organismic science" interpreted the movements executed by inanimate objects. The falling of a stone and the rising of flame may be interpreted as follows: Just as a mouse has its hole in the ground while an eagle nests on a mountain crag, so a stone has its proper place on the earth while a flame has its above on one of the spheres that revolve around the earth. Each body has its natural position, where it ought to be in accordance with its nature. If a body is removed from this position, it executes a violent motion and seeks to return there as quickly as possible. A stone thrown up in the air tends to return as fast as possible to its position as close as it can get to the center of the earth, just as a mouse that has been driven from its hole tries to return there as soon as possible when the animal from which it fled is gone. . . .

It is of course possible that the stone will be prevented from falling. This occurs when a "violent" force acts on it. According to the ancient philosophers: "A physician seeks to cure, but obstacles can prevent him from achieving his aim." This analogy presents the organismic point of view in probably the crudest form.

[1] Philipp Frank, *Einstein, His Life and Times*, pp. 27-28.

There are also motions that apparently serve no purpose. They do not tend toward any goal, but simply repeat themselves. Such are the movements of the celestial bodies, and they were regarded therefore as spiritual beings of a much higher nature. Just as it was the nature of the lower organisms to strive toward a fold and flee from danger, so it was the nature of the spiritual bodies to carry out eternally identical movements.

The organismic conception had its basis in teachings of the Greek philosopher Aristotle. Although it was basically a "heathen" philosophy, it is found throughout the entire medieval period with only slight modifications in the doctrine of the leading Catholic philosopher Thomas Aquinas, as well as in the teachings of the Jewish philosopher Moses Maimonides, and the Mohammedan Averroës.

Aristotle did not of course "invent" organismic science any more than he invented Aristotelian logic, any more than Euclid invented Euclidean geometry. However, it is proper to attribute the basis of organismic science to his teachings, because he was the first to give this system a *formulation.* He said in effect: This is the way the events in the world about us should be explained. It was the same as with codifications of laws. We speak of Hammurabi and Moses as "lawgivers." We speak of Solon's Code, the Napoleonic Code, etc. Yet Solon and Napoleon did not invent the greatest part of those legal systems. They, too, gathered prevailing practices and *announced* them in concise, consequential form. In philosophy, the importance of such formulations should by no means be minimized. They are instrumental both in making possible rapid advances in knowledge and in seriously hindering such advances.

A formulation of a metaphysics, such as Aristotle's teachings about the "natural position" of objects, is really a definition of the word "why." If one reflects for a moment, one finds that the question "Why?" has most meaning (is most justified) when it applies to phenomena which seem in some way extraordinary. Professor Frank's example of the man suddenly dashing off is an excellent one. Ordinarily people do *not* suddenly dash off. Therefore, it is proper to ask "Why did that man dash off?" Now, when the additional fact is known that somewhere gold coins are being distributed gratis, the situation is seen in a different light. If it is assumed that people *do* dash off when they learn that gold coins are distributed gratis, then the situation ceases to seem unusual and further "whys" are out of order.

Let us take another example.

Suppose a desert nomad, who raises cattle and has never seen a cultivated plant grow, watches a man pierce grassy turf with a plow and turn the earth over.

"Why are you doing this?" he asks. "God made the grass grow with roots down and green up. Is it right to turn God's work topsy-turvy?"[2]

Now we will suppose that the nomad's curiosity is stronger than his sense of propriety (otherwise fruitful exchange of ideas would end right there, and we would have another of the unhappy cases described in Chapter 1). So when the plowman tells him that he wants to soften the earth, the nomad pursues his questions further.

"Why do you want the earth softer?"

"Because I am going to put these seeds into it."

"What for?"

"Wheat will grow."

---

[2] Shortly after the revolution a pioneer detachment in the U.S.S.R. once came to some nomad tribes of Central Asia to teach them farming. After preliminary parleys, at which it was not quite clear to the nomads what the business of the strangers was, the pioneers decided to proceed and plowed up a field. The next morning there was no sign of the plowed field in the steppe. It was solid green. It turned out that during the night the natives had turned the clods over into their original position. They explained that it was God's will for the grass to grow upward, not downward.

"What is wheat?"

"These same seeds."

"Do you mean to tell me that you put these seeds into the ground just to have them come out again?"

"Yes, because many more will come out than I put in."

"And what will you do with them then? Put them back into the ground?"

"Some of them. The rest I will grind into a powder, mix the powder with water and yeast and salt, put the mixture over a fire."

"Why will you be doing this? Explain."

"I will be making bread. Look, this is bread (extensional definition). Have some. It is good to eat and nourishing."

Only then, and only if bread is to his taste, will the nomad be "satisfied." If he "sees the point" of eating bread, the plowman's behavior becomes understandable. The "whys" cease.

The first "whys" concern with the most unusual events and are "answered" if new facts are uncovered which make the event seem usual. The nomad has never seen anybody plow, so he seeks explanations. But he has seen people exerting themselves in order to get food. The plowman's behavior is explained to him as a food-getting behavior. It is new to him, but he *understands* it, because he classifies it as "food-getting behavior," of which he has seen several other instances.

The explanation need not necessarily be in terms of commonplace direct experience. It may be in terms of an *extrapolation* of such experience, sometimes quite farfetched. The exercise of such extrapolation we call imagination. Intolerance can sometimes be traced to an inability to extrapolate (a lack of imagination). Charles M. Doughty described the way he explained the workings of the telegraph to an Arabian chieftain.[3]

[3] Charles M. Doughty, *Travels in Arabia Deserta,* pp. 651-652.

"The telegraph is what? and we have seen it but canst thou not make known to us the working, which is wonderful?"

"It is a trepidation—therewith we may make certain signs—engendered in the corrosion of metals, by strong medicine like vinegar."

"Then it is an operation of medicine, canst thou not declare it?"

"If we may suppose a man laid head and heels between Hayil and Stambul, of such stature that he touched them both; if one burned his feet at Hayil, should he not feel it at the instant in his head, which is at Stambul?"

The chieftain has never seen a man who could stretch from Hayil to Stambul. But he can *imagine* such a thing, and he is "satisfied" with the "explanation."

When we watch a primitive tribe go through curious contortions, we may ask what they are doing. If we are told that they are having a war dance, we consider it a satisfactory answer, because we have heard of war dances. The phenomenon is classified as a "familiar" one even though we have never seen a war dance before.

We see an object seemingly suspended in the air. At once we are curious. We go to examine it. This too is a "Why?" We find that it is suspended by a fine wire. We are satisfied. An unusual event becomes a usual one.

This, then, is our strongest motivation for asking "Why?" *It is a striving to restore a disturbed balance, to reduce the unfamiliar to the familiar, the "unnatural" to the "natural."*

A metaphysics is essentially a framework in which the so-called "natural" phenomena are to be described. Aristotle's framework was the assumption that every thing has a "proper position according to its nature." Having made this assumption, he then proceeds to describe just what things "belong" where. Now the questions about why stones fall and flames rise and planets move in regular

103

paths are answered by pointing out that they are *supposed* to behave just that way in accordance with their "nature."

A metaphysics, such as Aristotle's or any other, not only provides a method for answering the question "Why?" but also determines a general notion of the nature of knowledge itself and therefore of the ways of getting it. Aristotle pictures the world as consisting of "things." Each thing possesses a "nature." The business of the philosopher (the seeker of knowledge), according to this view, is to try to find out what that "nature" is. He can do it by observation and "reasoning." Methods of reasoning are explicitly described, but techniques of observation are not specified. Controlled experiment is practically unknown. Language is taken for granted as being adequate to describe "reality."

We have said that a formulation of a metaphysical system can serve both to accelerate and to hinder the progress of knowledge. It helps the progress of knowledge when it is young, when it is a rallying point for fresh, progressive ideas. Its adherents are then in the vanguard of the pursuit of knowledge. From its camp is organized the intellectual struggle against the old system, which has outlived its usefulness.

Aristotle's formulation about "the proper way for each thing to behave" was at the time of its origin a great advance over an even more primitive metaphysics, which attributed the "causes" of phenomena to the whims of gods and demons. The implication of this more primitive view (which, just to give it a name, we will call "demonism") is that hardly anything consistent can be predicted about nature. Everything happens because some god feels grouchy or benevolent. The only way to influence events is to get on the good side of those characters. The notion that events have "natural" causes, on the other hand, admits that prediction of natural phenomena is possible if one studies the "nature of nature." The great revolutionary implication of Aristotelian metaphysics was that it asserted the *possibility* of science and prediction, that is, that prediction was not a monopoly of a group of priests but was within the reach of anyone who would take the trouble to study nature.[4]

The views of Hippocrates (*c.* 460-*c.* 370 B.C.) on medicine, although anticipating Aristotle's formulations, were essentially in agreement with organismic metaphysics. Many of his ideas might have been totally erroneous, but the notion that health and disease are to be attributed to "natural causes" makes a medical science at least *possible*, while under the more primitive demonistic assumptions such a science is impossible.

A metaphysical formulation becomes a drag on the progress of knowledge when it is the rallying point of the old system. Its adherents are then the people who have vested interests in the preservation of old ways of thinking.

Such was the role of the Aristotelian physics (based on the Aristotelian metaphysics) during the Renaissance, when it was the official world view approved by the Church. At that time a new formulation was in the making, namely, the beginning of the so-called "mechanistic" science, whose great exponent was Galileo Galilei.

Mechanistic metaphysics did not assign to each object in the universe a "proper behavior in accordance with its nature." It sought to explain physical phenomena by *a few general principles*, called the laws of mechanics. Isaac Newton, who gave the mechanistic formulation its final form, did it in such a way that the motion of *any* object could be described or predicted (in principle) once the forces acting on it were known and its motion was known at some initial moment. The "nature" of the object made no dif-

---

[4] However, the real *democratization* of knowledge became possible only when experimental science appeared and the experiment was promoted to the position of supreme judge as to what is "true" (see Chapter 5).

ference. It became meaningless. Or, if you wish, on the contrary, it acquired precise meaning only in the context of masses, forces, and velocities associated with the object.

Let us look at some of the implications of the two views. Suppose the question is asked, "Why do stones fall to the ground, but birds are able to fly?" The organismic philosopher might well seek to answer this question by asking other questions about birds and stones, questions which are in his repertoire, determined by his metaphysics.

"Let us first see," he would say, "what is the nature of birds and the nature of stones."

His answer to the original question is determined by his approach.

"Birds fly," the organismic philosopher goes on to say, "because they seek their proper position in the nests, which are above the ground; but stones fall because they seek *their* proper position as near as possible to the center of the earth."

The mechanistic scientist, on the other hand, would start with an entirely different question:

"What forces are acting on stones and on birds?"

This question leads him to certain investigations and experiments and finally to the answer:

"A stone falls, because the predominant force on it is the force of gravity; but other forces are acting on the bird with outstretched wings, and these forces cancel the force of gravity and propel the bird forward. When the bird is flying in a straight line with constant velocity, all the forces acting on it are canceled. It is natural for *any* body to move in a straight line if the forces acting on it are all canceled (the law of inertia)."

To the question whether an inanimate object could be made to fly in the manner of birds and perhaps carry people, the organismic scientist might well reply, "No, it is against the nature of inanimate objects to behave like animate ones. They will always seek their proper place near the center of the earth and hence fall." The mechanist, if he is true to his philosophy, will reply, "Yes, a flying machine is possible. All we need to do is investigate the forces such as act on birds in flight, and learn to duplicate them and apply them to our machine."

One more example. Pumps were known and used before the mechanistic outlook was formulated. The organismic explanation of the working of the pump went something like this: "Inside the pump vacuum is created. It is well known that nature dreads vacuum. Hence the water must rush in to occupy the empty space."

The explanation was all right (that is, it worked) provided the water was not pumped too high. Then people noticed that when wells over thirty-four feet deep were dug, no pump would be strong enough to carry the water all the way up. No matter how "vacuous" the space was above the thirty-four-foot column of water, the water did not rise. To patch up the organismic explanation, one could say something like this: "Nature dreads vacuum, but not when it is at a height of over thirty-four feet." Let us look now at the mechanistic explanation.

"If air is removed from a tube, the air pressure inside becomes less than the atmospheric pressure outside. Hence outside air is able to drive the water up the tube. But when the column of water is about thirty-four feet high, its own pressure on the water in the reservoir equals the atmospheric pressure on the free surface of the water. The two pressures thus cancel each other, and there is no force to cause the water to go any higher."

Note that our organismic philosopher does not necessarily give up when he is confronted with a phenomenon which defies his previous explanations. He can still "explain." But the trouble with his explanations is that they *have to be invented on the spot.* They are something like the new rule that an unsportsmanlike team tries to introduce while the game is going on if it is losing the game.

The mechanistic explanation is not only in strict accordance with *previously* set up rules but also suggestive of new ideas. If the height of the column of water supported by atmospheric pressure depends on this pressure, can we not measure atmospheric pressure by looking at the height of the column of water it will support? And if the material is much heavier than water, say mercury, the column will not be nearly so high, in fact, about thirty inches. That makes a nice portable barometer possible. You can't invent a barometer on the assumption that "nature dreads vacuum."

The sensational success of the mechanistic point of view was that not only could observed physical phenomena be explained consistently with the few general principles set down in advance but phenomena *not yet observed* could be successfully predicted.

Now, a man who can predict successfully is bound to become popular in almost any human society, especially if he can predict some good news for a change. So great is the desire of human beings to know what is coming, that even a moderate amount of success in predicting lends a great deal of prestige to the predictor, which is probably the secret of success enjoyed by medicine men, priests, shamans, astrologers, and assorted charlatans in prescientific societies. It is the success of shrewd men who have by keen observation learned to predict some phenomena in a rough-and-ready way and, having awed their followers, claim infallible ability to predict all events with an ever-ready explanation of failure made up on the spot.

It was inevitable that in the field in which the mechanists could predict most successfully and most spectacularly (physics) they finally won a decisive victory over the organismic school of thought. In a world of rapidly growing commerce, navigation, and production, a physical science became necessary to the rising class engaged in all this new activity, merchants, seafaring men, engineers, and manufacturers. If the Church stood in the way, so much the worse for the Church. Came the Reformation. Came the French Enlightenment. If the aristocracy and the monarchy stood in the way, so much the worse for them and for their "natural order of things." Came the French Revolution. Organismic metaphysics was doomed. The mechanist view became the framework of physical science.

Some seventy years ago cracks began to appear in the mechanistic edifice. Another metaphysical revolution was in the making. We shall have more to say about it in the succeeding chapters. When its full history is written, it will offer a story quite as thrilling as the Mechanist Revolution. The new movement has appeared in several streams under several names.

The precursor in physics (the most advanced field in human endeavor, which is therefore the breeding place of revolutionary movements of thought) was Ernst Mach. Mach's influence spread into many channels. In Vienna there were the logical positivists. In Russia the so-called empirio-criticists; in England the semanticists. Isolated men of genius like Einstein, the Relativist, and Poincaré, the Symbolist, have contributed weighty blocks to the new magnificent edifice still being constructed. Some people, including the author of this book, credit Alfred Korzybski with giving the new metaphysics a general formulation. The implications of this new system will be described in succeeding chapters.

Physical science, that is, the science that deals with explanations and predictions of "physical phenomena" observable in specified times and places, has enjoyed ever since the Mechanist Revolution a continuous accumulation of success. We have seen how a difference in outlook changed the character of the questions that scientists were asking about the world around them, and the changed character of the questions was responsible for the rapid progress in knowledge about the physical world. Along with knowledge came the ability to control the world.

The *language* of science kept changing. New and ever-renewed language made it possible to ask new, more meaningful questions. But how about language in general? Did it also undergo profound changes? How deeply did the new scientific outlook seep through? Not very deeply. The language of ordinary life, dealing with human relations, with attitudes, likes and dislikes, with fears, hopes, and guesses about the future, the language of law, dealing with relations between subject and state, employer and employed, the language of religion dealing with "moral values," with opinions regarding the future of mankind, with the so-called "nature of man" and the "meaning of life," these languages changed little. Even the languages of the other disciplines of science, for instance the biological ones, changed more slowly than the language of physical science. They lagged behind. When organismic ways of talking had already been purged from physics and astronomy, physicians still talked about the Four Humors and other organismic nonsense. The language of physics was always the most advanced since the Mechanist Revolution.

The modern physicist can read Aristotle's *Physics* only with a smile. He would no more think of trying to learn any physics from it than a modern geographer would try to learn geography from Columbus' map of the "Indies." The modern physician must dismiss most of the medical science of fifty years ago. But people of all kinds still find moral inspiration and satisfaction from texts written over two millenniums ago. The basis of our law is still an eighteenth-century document. Some of our statesmen don't see anything silly in the politics of Caesar, of Richelieu, or of Gladstone. In fact they learn a great deal of their trade from those and similar authorities.

This may imply either of two things. It may mean that our religious convictions, legal systems, and politics have been so successful in accomplishing their ends during the past two thousand years that there has been no need to change our outlooks about them. Or it may mean that the outlook has not changed for other reasons.

I will leave the first hypothesis to those who are willing to defend it and choose the second.

As the reader may have guessed, I am interested in learning how obsolete structure of language preserves obsolete metaphysics.

CHAPTER 12

Our Aristotelian Heritage

If a man in our day made notable contributions to biology, psychology, ethics, aesthetics, dramatic criticism, musical criticism, and logic, we should certainly consider him a genius of the first magnitude. Aristotle *started* all these subjects practically single-handed.

It is true that gifted men before Aristotle thought profoundly about the world and made discoveries which even today are scientifically sound. But Aristotle had a genius for *organizing* knowledge. It was he who thought of compartmentalizing knowledge into *disciplines*, so as to make possible a division of labor among the gatherers of knowledge. He marked out areas of inquiry, and his divisions still persist to a large extent in our own learning.

Perhaps the greatest scientific achievements of Aristotle were in biology. It was here that he proceeded most "scientifically," making extremely keen observations. Probably having ample means at his command, he organized at Athens the Lyceum, an extensive institution of learning. The biology department must have been especially heavily endowed, because we are told that hundreds of field workers were employed in obtaining zoological and botanical specimens.

Aristotle's great talent appeared to be in the ability to find common characteristics in seemingly diverse objects. He found that a great deal could be understood about animals if they were classified "properly."

Our Aristotelian Heritage

It is natural for a thinker to pursue the lines of thought that have proved successful. So we may suppose that Aristotle came by his view of the world (his metaphysics) by generalizing his successful approach to biology.

This view considers the world as a collection of objects. The objects are characterized by certain "properties." If a number of objects have a property in common, they can be thought of as a "class" of objects. The properties in common then become the properties of the class. Classes having properties in common can be organized into larger classes, etc.

Studying nature means studying the properties of objects and classes. The discovery of the properties of anything enables one to place it in a certain class (inductive reasoning). On the other hand, if one knows to what class an object belongs, one can say what its properties are (deductive reasoning).

Here is a cat. What can we say about it? As we observe it, we notice that it moves about seemingly "at will." This places her in the class of living beings. She has fur and is warm blooded. That makes her a mammal. We have arrived at the judgment *Cats are mammals* (by inductive reasoning, that is, from particular properties to general classification). Now we reason further.

Mammals give birth to live young and nurse them (arrived at inductively from previous numerous observations of mammals).

Cats are mammals (arrived at inductively from the observations of some properties of cats).

Therefore, cats, and in particular this cat, must give birth to live young and nurse them (conclusion by deduction).

Let us try to imagine how Aristotle would answer our fundamental questions about communication and the sources of knowledge.

1. *What are assertions about?*
2. *What do you mean? How do you define your terms?*

113

3. How do you know that what you are saying is true?

One might guess that he would give these answers.

To the first question he might reply:

"Assertions are made about the real world, which consists of objects and their properties. The important assertions are those which describe the properties of objects and classify them according to those properties. Here are some samples: Grass is green. Water is a liquid. Barbarians are uncultured. Democracy is a desirable (or an undesirable) form of government."

To the second question, Aristotle's answer might be:

"Naturally I define my terms by Aristotelian definitions. Such definitions are informative. By placing an object in a certain class, I have said a great deal about it, namely, I have implied that it is endowed with all the properties of the class. By giving the properties peculiar to the object, I have indicated how to distinguish it from the other members of its class. In fact, if my definition is complete, I have told all about the object that is worth knowing."

To the third question he might reply:

"The truth of an assertion can be established if the assertion is self-evident or can be deduced logically from other assertions known to be true."

The tremendous influence of Aristotle is reflected in the fact that most people today do not see anything remarkable in these answers. They seem "natural," "common sense," even "obvious." A great many "facts" which Aristotle believed in have since been shown to be false, such as his contention that a woman has fewer teeth than a man, or that the brain serves to cool the blood, or that the earth is the immovable center of the universe. But few people are prepared to challenge Aristotle's views on communication and epistemology. They are still accepted in many quarters as eternally true. As a matter of fact, they were progressive when they were uttered (if compared with what passed for communica-

114

tion and knowledge outside of Greece) but are in many respects obsolete today!

A world view, like a technological invention, may be of overwhelming importance when it appears. But its very impetus induces changes in thinking, feeling, and behaving, which eventually make it obsolete, that is, inadequate to meet the new problems it has called into being. Scientists and engineers have learned to recognize this and to change their ways whenever it becomes necessary. That is why science and technology are able to move forward, and that is why scientists can come to agreement about ways of coping with their special problems.

This is not usually true of people dealing with matters relegated to "philosophy." Philosophical "truths," instead of being steppingstones to be walked over, become monuments to be gazed at. So it has become with Aristotle's views, or, rather, with the tacit implications of his views. They were so important and far-reaching that they have paralyzed intellectual progress in many fields for many centuries.

Aristotle was not only the most systematic thinker of his time (and of the next fifteen centuries), but he also could communicate his methods of systematizing thinking. People had reasoned logically before, but Aristotle showed what people were doing when they reasoned logically. He created logic *as a system of inquiry*, perhaps his greatest, most lasting contribution to knowledge.

Aristotle's logic consisted of rules for the use of language. The language he spoke was Greek, one of a large family of languages called the Indo-European. Fundamental in the structure of the languages comprising this group is the so-called subject-predicate form of the sentence. A simple sentence is supposed to ascribe some property (or action) called the predicate to some object (or class of objects) called the subject. Since properties are the basis for classifying objects, and are themselves derivable from the

115

class to which an object belongs, it follows that knowledge can be organized into assertions which place objects in their proper classes.

Cats are mammals.

Man is mortal.

Stones are hard.

From the point of view of Aristotelian logic, this form of assertion is the most convenient to handle, and *it is assumed that all assertions are translatable into this form.* So every assertion (according to the Aristotelian view) is really a classification. The general form of such assertions is "A is B." Here A is the subject (whatever it may be) and B the predicate. It may also be put in the negative form, "A is not B," which means that A belongs to a class which lies outside of the class B.

Now, Aristotelian logic consists of the following rules.

1. *"A is A" is always a true assertion.*

This means that we may be sure we are making a true assertion (although perhaps not an interesting one) when we say "Cats are cats," "Water is water," etc.

2. *Both assertions* "A is B" *and* "A is not B" *cannot be true.*

In other words, if we contend that A is B, we cannot contend that A is not B, where A and B have the same meaning as before. We cannot assert that men are mortal and that men are immortal.

3. *One of the assertions* "A is B" *or* "A is not B" *must be true.*

That is, if we have admitted that "A is B" is a false assertion, then we must admit that "A is not B" is a true one, and vice versa. If we have come to a conclusion that "the earth is a moving object" cannot be a true assertion, then we must conclude that "the earth is not a moving object."

Since assertions about parts of classes also are useful, the general forms of assertions are extended to four types:

"All A are B," "No A is B," "Some A are B," and "Some A are not B."

The backbone of Aristotelian logic is the syllogism. A syllogism consists of three assertions, one about A and B, one about B and C (these are called the premises), and one about A and C (the conclusion). The rules of logic state what conclusion (if any) can be drawn from any two premises.

For example if *All A are B* and *All B are C* are both true assertions, then *All A are C* is necessarily a true assertion. (If all cats are mammals, and all mammals are vertebrates, then all cats are vertebrates.)

Another example is *No A is B, some C are B;* therefore, *some C are not A.* (No mammal has feathers; some animals have feathers; therefore, some animals are not mammals.)

In all, there are nineteen such valid combinations, called the nineteen modes. Medieval scholars have invented fancy names for the modes to facilitate memorization. The two examples cited belong respectively to the "Barbara" mode and the "Ferioque" mode.

It is important to note that some combinations of premises warrant no conclusion. For example, if "Some A are B" and "Some B are C" there is nothing that follows from this by Aristotelian logic. One cannot say "Some A are C," as we can verify if we substitute "Irishman" for A, "Redheaded people" for B, and "Frenchmen" for C. These combinations were, therefore, excluded by Aristotelian logic. If one takes the point of view that an assertion must be either true or false (see Rule 3 above), then, if a combination of premises does not allow either to make an assertion or to make its denial, such a combination does not seem to be of much use. As we shall see in Chapter 20, this is a serious shortcoming of Aristotelian logic.

None of the other combinations of premises where both begin

117

with "some" warrant any conclusion. Therefore, in order for the Aristotelian syllogism to function at all, at least one of the premises must assert "All X are Y" or "No X is Y." This has interesting consequences if one wishes to consider sources of knowledge.

The truth of the conclusion in the syllogism rests on the truth of the premises. What does the truth of the premises rest on? If the premises are conclusions derived from other syllogisms, the answer to our question is merely postponed. If we agree that the ultimate source of knowledge is experience, then, if we trace the ancestry of some assertion through the various syllogisms through which it has been derived, somewhere we must come to something that is not a syllogism. In other words, the ultimate justification of a premise must be experience. And we have seen that at least one of the premises in each syllogism must be in the form "All X are Y" or "No X is Y." Therefore, to make use of a chain of syllogisms for arriving at new truths we must have concluded *from experience* an assertion in the form "All X are Y" or "No X is Y." Let us see what that involves.

Suppose "All X are Y" stands for "All men are mortal." That is supposed to be known by "experience." The experience consists of a number of observations, namely, that Jones has died, and Smith has died, and Wylczinski, and Cohn, and Tartini, and Koomaraswami, etc., etc. How does that experience map on "All men are mortal"? All we have observed is that *some* men have died, and assertions beginning with "some" cannot serve for both premises in a syllogism.

The reader should not conclude that I doubt the value of "All men are mortal" as a working hypothesis. I am merely pointing out that it cannot be deduced *categorically* from experience. Similarly, the fact that no man has ever been seen with horns does not logically guarantee that one will not appear tomorrow, although any of us will give odds that he will not.

118

When ardent adherents of the Aristotelian outlook are faced with this criticism of the reliability of the syllogism, they sometimes resort to the following argument:

"It is not necessary to observe the death of all men to conclude that all men are mortal. Man's mortality is deducible from the *nature* of men. The mathematician does not have to verify the Pythagorean theorem on every right triangle. He deduces the theorem from the *nature* of the right triangle. Even the most empirically minded scientists (modern Aristotelians often bemoan extreme empiricism, i.e., heavy reliance on observation and experiment) do not make an infinite number of observations. Having observed that hydrogen and oxygen in the presence of a spark consistently combine to form water, they conclude that it is their nature to do so and can therefore assert that it is generally true that they will so combine."

The argument is a triple one. It treats the genesis of mathematical proposition; the reliability of conclusions made from many observations; and the "nature of things." The first two matters will have to be postponed.[1] But we shall take up this Aristotelian predilection for the "nature of things." It lies at the root of organismic metaphysics, our heritage from Aristotle, and in turn springs from the conviction that knowledge about the world can be built from assertions in the form "A is B."

Let us go for a while where one of those "nature of things" arguments leads us.

REFUTATION OF THE BELIEF THAT THE EARTH IS ROUND

Observations show that if water is sprinkled on a ball, it will run down the sides and drip off the bottom. This experiment was performed thousands of times, and never has an instance been observed in which water would fail to run off the surface of the

[1] See Chapters 19 and 20.

ball. We conclude that the nature of round objects is such that they cannot hold any considerable amount of water on their surfaces.

Now, it has been observed that the surface of the earth is covered by vast amounts of water. If the earth were round like a ball, as is maintained by scientists, it could not hold all this water. Therefore the earth cannot be round.

When we said in Chapter 3 that too much training in logic sometimes makes it difficult for people to agree, we had examples like the above in mind. Not many "logicians" may be willing to defend the opinion that the earth is flat, but some of the opinions they do defend are often just as obsolete.

So prevalent is the notion that Aristotle's laws of logic represent "eternal truths," rather than just rules for the use of a language based on syllogisms, that the prestige of an assertion may sometimes be established if only the assertion is somehow exhibited as a conclusion of a syllogism. The fact that the truth of the conclusion stands or falls with the truth of the premises is often forgotten. The fact that the symbols used in the syllogisms are often extremely high-order abstractions is not even generally known.

Reasoning by strict logic is something like an accurate reading of a map. It will help us arrive at correct conclusions about the territory, *if the map correctly represents the territory*, but not otherwise. And we have seen in Chapter 10 how difficult it is to make accurate maps.

CHAPTER 13

Our Aristotelian Heritage (Continued): Allness, Identification, Either-Or

> And out of the ground the Lord God formed every beast of the field, and every fowl of the air; and brought them unto the man to see what he would call them: and whatsoever the man would call every living creature, that was to be the name thereof.
>
> Genesis 2:18-19

Logic makes possible the full utilization of the two principal functions of language:[1]

(1) *Communication* (transmitting experience from person to person).

(2) *Heuristics* (solving problems).

Logic is an indispensable component of heuristics. It helps us "figure things out." By means of it we can acquire knowledge without directly experiencing what we find out. Sherlock Holmes with his uncanny deductions, the anthropologist reconstructing the entire appearance of the pre-ice age man from a few bones, the physicist predicting the properties of an element not yet discovered, all use logical tools.

Logic, however, is not the language itself. Logic is a set of rules about how language is to be used. For example, the nineteen modes of the Aristotelian syllogism tell us how to use a language

---

[1] A third important function, the *expressive*, is often attributed to language. It will be partially considered in Chapter 21.

121

consisting of assertions in the form of "All A are B," "No A is B," etc., so that given the truth of two such assertions, we may assert the truth of a third one.

Mathematics is another system of logic. It is a system of rules applied to assertions in the form of equations, inequalities, and other relations, so that given certain assertions we may derive others from them. For example, if it is asserted that the difference of two numbers is equal to the difference of their squares, then we can assert that either the two numbers are equal or their sum is 1.

Logic, being only a system of rules, does not enable us to discover new knowledge *independently*. To discover the truth of new assertions by logic, we must *assume* that certain other assertions are already known to be true. Thus, in a syllogism, the two premises must be given before something else is proved; Sherlock Holmes needs clues before he embarks on his deductions: the physicist assumes that his "laws" are valid before he makes his predictions.

Even if our logic is perfect, the truth of our conclusions is only as certain as the truth of our premises. We have seen that assertions about things can be considered true only if they are traced to someone's experience. But even so, certain assumptions invariably accompany the assertions that are *generalizations* of experience. We say "Grass is green." We mean it was green every time we looked at it. We *assume* it will be green the next time we look. We say "Man is mortal." We mean A, B, C, . . . X have died. We *assume* a certain constancy, a certain assurance that what has happened once will happen again, that objects and persons are practically the same over long periods of time, that each thing has a "nature" and behaves in accordance with it.

These convictions perpetuate themselves in the structure of our language, where subjects and predicates connected by "is" play such an important part. Organismic metaphysics is still prevalent in these convictions. It still forms the basis of the maps we make of the world.

Little A behaves as he does because he *is* spoiled.

Gaminos have a low standard of living because they *are* lazy.

Mixed bathing in the nude is prohibited because it *is* immoral.

My husband doesn't like my hat because he *is* mean.

Our social system is the best in the world because it *is* a democracy.

X should be elected because he *is* an X-ist.

Y should be dismissed because he *is* a Y-ist.

Z should be sent to jail because he *is* a criminal.

Every one of these utterances contains a "because." Presumably, then, they are answers to "Why?" *And every one of them is a classification.* Things behave as they do because things *are* as they *are.* We should behave so and so toward so and so, because so and so is a so-an-so.

Sometimes it is useful to judge that way. I avoid rattlesnakes because they are poisonous; I eat greens because they contain vitamin C: I follow W's advice because he is a physician; I vote against a candidate because he is affiliated with the Ku Klux Klan. But I *try* to keep in mind that rattlesnakes under certain conditions can be made harmless; that greens can lose their vitamins; that W can go insane; that even a klansman can renounce his affiliation. It is important to recognize that things are different under different conditions. The strict Aristotelian classification habit does not allow this recognition to develop. "It is in the *nature* of balls to shed water from their surface."

ALLNESS

This shortcoming of the Aristotelian orientation has been called *allness* and is attributed to the habit of identifying a thing with the class in which it has been placed (by definition) or with a property ascribed to it (by induction).

We learn about the world around us by observing it. When we have observed that a number of properties in some class of objects consistently go together, we place these objects in a class. Then we need observe only one of the properties to classify the object. This saves time and trouble. For example, if we have noticed after eating many apples that greenness and sourness always go together, we need only note that an apple is green in order to decide that it is sour. We save even more time if we are so convinced that the properties go together that we are satisfied with just one observation. Having noted on one occasion that the No. 5 streetcar takes me downtown, I will unhesitatingly take No. 5 whenever I want to go downtown.[2]

While other animals need several experiences for associating one event with another, we with our verbalization of experience and our symbolic trigger mechanisms can inscribe the association indelibly in our memories the first time it occurs.

"Aha!" we say. "No. 5 goes downtown."

This is "inductive reasoning" cut to the bone. It may be called a trigger induction. We do not always recognize the fact that there is nothing in the scheme of things to guarantee the correctness of conclusions based on trigger inductions. We forget that when we make such inductions we are doing so entirely at our own risk. And we often fall victims to allness.

I have heard the following "proof" offered in all seriousness on an "educational" radio program.

REFUTATION OF THE BELIEF THAT MANKIND IS MORE THAN 6,000 YEARS OLD

Statistics show that during the past 150 years the population of the world has approximately doubled. On the basis of doubling

[2] Strictly speaking, I base my assurance on many previous observations that streetcars marked by certain numbers always take the same routes. But it is not always clear whether such previous observations have actually been made.

124

the population every 150 years, the present population would have been reached if there had been just one couple living about six thousand years ago. This is a corroboration of the account of the origin of mankind given in Genesis.

The habit of looking for properties with which to pigeonhole an object reduces our powers of observation. We no longer examine the world innocently with the keen pleasure that goes with satisfying curiosity, the way young children do. We have eyes only for the "classifying" properties. We become blind to the world. Rather than look at the infinitely varied, eternally interesting universe, we consult our inner maps, often constructed from hundreds of trigger inductions, proudly referred to as "experience."

"You may not believe there's anything to dreams," says Mr. P whom we met in Chapter 3, "but I know for a fact that dreams come true. Why just last year Mrs. P dreamt that her mother was going to visit us, and a couple of months later she did."

Prejudices, hatreds, conflicts based on prejudice and hatred are perpetuated by allness orientations. Glaring examples of violent semantic disturbance, obviously involving allness reactions may be found, among other places, in the utterances of Adolf Hitler, Westbrook Pegler, etc. The following excerpt is from an interview of the German physicist, Max Planck, with Hitler. In 1933 Planck, paying his respects to the new head of state, attempted to intercede for some of his Jewish colleagues. Said Hitler:

"Against the Jews as such I have nothing. But the Jews are all Communists and these are my enemies. Against them my fight is directed. . . . Jew is Jew."[3]

At this point we are not prepared to discuss whether prejudices and hatreds are "caused" by bad language habits. We do think

[3] Quoted from the *New York Times*, Jan. 9, 1949.

that prejudices are *perpetuated* by the categorical "is-language" of classification. Ignorance of the fact that classifications are artifacts (see Chapter 9) allows people to internalize them. The reason tall people have in general no serious enmity toward short people and do not fear that, unless something is done about it, the short ones will "take over the country" is because the classification of people into tall and short is not an integral part of our language habits.

IDENTIFICATION

Closely allied to the allness orientation is *identification*, that is, confusing words or other symbols with the things they stand for. To a person preoccupied with the map, having forgotten the territory for which it is supposed to stand, north is always up, Italy a boot, and the British Empire eternally pink. Figuratively speaking, such a person thinks he is traveling when he passes his finger along the globe. There are people in Wisconsin, in Pennsylvania, and in England who stick pins into the images of their "enemies" and believe that they have permanently damaged them by doing so.

Such habits are extremely persistent. They not only influence our judgments but determine to a great extent how we evaluate information and experience. They influence the extent of our inquiry about the world. Such great importance is attributed to names of things (since names are indicative of classification, and knowledge is considered as the ability to classify "properly") that the question "What is it?" can often be satisfied simply by giving the name, so that an incentive for *experiencing* an event is destroyed. Knowledge stops with the word. The gap between word and experience is not bridged.

My mother tells me that when she went to school in old Russia, geography seemed to her a dry study. In view of the way it was taught, this does not appear surprising. It was largely concerned

126

with names and definitions which had to be learned by heart. "An island is a body of land entirely surrounded by water"; "An isthmus is a narrow stretch of land connecting two continents"; etc. Then there were deadpan enumerations of the islands, peninsulas, rivers, and mountain ranges. When a pupil was called upon to recite "the islands of Europe," the idea was to rattle off "Nova Zembla, Spitsbergen, Great Britain, Ireland, Iceland, Sicily, Sardinia, Corsica, and Crete" *in that order.* If the teacher asked what the other name for Crete was, the pupil was supposed to say "Candia." If asked "the peninsulas of North America," he said, "Alaska, California, Yucatan, Florida, and Labrador."

My mother says she found it difficult to get used to the idea that Florida was unlike Labrador. She had been trained always to say their names in the same breath.

A great part of our elementary educational process still consists in the teacher's asking questions and the pupil's answering them, the questions being predominantly of the type "What is . . . ?" "Where is . . . ?" "How much is . . . ?" and "When was . . . ?"

The popularity of quiz programs and games reflects the same preoccupation with *answers*, and the great part of the answers have to do with the knowledge of *names* of persons, places, and things.

The belief in the strength of the Word is indeed widespread. We find it explicitly stated in the opening sentence of the Gospel of St. John. We find it in the frequent incidence of word magic in all cultures from the most primitive to our own. We find it in the quotation from Genesis at the beginning of this chapter and in the endless dissertations of the scholasticists. It is by no means always a hidden unconscious belief. Often it is quite shamelessly stated. Swami Hariharanand Sarasvati, a Hindu scholar, writes:

The things *named* and their *names* are both parallel manifestations resulting from the unison of Brahman (the undifferentiated principle) and the Maya (appearances) just as waves appear in the sea. From Brahman united with Sakti (Energy-Maya) is issued in the order of

127

manifestation of the world on the one hand the Principle of Naming . . . and on the other the Principle of Forms, and out of it all the world, living beings, etc.

But between those two aspects of manifestation, the relation remains close, there is fundamental identity between the principle of names and the principle of forms, as well as between words and objects.

One need not go to India or search among the archives to encounter such views. A member of the faculty of a prominent center of learning published a book in 1948, in which he states:

I should urge examining *in all seriousness* that ancient belief that a divine element is present in language. The feeling that to have power of language is to have control over things is deeply imbedded in the human mind. We see this in the way men gifted in speech are feared or admired; we see it in the potency ascribed to incantations, interdictions, and curses . . . knowledge of the prime reality comes to man through the word; the word is a sort of deliverance from the shifting world of appearances. The central teaching of the New Testament is that those who accept the word acquire wisdom and at the same time some identification with the eternal . . .[4] [My italics. A. R.]

Mr. Weaver also quotes the passage from Genesis cited at the beginning of this chapter; but he does it "in all seriousness."

Quite a number of people share with Mr. Weaver and the Swami the belief that something is discovered about a thing when it is named. Anthropologists have made extensive studies on languages from Hottentot to English and have discovered in almost all of them taboos against the use of names ranging from the name of one's mother-in-law to the name of God. Word magic is not surprising in primitive ways of thinking, since it is prevalent in the child's way of thinking. The child discovers in his second year that pronouncing the magic word "mama" makes mother

[4] Richard M. Weaver, *Ideas Have Consequences.*

128

materialize. Belief in prayer and invocation, oath and curse, is rooted in the persistence of the child's awe of word magic.

And so a gentleman dies bequeathing a small fortune to some one who will give "the best" definition of a joke. The papers find it amusing but not more so than if he had bequeathed the money to the inventor of a self-lighting cigar. Somewhere in the scheme of things there is a "best" definition of a joke. It is the eccentricity of the gentleman's quest and not its absurdity that amuses the reporter. And he calls Hayakawa, the semanticist (aren't those people experts on definitions?), and asks him to give it a try.

And so people write to Dorothy Dix and ask for "true" meanings of "love," "jealousy," "loyalty," etc., as if these noises and ink marks were something other than vehicles for transmitting different experiences of different people.

And so a century ago Pushkin, the poet, aged thirty-nine, and Lermontov, the poet, aged twenty-six, and Galois, the outstanding mathematical genius, aged twenty, were killed in duels, because of the trigger effects of the symbolic stimulus "honor."

And so Neptunians and Plutonians are ready to start shooting at each other as soon as certain words are printed or pronounced.

We repeat, we are not pointing out the "causes" of wars, because we have not even defined "cause." We merely express the opinion that the millions of Neptunians who have never seen a Plutonian and vice versa could not be organized to exterminate each other if they did not confuse symbols with things. There are many other things people could not be organized to do if they did not confuse symbols with things. They could not be organized to pay more attention to labels than to the contents of packages; nor vote straight tickets; nor fear social experiments; nor participate in lynchings.

Politicians, cartoonists, and advertisers are aware of this. They earn their livelihood by manipulating the symbols to which identification reactions have been established: the label of "socialism" stuck to a public health bill; the caricature of the wild-eyed professor in his cap and gown; the bear walking across Europe; Old English type on whisky bottles; the girl in the bathing suit; a thousand assorted stereotypes all pigeonholed into an orderly and nonexistent world.

EITHER-OR

The third affliction of our Aristotelian language culture may be called the "either-or" (two-valued) orientation. Its source can be easily traced to the second and third Aristotelian "laws of thought."

(2) *"A is B" and "A is not B" cannot both be true assertions*;

(3) *One of the assertions "A is B" or "A is not B" must be true.*

Perhaps it would be more accurate to say that these "laws of thought" are formulations of the already existing semantic reactions.[5]

Nothing can be said against the *formal* aspect of these rules. Rules are agreements on the use of language, nothing else. But rules for using language internalize into a metaphysics and tend to perpetuate themselves even when the language becomes obsolete. The rules then leave us in possession of archaic maps with which we are to navigate the uncharted areas of the modern world.

When we make judgments and assertions, we do not make them about A's and B's. We substitute other symbols for them, symbols which are supposed to have a counterpart in reality. Thus A can stand for "a man" and B for "good." Then Rule 3 becomes "A man is either good or not good." But "not good" in our language

---

[5] "Semantic reaction" is a term introduced by Korzybski to refer to behavior "on the colloidal level" in response to symbols and symbolic patterns. The "colloidal level" refers to the submicroscopic structure of the nervous system. Semantic reactions are thus able, according to Korzybski, to effect lasting structural changes in our nervous systems.

habits is not just a formal negation of "good." For all practical purposes it means "bad." And so we are led from a linguistic rule to this "profound observation" about humanity: "A man is either good or bad." No mention is made of the circumstances in which a man may find himself. No mention is made of the many periods of his life, nor of his relation to his family, associates, employees, nor his attitudes toward his duties or his opinions or his rights. He is either good or bad. Not everyone thinks so naïvely. But such tendencies are observed in most of us.

In science, where the old metaphysics is untenable (because in science assertions are checked against experience), the old ways of speaking and evaluating have been discarded. No physicist will derive much meaning from St. Thomas Aquinas' assertion that a thing is either cold or hot. The physicist uses a thermometer. He doesn't pigeonhole temperatures; he records them as numbers. His descriptions of events are then relations between numbers, which range over an infinity of values. But comparatively few people have training in science, and nonscientific ways of speaking pervade all aspects of human activity. Even the scientists, although forced to use scientific language in their work, unfortunately do not work all the time. They come in contact with their wives (or husbands), their preachers, their lawyers, their landlords, with whom they have to transact the business of daily life. And most of this business is conducted on a basis far from scientific.

Little J was either a "good boy" or a "bad boy" today and has to be either rewarded or punished. (It is fortunate if the qualification "today" is made. In some families little J is either a "good boy" or a "bad boy" *in general*.)

The prospective business partner is either "honest" or "dishonest."

Daughter is either "in love" or "not in love" with the boy who comes to see her.

"Good people" go to heaven. "Bad people" don't.

131

CHAPTER 14

Elementalism, Absolutism

The person who asks "What happens to the hole when you eat the doughnut?" exhibits elementalism.

Elementalism is a tendency to take seriously the divisions and dichotomies implied by language, to believe in the existence of separate independent "qualities" or "categories," simply because words have been invented to stand for them. It is easy to see how elementalism arises out of false-to-fact identifications (taking separate words to *be* separate things); out of allness (believing the word to have said all about the thing); and out of either-or orientation (the habit of thinking in terms of mutually exclusive opposites).

Like the other Aristotelian semantic reactions, elementalism has its roots in ways of thinking which are *within limits* useful. The world is enormously complex. To begin orienting ourselves in it, we must tentatively break it up into separate components in order to fix our attention on each of them in turn. While we study one aspect of some event, we do not want the others to keep changing. We would like to forget about them for a while, so that they do not interfere with our observations. We can do that *if they remain constant*. So in our way of talking about them, we make believe they remain constant.

Wondering where the hole in the doughnut has gone is the result of such make-believe. We have *fixed* the hole in our imagination as something independent, and so we unconsciously assume it can remain "itself" while we eat the rest.

The scientific experiment is a procedure in which an attempt is made to keep some aspects of an event constant, while the other (variable) aspects are studied. The pains scientists take in setting up their experiments and the skepticism that good scientists invariably show toward the results of most experiments indicate that they are aware of how difficult it is to keep all the conditions (except the chosen few to be studied) constant.

As a typical example of this kind, we may take the classical experiment on gas pressure performed by Boyle in 1659. Boyle discovered that in most gases pressure varies inversely as the volume, *provided the temperature is kept constant.* This allowed him to *disregard* temperature and to speak only of the relations between pressure and volume.

The controlled experiment thus provides a way to make the world behave to a certain extent like the map we make of it. We have separate words for pressure, volume, and temperature. If we take words to be things, we suppose that these can have separate existence. In the real world, however, the aspects of events for which the words "pressure," "volume," "temperature" stand are intimately connected. They cannot be considered apart from each other unless an artificial environment is created in which some are held constant.

Physics, far in advance of the other disciplines of science (because the physicists were forced earlier than other scientists to abandon Aristotelian language habits), keeps discovering the intimate connections between different aspects of the world, formerly believed to be separate, independent categories. Heat and work; electricity and magnetism; time and space; mass and energy have become, in modern physics, thermodynamics, electromagnetism, space-time, and mass-energy, respectively.

133

Purged from the physical sciences, elementalistic notions remain entrenched in linguistic habits where looser hygienic standards prevail. They pervade, of course, the whole range of our daily language but are far from limited to those areas. They invade sections of social science, a great deal of psychology, and most of what passes for philosophy. The areas where the disinfection of linguistic habits is usually taboo (theological and political doctrines) are the real pestholes of elementalism. But we will not confine our examples to those regions.

In mathematical physics, the notions of "cause" and "effect" were abandoned years ago as practically useless, but without them large parts of metaphysics[1] and theology lose their *raison d'être*.

Modern genetics has shown how impossible it is to separate (except verbally) the notions of heredity and environment. Yet heated discussions are carried on ranging from high school debates to sociological dissertations on heredity vs. environment.

Newspaper columnists and preachers write and talk about scientific vs. "humanistic" values, which they often equate respectively to "material" and "spiritual."

Schools of psychiatry discuss action on the "emotional" level and action on the "intellectual" level.

People who are concerned with problems of aesthetics worry about the relative importance of "content" and "form."

Increased frankness in sexual matters to some extent increased the recognition that the "physical" and the "spiritual" are merely aspects of the behavior complex that is associated with a sexual union. But not so long ago Tolstoi was much concerned with the question of physical vs. spiritual love, and Titian once painted a picture on the subject.

We will examine two such popular dichotomies, the "emo-

---

[1] "Metaphysics" is used here in its traditional meaning: a system of inquiry seeking to uncover "the nature of ultimate reality."

Elementalism, Absolutism

tional" vs. the "intellectual" attitude (terms used in describing personalities) and "ends" vs. "means" (of interest in problems of ethics).

EMOTION AND INTELLECT

Example 1

Little A and Little B are each given an identical problem, say a jigsaw puzzle. Little A studies the picture carefully, notes the distribution of colors, seeks out the pieces that fit, and puts them together. His pattern begins to take shape, and he is absorbed in his problem.

Little B starts to fit some pieces together. They don't fit. He tries to force them. They still don't fit. One piece breaks. Little B sweeps the pieces off the table, lies down on the floor, and starts kicking and yelling.

Example 2

You are in a theater. You see smoke creeping into the auditorium from under the curtain. You have a choice of action. You can revert to the primitive generalized reaction to danger, that is, yell "Fire!" and run (it does not matter where, just run: danger means run). Or you can react in a *specific* way. You can get up on the stage and speak through a microphone:

"Ladies and gentlemen, I will ask you to rise and to follow instructions. The people nearest the center aisles will now proceed to the rear exits. Those near the outside aisles to the side exits. There is no danger. The fire department has arrived and has everything under control. The orchestra will please play 'There Will Be a Hot Time in the Old Town Tonight.' "

If that gets a laugh, you are a hero. Whether your name will appear in the paper as the man who forestalled a panic or among a long list of victims depends on whether you have succeeded in *narrowing down* your reactions to *specifically useful ones for the situation.*

The man who yells "Fire!" and runs is generally described as behaving "emotionally," while the man who makes the speech is said to behave "intellectually." Similarly, Little A, who works at his puzzle, is supposed to be "intellectual," while Little B, who has tantrums, is "emotional," or, to use a more old-fashioned term, "nervous." Yet it is difficult to see to what these old-fashioned categories refer. If they are supposed to differentiate between the inner feelings accompanying the two kinds of attitudes, they are not very useful. The "inner feelings" of two different individuals cannot be compared, because each "inner feeling" is observable only for the individual who is experiencing it. One could compare the verbalizations of these inner feelings. But this is hardly more reliable in view of the inadequacies of our language in this area. A more promising procedure would be to compare the physiological symptoms accompanying each type of behavior. In principle, it would be possible to measure the gland secretions, rate of pulse and respiration, shape and rate of brain waves, etc., of Little A and Little B and of the men who react differently to danger. If certain forms of overt behavior were consistently accompanied by certain physiological processes, one could perhaps classify behavior into "intellectual" and "emotional."

It is not likely that one would find such consistencies. The man who gives an over-all appearance of calmness and deliberation and so appears to be acting "intellectually" in the popular sense may exhibit physiological processes similar to those of the man "in a panic." A murderer may be "calmly" telling an involved, carefully thought-out alibi, while the lie detector tells an entirely different story about him. A person engrossed in mathematical research, usually believed to be one of the most "detached," "intellectual" forms of activity, may have strong "feelings" in the process quite

136

similar (if judged by verbalizations and/or physiological measurements) to those of a composer creating a symphony, who is popularly considered to be engaging in "emotional" activity.

The organism does not have definite, independent seats of "emotions" and "intellect," as the verbal dichotomy of these terms has led people to believe. Given a situation, the *whole organism* reacts to it in some way. There are visceral changes (changes in the blood supply to various areas); there are nervous impulse patterns; there are gland secretions. All are intimately related; all participate and interact.

A more useful way of classifying reactions to environment is to range them from "diffuse" to "specific." A specific form of behavior is one which is directed toward the solution of a definite problem confronting the organism. It is behavior which includes as little as possible unnecessary incidental activity. In other words, efficient behavior is specific behavior.[2]

When an animal is confronted with danger, say a hostile animal, whom it is necessary to fight or from whom it is advisable to flee, certain physiological changes occur. A substance called adrenalin is secreted by appropriate glands. Blood supply is diminished in the stomach and increased in the muscles. In fact, changes occur which will make the defense *effective*, whether the defense will be fighting or running. We recognize some crude, overt manifestations of these changes, and by comparison with similar symptoms that occur in us we call them "rage" (preparation for fighting) and "fear" (preparation for running). In appropriate circumstances these forms of behavior solve the problem for the animal (defense against the enemy). Therefore, these are more or less specific reactions for that animal. The whole body mobilizes its economy for the most effective form of behavior.

[2] For further elaboration, see Russell Meyers' "The Nervous System and General Semantics."

It is probable that the man who cries "Fire!" at the theater experiences metabolic changes similar to those of a fleeing animal. But his behavior does *not* solve the problem. His cries may start a panic in which he too will perish. The man who prevented the panic acted specifically. We don't know what sort of activities took place inside of him. Probably they were much more complex than those accompanying "fear," but we know they were *specific*, judging by the results.

In general, any acquired skill consists of the narrowing down of reactions to stimuli so as to channelize them into effective action. Usually it means the elimination of useless actions. The baby learning to grasp, the boy learning to write, the man learning to ski or to play the piano or to operate a lathe, all learn by eliminating the unnecessary, diffuse activities that accompany their first attempts. That is why the expert does not tire of prolonged activity as the novice does. The experienced boxer or golfer does not necessarily have stronger muscles than the beginner. He has merely learned to use them to more *specific* purpose, to punch harder or to drive farther. *Skillful activity is specific activity*, whether it involves viscera, glands, or the cerebral cortex. We are pretty safe in saying that in any overt activity of the organism all these are involved.

It so happens that the visceral and glandular activities associated with "fear" and with "rage" have lost most of their biological usefulness for human beings. It does not do us any good to have blood pumped away from the brain and into the leg muscles, because the things that can do us most harm today cannot be escaped by running away. We can't run away from cancer, from a depression, from a war, from high prices, from racial discrimination, from intellectual persecution, from frustration, as we can from a rhinoceros. Those dangers require an entirely different set of reactions than the reactions induced by fear and rage. *Yet we*

138

still continue to react to the danger of a push-button war as our pre-ice age ancestors reacted to the danger of invasion by a hostile tribe. To them fear and rage may have been useful for survival in the inevitable conflict. With us these reactions only serve to *make* the conflict inevitable. It is on that basis that we advocate training in semantic reactions in which these "emotions" are eliminated. They should be eliminated from the repertoire of human responses to environment *not because they are emotions,* but because they are *not specific enough* for most of the problems confronting us.

Note that the classification of reactions into diffuse and specific is not elementalistic like the intellect-emotion dichotomy. Reactions are not *either* diffuse *or* specific. They are *more or less diffuse and more or less specific.* The measure of specificity is effectiveness.

MEANS AND ENDS

The ends-means dichotomy has resulted in a long-standing debate question, "Does the end justify the means?" It is assumed that there is some way of comparing the ends achieved with the means employed. The question refers presumably to such bookkeeping.

The scientist generally recognizes the inseparability of "means" and "ends." When the biologist wishes to examine a cell through a microscope he knows that staining the cell with some dye makes observation easy. But he is also aware that *he is not observing the original cell,* but the *stained* cell. The means he has employed to make observation possible have changed the thing he observes. Some of the most tantalizing problems in experimental science are concerned with the necessity of making the thing observed relatively unaffected by the technique of observation. This is another instance of how scientific experiments amount to efforts to make a little section of the world elementalistic, so that we can study it with our elementalistic maps.

But the language of "ethics" does not keep pace with our changing outlook on the "physical" world. The means-end dilemma is still in the either-or stage. People concerned with "morality" think they are asking a profound and dramatic question when they pose it this way: "Suppose you could save the life of ten people by killing one innocent person, would you do it?"

This dilemma is the theme of countless legends and is prominent in modern literature. Answers are usually either an emphatic "yes" or an equally emphatic "no." On the affirmative side are people concerned with making history (or those who think they are making history). Revolutionary leaders who order mass executions and mass deportations of populations in the name of building a better social order justify their behavior by pronouncing the words "The ends justify the means." On the negative side are people who wish to avoid any conflict under any circumstances (nonresisters) and those concerned with fixing patterns of behavior in human beings once for all (religious moralists). Among the latter are the people who may insist that it is wrong to destroy a fetus in order to save the mother's life, because although the end is praiseworthy the means are immoral, and "The end does *not* justify the means."

Both parties are victims of an elementalistic orientation. "Ends" and "means" are viewed as having separate, independent existence like "cause" and "effect," "body" and "soul," and similar elementalistic fictions. The moralists assume that by refusing to employ means which they consider "immoral" they are somehow exonerating themselves from responsibility. It is difficult to see why the doctor who neglects to save a woman's life by refusing to perform an abortion is any less responsible for her death than he would be for the death of the fetus, if he did operate. On the other hand,

140

the apologists for any means to achieve desired ends forget that the separation of "means" and "ends" is merely a verbal convenience. They forget that the means they employ are *included* in the ends.

The question is not whether the establishment of a new social order is "worth" the sacrifice of so many lives in a reign of terror. The question is how a reign of terror will be reflected in the new social order; what sort of men will be attracted to leadership; what sort of semantic reactions will be developed in the population; how these reactions will necessitate other unforeseen measures, etc.

ABSOLUTISM

Failure to recognize the intimate connection between the observer and the observed may be called "absolutism."

When we say "hot" we mean hotter than our skin, and when we say "cold" we mean colder than our skin.[3] But our language does not say that. In it "hot" and "cold" exist independently of observers. The same holds, of course, for large and small, up and down, fast and slow, etc.

Physics long ago threw away these egocentric, personalized notions and has substituted for them systems of measurements. By saying 50 centimeters long instead of "long," the physicist communicates more effectively. The expression "50 centimeters" has constant meaning (is associated with similar experiences) to more people than the word "long." One of the most astounding discoveries ever made by man was the recognition that even such expressions like "50 centimeters" and "three hours" do not have an *absolute* meaning, but depend on the circumstances under which the measurements are made. In principle, the concepts of

---

[3] A neat experiment illustrates this. Take three vessels of water and fill them with cold, lukewarm, and hot water. Put your left hand in cold water for a while and your right hand in hot water. Then put both hands in the lukewarm water. It will seem "warm" to your left hand and "cold" to your right.

length, time, mass, energy, long considered absolutes even by physicists, are relative, somewhat like the notions "right" and "left." They are more useful, of course, than right and left, because they mean the same thing to many more people (in fact, to all the people on this planet). But when a change in the frame of reference must be *imagined*, as it has to be in certain calculations, the lengths of objects and the time intervals between events take on different values.

The dealers in "absolutes" such as good, evil, justice, injustice, morality, immorality, honesty, dishonesty could learn much from the physicists, if only they turned their attention to the fact that physicists can understand each other better than most people in spite of the seemingly esoteric character of their language. Theirs is a language which keeps replacing elementalistic and absolutist notions by nonelementalistic and relativist ones. In this language things which man has rent asunder are joined and idols are constantly knocked off their pedestals.

CHAPTER 15

CHAPTER 15

The Non-Aristotelian Formulation

Of all animals, man has the greatest potentialities for learning new forms of behavior. But we can do even more, something no other animal can do. We can transmit what we have learned to others removed in space and time. We are *time-binding* animals.[1]

We have seen how we practice time-binding by means of language. We "fixate" our experiences in language and then communicate them to others. We also use language heuristically to explain to ourselves what we experience. Much depends, therefore, on the way language functions. But the functioning of language depends on our knowledge of the distortions that inevitably enter our verbalizations. It is not the distortions themselves but our *ignorance* of them that is responsible for the bad functioning of our linguistic maps. If our watch runs fifteen minutes slow, the thing that makes us miss appointments is not so much that it is running slow as the fact that we don't know about it.

In one area of human experience there is an ever-present healthy attitude of skepticism toward the language that describes it—in science. Then, if we consider our time-binding function, the most important uniquely human function that we possess, we must conclude that when we behave like scientists we behave at

[1] "Time-binding" is a term introduced by Korzybski to describe the ability peculiar to human beings, of transmitting *accumulated* experience to succeeding generations (Cf. A. Korzybski, *Manhood of Humanity*).

143

our best (from the point of view of functioning like human beings). If, instead of making language serve our needs, we become slaves to it or to people who can manipulate it cleverly, we are behaving at our worst. Somewhere between these extremes ranges the behavior of our daily living.

What can we do to function better?

Alfred Korzybski has constructed what he calls the first non-Aristotelian system. Before we proceed to describe it, certain possible misunderstandings should be forestalled.

A non-Aristotelian system is not *anti*-Aristotelian. That is, it does not simply negate the rules Aristotle has formulated for the use of language. It simply points out that the rules are inadequate, because the language itself, to which they are applied (the language of syllogisms), is inadequate for describing the world we know today.

The use of the term "non-Aristotelian" is historically justified. Long before Korzybski's formulation of the non-Aristotelian system, non-Euclidean geometries were invented, and modern physics, which includes the theory of relativity and quantum mechanics, is often referred to as *non-Newtonian* physics. Non-Euclidean geometries and non-Newtonian physics are not anti-Euclidean or anti-Newtonian. They are more general than the older systems and include them as special cases. Thus the geometry that describes the surface of a sphere may be formulated as a Riemannian (non-Euclidean) geometry. In small regions of the sphere (which can be considered almost flat) Euclidean geometry can be applied successfully. The same is true of physics. If we are dealing with high velocities (such as are sometimes reached by subatomic particles), we must use Einstein's laws of motion to predict accurately, but where velocities are of ordinary magnitude, Newton's physics is quite adequate. All our engineering practice, except where nuclear physics is involved, still rests solidly on Newtonian physics and does very well.

144

The Non-Aristotelian Formulation

The language used in physics and in all other branches of science which are becoming exact (and this includes always more of science) is mathematics. Mathematics is a language not of classifications and identifications (as the language of syllogisms is) but one of *relations*. The logic of mathematics consists of rules by means of which new assertions can be derived from those admitted. In this way the logic of mathematics is analogous to the logic applied to the Aristotelian assertions (All A are B, etc.). But since the language (mathematics) is different, so is the logic.

We will give an illustration to show how the rules of Aristotelian logic are not applicable to mathematical "assertions." The point is that in mathematics certain "assertions" may be labeled "true" and other assertions "false," but still others may be made which are *neither true nor false* as they stand. Furthermore, there are various systems of mathematics. An assertion may be true in one system and false in another. Here are a few examples.

"$x + 3x = 4x$" is a true assertion in ordinary algebra.

"$1 + 2 = 4$" is a false assertion in ordinary arithmetic. But "$2x + 3 = 7$" is neither true nor false as it stands! It *becomes* a true assertion if x assumes the value "2"; for any other value of x, it is a false assertion. If we had been iron bound by the "eternal laws of thought" that an assertion must be either true or false, we could never have invented assertions in the form "$2x + 3 = 7$"; mathematics and science would have been impossible.

Another example is the assertion "$x^2 - 5x + 6 = 0$." If we are asked to draw a conclusion from the truth of this assertion, we can only say, either $x = 2$ or $x = 3$. If an Aristotelian zealot insists that x cannot equal both 2 and 3, we can only feel sorry that his rigid logical framework prevents him from adequately understanding the spirit of mathematical logic. We do not mean that x equals both numbers. We mean that a state of knowledge is reached at this point which enables us to say that x must equal one or the other. To a strict Aristotelian, this is not true knowledge. He has

145

to assert "A is B" or "A is not B." But in many areas of scientific inquiry "partial" knowledge (the range of possible values of a variable) is of the greatest importance.

Another example is the mathematical assertion $a \times b = b \times a$. It is a true assertion if the numbers of ordinary arithmetic are substituted for a and b, for example $3 \times 7 = 7 \times 3$. It is also true in much broader domains of numbers than those used in ordinary arithmetic. But if a and b represent the so-called "hypercomplex" numbers (of which ordinary numbers are a special case) the assertion is *not* in general true. There is an area of knowledge (quantum mechanics) in which events are best described in terms of such hypercomplex numbers. To be able to use them, one is forced to discard the notion that the rules of arithmetic, as taught in elementary schools, are "eternally true." One recognizes in them simply rules for the use of a particular language, the numbers of ordinary algebra. In different languages different rules apply. This is what was meant by the statement that physicists (and mathematicians) were forced by the progress of their inquiries to discard Aristotelian habits of thinking. We shall come back to this question in Chapter 19.

Non-Aristotelian systems already exist in science, namely, in the several kinds of mathematics used to describe our world and the logical rules applying to them. We cannot yet use mathematical language for most communications of daily living. Science has studied only comparatively simple classes of events. Our world is too complex for our present state of knowledge to be described exclusively in mathematical terms. Somehow we must get along with a language inherited from prescientific ages.

It is in regard to the use of these languages (pervaded by Aristotelian notions) that Korzybski applies his famous negative postulates. One could take them as warnings that go with dangerous pieces of machinery. The postulates are embodied in the principles

146

of non-identity, non-allness, multi-ordinality and self-reflexiveness. Each will be discussed in its proper place.

The principle of non-identity is a recognition that when we verbalize our experiences we necessarily map different experiences on one word (see Chapters 7, 8, and 9). When we forget about this in evaluating words we violate the principle and make false-to-fact identifications.

Here is a simple example. We see a particular cat, Minnie. We call it a "cat." We see another cat, Mitzi. She also "is" a "cat." Since a "cat is a cat" in our language, we may think that Minnie is Mitzi. This does not mean that we will admit *verbally* that "Minnie is Mitzi," because this assertion is not in the form "A is A." But we often act *as if* every cat were just "cat" to us. With cats the consequences may be no more serious than getting a scratch (Minnie likes to be petted, but Mitzi doesn't). When, however, groups of people are classified by some label, the consequences may be serious. Remembering that "the word is not the thing" serves to prevent the *confusing of orders of abstraction*.

"Minnie is Mitzi" sounds false, but "Minnie is Minnie" sounds right. Yet even this assertion must be taken with a grain of salt according to the principle of non-identity, because Minnie today is certainly not Minnie yesterday. She may be for all practical purposes, but it is well to keep in mind that she is not *entirely* so. She may have had kittens or contracted hydrophobia.

Although the principle of non-identity does not contradict the *formal* aspect of Aristotelian logic (it doesn't blandly say, A is *not* A), it does imply the rejection of Aristotelian metaphysics (see Chapter 11), according to which the world is a static collection of objects with properties and "natures." Korzybski subscribes to a more modern metaphysics, according to which the world consists of events and processes, rather than "things." Like the Aristotelian world, this world is also orderly and can also be studied with profit. But the things that must be sought out to get knowledge in this world are not the "natures" of things (as the Aristotelian philosophers thought) but regularities in the occurrence of events. Just as the most significant assertion in Aristotelian metaphysics was "All A are B," so the backbone of non-Aristotelian method of inquiry is the assertion "If P occurs, then Q will occur." Actually this is a simplification. The fundamental assertion is rather "If P, Q, R . . . occur, then the probability that S will occur is *so much*." The detailed discussion of this method must be postponed until the role of probability in scientific assertions is described (Chapter 20).

What, then, are the "events" in terms of which the whole world is described? According to our rules of definition, we must proceed operationally. This definition will be a long one, and the operations will all have to be performed mentally. The reader is asked to be patient and to come along into the four-dimensional space-time world, in which "events" are imbedded like raisins in bread.

THE SPACE-TIME WORLD

When a telegraph line inspector reports damage to the line, he specifies the *number* of the pole, and the repair gang knows where to go.

A ship at sea gives its position by two numbers, latitude and longitude.

An apartment in a city can be designated by three numbers, the position of the building in the city (which involves information equivalent to latitude and longitude) and the number of the floor.

But when during the war enemy bombers were reported approaching, they had to be specified by at least *four* numbers, position related to a point on the ground (that is, latitude and longitude), altitude, and the *time of passing*. Other numbers were

148

usually given besides, for example, velocity and direction of flight, but these referred to *future* events (to indicate where the bombers would probably be at a future time) not to the event itself.

Actually it always takes four numbers to specify an event. Some of these numbers (co-ordinates) may be obvious or unimportant and therefore omitted. For example, the ship at sea does not bother to give its altitude, because any point on the ocean is obviously at sea level. An apartment is not specified by time, because it is assumed that it will not appreciably change for a while. We may omit any of the co-ordinates in describing an event. Nevertheless, we must remember that four co-ordinates are required to indicate an event, three of space and one of time. It is possible to view the world as a vast collection of events taking place at more or less certain moments at more or less certain locations.

There is good reason for saying "more or less certain" instead of "certain," but to explain it would require a discussion of theoretical physics, which does not concern us here. We have played safe by inserting "more or less certain" in describing events, but we will develop our outlook *as if* every event could be exactly specified by four co-ordinates. In other words, we will take the space-time continuum to be a reasonable *approximation* to reality.

Actually, even if the space-time continuum picture of reality were "exact," an event could still be only roughly represented by co-ordinates, because events have extension both in space and in time. Similarly, Chicago is only roughly indicated by its latitude and longitude, because it is not a *point* on the earth's surface. Happenings which are commonly known as "events," such as eruptions of volcanos, hatchings of eggs, revival meetings, football games, eclipses of the sun, in short, everything that ever happens, should really be regarded as complex sequences of combinations of tiny atomlike "point-events." When such a view is adopted, it becomes clear that so-called "objects," such as chairs, cuspidors,

149

ambassadors, etc., are also combinations of "point-events." It is more accurate to speak of these things as "happening" rather than "being."

From this point of view, Minnie is not an "individual" as her name makes her out to be. If she is taken to be a lump of matter, she is a large collection of living things called cells. The cells themselves have structures, that is, differentiated parts. Analyzed into its chemical constituents, the cell is seen to consist of several different kinds of molecules (still smaller particles), which too have structure. Molecules consist of atoms, and atoms of even tinier subatomic particles. We don't know what comes after the "subatomic particles," but it is useful to imagine that we can carry this division indefinitely. Just as we imagine that we can subdivide a line into infinitesimally fine particles (points), so a surface can be imagined to consist of thin slices (lines), which in turn consist of points, and solids can be thought of as consisting of surfaces. But all this analysis is really not of the lump of matter as it exists in time but of its instantaneous "photographs." To talk about the "real existence" of a lump of matter, we must add another dimension, time. Then, even a "space-point" can be thought of as sliced up into "instantaneous points." These instantaneous points (space-points at specific instances) we will call point-events.

If we assume that the real universe consists of a vast collection of point-events, then it appears that no two events are the same event. This may appear so obvious that it seems superfluous to say it. We shall nevertheless say it again and even put it in italics: *No two events are identical.* This is another form of the principle of non-identity.

Let us see what this means. We have seen that point-events are designated by four numbers, three co-ordinates of space and one of time. Let us take the point-event E_1, characterized by co-ordi-

150

nates (x_1, y_1, z_1, t_1). Another event, E_2, will be characterized by another quadruple of numbers, (x_2, y_2, z_2, t_2). They cannot *all* be respectively equal to (x_1, y_1, x_1, t_1) because if they were we would be talking about the same event, E_1. It suffices only for one of these four numbers, say t_2, to be distinct from the corresponding co-ordinate, t_1, of E_1 for the event E_2 to be distinct from E_1. This means that even if we are talking about such a simple thing as a "point in space" we cannot call it the "same" point if we mention it at another time, since its fourth co-ordinate (t) is always changing.[2]

We have seen that Minnie with young kittens is not the same as Minnie without kittens (for one thing she gives milk, which she did not do before). Let us think of this for a while. If we feel that we are only "pretending" that Minnie is not the same, that "really" she is the same old Minnie, we are not holding to the assumption we have made, namely, that the universe consists of point-events and no two point-events are the same. Let us resist the temptation of slipping into the old ways of thinking, if we wish to see the consequences of the non-Aristotelian assumption.

Minnie, of course, is a much more complicated system than a point-event. If all the point-events that make up Minnie are different, then Minnie must always be changing with time. The

---

[2] In ordinary space, two points are considered distinct if the distance between them is greater than zero. If the distance is zero, this implies that all the co-ordinates of one point are equal respectively to the corresponding co-ordinates of the other. If the notion of "distance" is generalized to the space-time world, this rule does not always hold. In the theory of relativity the analogue to distance is taken to be the "interval," between two point events, specified by the expression $\sqrt{(x_1-x_2)^2+(y_1-y_2)^2+(z_1-z_2)^2+(\tau_1-\tau_2)^2}$ where τ is "time" multiplied by a certain constant. Because of the nature of that constant, it is possible for the interval between two events to be zero without the corresponding co-ordinates being equal. Whether in that case the events are to be called "distinct" or "identical" depends on how we define "identical" events. The problem does not arise, however, except in cases involving speeds equal to that of light.

secretion of milk when kittens come is only a more conspicuous manifestation of the changes constantly going on in her. Really she is not the same at any two moments. In any interval of time, there is a whole sequence of Minnies. Or, if you wish to put it in another way, at any moment of time, we observe only a *cross section* of Minnie.

When we persist in calling the totality of Minnies just Minnie, we are abstracting. We are ignoring those characteristics which are always changing and are paying attention only to those which remain *invariant*. If we did not do this, we could not live. We could not react to the world on the basis of past experience, because if we did not identify "similar" experiences we could not "recognize."

And so we are identifying that complex collection of events which we could never describe (because a description, no matter how detailed, could not mention all the innumerable point-events) by a short noise, "Minnie." This enables us to *communicate*. If a friend of ours has performed the same feat (i.e., reduced the collection of events that compose Minnie to a single word, "Minnie"), we can establish a bond of communication with our friend. We abstract from the complex of events Minnie to form the noise Minnie. Our friend translates the noise Minnie into *his* recollection of that complex of events.

The modern physicist often pictures the world as a four-dimensional collection of point-events, the space-time continuum. No two events are identical. In order to react at all to our environment, to study it or to communicate about it, we must abstract, that is, we must assign the same names to different collections of point-events. As long as we keep this in mind and behave accordingly we do not confuse words with things, we subscribe to the non-Aristotelian principle of non-identity. If we take our abstractions at face value, as if they *were* reality, we are making false-to-fact identifications.

Thus the principle of non-identity does not say that we should not make identifications (linguistically). It says that we should always remember that the identifications are *only* linguistic.

CHAPTER 16

The Non-Aristotelian Formulation (Continued)

The key problem is to eliminate, first, the semantic disturbance called identification or the confusion of orders of abstracting and similar disturbances of evaluation.

Alfred Korzybski, *Science and Sanity*

A map or language, to be of maximum usefulness, should, in structure, be similar to the structure of the empirical world.

Alfred Korzybski, *Science and Sanity*

Now let us summon a non-Aristotelian and ask him the three questions, the answers to which seem so important for understanding communication:

1. *What are assertions made about?*
2. *How do you define your terms?*
3. *How do you know that what you are saying is true?*

To the first question, the non-Aristotelian might reply something like this:

Assertions can be made about point-events and about seeming invariants of complexes of point-events (so-called objects). When labels are affixed to abstractions which our nervous systems make of objects and to abstractions of higher order (words), assertions can be made about them. Furthermore, assertions can be made

154

about *assertions*, which, in fact, I am doing now. And if someone chooses to comment on what I am saying, then he will be making assertions about assertions about assertions. In principle, there is no limit to this process.[1] Again, assertions can be made about abstractions from events *inside* the speaker. Such assertions should be recognized as opinions, expressions of taste, or value judgments.

The kinds of assertions made and the things they are made about form a hierarchy of abstraction, an "abstraction ladder." The principle of multi-ordinality (see Chapter 15) is the recognition of the distinction between the different rungs of the ladder.[2]

To make language effective both as a means of communication and heuristically, the users of language (both transmitters and receivers) should be constantly aware of the level of abstraction of their discourse. Failure of communication and distortion of "reality" through language can be often traced to the confusion of the orders of abstraction.

Words are abstractions made of things; reports are abstractions made of experience; inferences are abstractions made of descriptions. When people react to words as if they were things, to inferences as if they were descriptions, etc., they are confusing levels of abstraction. They are not using language to the best advantage and therefore not functioning at their human best.

The form of assertion fundamental in Aristotelian cognition, "A is B," is dangerous, because of the internalized meaning of the word "is." Because we associate identity with "is," we tend to identify different levels of abstracting, for example, when we hear "A cat is a mammal." Explanations to the effect that the assertion does not *mean* to identify cats with mammals are not relevant. The

---

[1] This is Korzybski's principle of self-reflexiveness (see Chapter 15).

[2] This abstraction ladder is represented by Korzybski in his so-called "structural differential." For detailed discussions of this device and its applications see his *Science and Sanity*, S. I. Hayakawa's *Language in Action*, Stuart Chase's *Tyranny of Words*, Francis P. Chisholm's *Introductory Lectures on General Semantics*, William Vogt's *The Road to Survival*, or Wendell Johnson's *People in Quandaries*.

155

meaning is not in the assertion but in the evaluation. The persistent confusion of abstraction orders is *observed* in the users of language. The thesis is that this confusion is correlated with the internalized structure of our language, which does not reflect the structure of the world.

Examples of bad use of language can be found in "philosophy." Traditional philosophy has been built on a delusion that it was making true assertions about "reality." It had neither the method for learning about reality (experimental techniques) nor the language to talk about it (mathematics). If only philosophy would leave the assertions about "reality" (events) to science and content itself to inquiries about language (theory of meaning, logic, logical syntax), it could become respectable again. Carnap and Wittgenstein should be credited with restoring a useful function to philosophy by recommending that it limit its researches to language about language.

Other examples of bad use of language are found in political doctrines, where "isms" are irresponsibly manufactured. High-order abstractions are treated in the discourse of journalists and demagogues as if they were on the object level. To aggravate the confusion, political cartoons are employed to spread identification of these high-order abstractions with persons or animals, especially with those able to precipitate fear reactions.[3] The language of political ideology is a powerful block to understanding and to systematic inquiry.

To the second question, the non-Aristotelian's reply might be: I define my terms by extensional definitions. I may use any of

---

[3] An all-time low was reached recently in an animated cartoon, used for propaganda purposes, in which an abstraction was made of all the "bad isms" personified by a monster, labeled simply Ism. By this technique, people are trained to respond with fear reactions to a *suffix*. Under the conditions of fear and rage inquiry and communication, the typically human activities, are inhibited.

the techniques if linguistically convenient, but the meaning of my definitions is extensional, in terms of referents on levels of abstraction closer to direct experience than the terms defined.

The structural differential as modified by Wendell Johnson (see footnote on page 155) prescribes an order to the levels of abstraction. On the "lowest" (submicroscopic level) are the "events" of the four-dimensional space-time world. The next (microscopic) level reveals "objects" visible through magnification. Then comes the "macroscopic" level, of which we are aware through our unaided senses. Then the first "verbal" level, the names of objects resulting from a primitive abstracting process, etc. Direct experience takes place on the microscopic and macroscopic "object" levels. My fundamental assumption is that *this level of experience can serve as the basis of communication between human beings,* and that the other levels of experience can by extensionalization be translated in terms of those levels. Thus the knowledge of "low-order" abstractions like "atoms" and high-order abstractions like "energy," "diplomacy," "insanity," etc., should all be defined in terms of experiences on the object levels. In physics this can always be done by operational definitions. In other fields of knowledge and discourse it remains to be done.

Extensional definitions disclose the level of existence of the referent, to which a term refers. When I point to an object which is supposed to be the referent for the word "Minnie" I have indicated that Minnie exists on the object level. The word "cat" is more abstract. To define it, I can point to Minnie, Mitzi, and a thousand other cats and *hope* that the next time the recipient of my definition sees something which I call "cat," he too will call it "cat." We do not know of anything that guarantees that he will do so, since, after all, the 1,001th cat, as an object, is different from each of the other 1,000 cats. But the method *works.*

So we use it and base our whole system of communicating on its working.

The word "mammal" is still more abstract. Mammals differ more from each other than cats do. Here it will not be sufficient to point to a thousand mammals to ensure that the 1,001th will be recognized as a mammal. The operational definition becomes *verbal*.

"Observe how the animal reproduces. If it gives birth to live young and nurses them, it is a mammal female. The males that copulate with such females also are called mammals."

The definition depends on the knowledge of "reproducing," "nursing," "copulation," etc. These, in turn, can be extensionally defined. So from high-order abstraction a chain of operational definitions leads to objects and events that can be defined only by *pointing* (the object level). There is no rule as to where speaking must cease and pointing must begin. But obviously if abstractions are to be connected with direct experience, somewhere along the line *this must take place*.

In my critique of philosophic, political, and theological discourse, I often judge certain terms meaningless. This does not mean that extensional definitions for such terms *cannot* be given, but that an extensional definition *has* not been given. To be sure, the devil can be extensionally defined. One can point to a picture of one. But this definition is not equivalent to the usual intensional definitions of the devil (Prince of Darkness, Tempter of Humanity, etc.). The term is therefore meaningless because no connection can be established between its verbal definitions and direct experience.

Some people maintain that the terms used in theology and philosophy are high-order abstractions and therefore cannot be connected with object referents any more than the highly abstract terms of physics can (such as entropy, energy, magnetic flux, etc.).

158

This they have a right to maintain. But to give those terms meaning, they should define them at least operationally (the way the high abstraction terms in physics are defined). Sometimes such definitions are attempted. A theologian asked to define hell may say:

"If you ask many people, whether they believe in hell, they will say 'yes.' Many people guide their actions in accordance with a desire to avoid going to hell. So hell is real to *them*. Therefore, it does have some measure of reality."

Indeed, the person who defines hell in this way is adhering to our standards of operational definition. We did imply that any definition is acceptable which connects the term with some observable events in space and time. People's behavior certainly consists of observable events. Therefore, an operational definition of hell must be admitted to have been given. There is no argument there. *Any* term may be arbitrarily defined, that is, connected with any class of events whatsoever. We allow complete freedom of definition, because we recognize that words do not have an inherent meaning. But once one has committed himself to a level of discourse by giving a definition, one must stick to that level. And if one does that, one will find that the way to avoid "going to hell" is simply not to react to the word as if it stood for anything *other* than a fiction. The person most important for "salvation" then becomes the semanticist instead of the priest.

A unicorn has a "level of existence." It exists on the British coat of arms and in mythology, but not in zoology.

Donald Duck has an existence—as a chemical precipitate on films and as a class of events inside the skins of people who have seen colored shadows of this precipitate projected on a screen, but not as a duck in a sailor suit.

"Un-Americanism" has a level of existence—in the reactions to this word of people who invented it and in the semantic dis-

159

turbances[4] for which it is responsible, but not as an extensionally defined activity that harms people like dope peddling, race prejudice, and witch hunting.

To the third question, "How do you know that what you are saying is true?" the non-Aristotelian's reply might well be:
We don't. Absolute truth is meaningless, because no definition of it can be agreed upon. Intensional definitions of truth do not tell how to distinguish truth from nontruth. Extensional definitions of truth have often been given, but they seem useless for obtaining knowledge about the world. Here are some examples:
"Truth is that which is eternal and unchanging and revealed through the Divine Word" (intensional definition).
"Truth is the totality of statements in the Bible [or Koran or Stalin's Collected Works] and the interpretations of these statements made by such-and-such persons" (extensional definition).
The former definition does not tell us how to distinguish truth from nontruth; the latter seems useless for obtaining knowledge about the world. Neither definition serves to improve communication. But concern with truth *should* help establish communication and promote a better understanding of the world. Therefore, no definition of absolute truth is acceptable.
We must define truth operationally. Since time-binding makes possible a constant extension of our repertoire of operations, truth is not static or absolute. The world is a dynamic state of affairs, and our knowledge about it is always changing. This means not merely that new "facts" are discovered, but also that new ways of talking about what we experience are discovered. One cannot expect, therefore, any assertion about the world to retain its truth value as the state of our knowledge changes. No assertion tells *all*

[4] Confusing levels of abstraction, which results in false-to-fact maps.

about the world or any portion of it (the principle of non-allness).
Hence my skepticism.

*The truth value of an assertion is measured by how much you
are able to predict on the basis of it.* In the literature of general
semantics, this notion of truth is referred to as the "criterion of
predictability."

The assertions you make about the world are your map of the
world. The question "How do you know that what you are saying
is true?" becomes more meaningful if asked this way: "How good
is your map?" This question is easy to answer: a map is the
better the more you can predict about the territory by means of it.
To speak the truth means to predict well. Good prophets have good
maps.

The non-Aristotelian is careful to distinguish between the levels
of abstraction of the content matter of assertions. He is aware
that the syntactic structure of assertions is not an indication of
this level. In our language "beer," "mother love," and "topological
group" are all nouns.

The non-Aristotelian defines his terms in such a way as to connect them (not necessarily by the definition itself, but by a chain
of definitions) ultimately to the levels of common experience,
the sensory or object levels. Definitions on that level are made
by pointing. Thus the gap between language and experience is
closed.

The non-Aristotelian uses only one criterion for truth: the
criterion of predictability.

A Note on the non-Aristotelian's Family Tree

In what follows, the non-Aristotelian will continue to state his
views. Let us make a brief digression to look at his intellectual
heritage.

The resemblances our non-Aristotelian bears to various thinkers from William of Occam to Alfred Korzybski are not coincidental. They are clear indications of paternity. One might name three currents of thought which merged in the outlook of the modern non-Aristotelian.

1. *The Materialist Current*

To this current Aristotle himself had contributed, since he was the first man who found out things by systematically looking at things.[5] Moreover, as we have seen, he sought to explain events by "natural" causes and clearly stated the principles of cause and effect to be residing in the interaction of material things.

William of Occam (d. *c.* 1349) also advanced the cause of materialism. He preferred to base his "reality" on individuals rather than on universals. He said in effect:

"What exists is Smith, Jones, and Kelly, rather than the 'concept' Man; this hovel, that cottage, and yon palace, rather than the concept Dwelling."

The modern non-Aristotelian, with his levels of abstraction (see Chapters 15, 16) assigns different *kinds* of reality to "objects" and "classes of objects." But he demands that judgments about a class should be translatable in terms of verifiable predictions about directly observable objects. This is essentially a materialist point of view.

English materialism of the seventeenth century is most vividly represented by Bacon and Locke. We have already seen how Bacon firmly stood on his position that the source of knowledge is ex-

---

[5] The beginning of experimental science during the Renaissance is often considered as a revolt against "Aristotelian" (purely speculative) science of the Middle Ages. But Aristotle himself was less Aristotelian than the scholasticists who venerated him. Although he performed practically no controlled experiments, he made some remarkably accurate *observations*, especially in biology.

perience (see Chapter 5). Locke stated this position in purely epistemological terms:

> Let us suppose the mind to be, as we say, white paper, void of all characters, without any ideas; how comes it to be furnished? . . . To this I answer in one word, from experience; in all that our knowledge is founded and from that it ultimately derives itself. Our observation employed either about external sensible objects, or about the internal operations of our minds, perceived and reflected upon by ourselves, is that which supplies our understandings with all the materials of thinking. These two are the fountains of knowledge, from whence all the ideas we have, or can naturally have, do spring.[6]

Basically similar notions concerning the origins of knowledge were entertained by the French Encyclopedists of the eighteenth century. Here is Diderot's view:

> Suppose a pianoforte endowed with the faculty of sensation and memory . . . would it not of its own accord repeat those airs which you have played on its keyboard? We are instruments endowed with the faculties of sensation and memory. Our senses are keys upon which surrounding nature strikes and which strike upon themselves. This is all . . . that occurs in the piano which is organized like you and myself.[7]

So far we have described the "crude" materialist point of view according to which "nature" simply "exists" in material things. An important advance was made by the *dialectical materialists*, who adopted Hegel's "dialectics" and applied it to the materialist outlook. The principles of dialectics, as stated by Engels in his *Dialectics of Nature*, begin to look conspicuously like the non-Aristotelian premises of non-identity and self-reflexiveness:

1. The law of transformation of quantity into quality.
2. The law of the interpenetration of opposites.
3. The law of the negation of the negation.

[6] John Locke, *Essay on the Human Understanding*, II, 1, 2.
[7] *Dialogue of D'Alembert and Diderot*, as quoted by V. I. Lenin in his *Materialism and Empirio-criticism*.

Hegel had stated them as "laws of thought," analogous to the Aristotelian "laws of thought." To harmonize them with a materialist outlook, the dialectical materialists declared them to be "laws of nature," since they had to stick at all costs to their guns in taking "matter" to be "primary" to "mind."

The important notion of nature being in a "state of flux" arose in the dialectical materialist view, which finally took its modern shape in the space-time continuum picture of reality. With the flux notion, the immutable "objects," "qualities," "categories," "species," etc., of Aristotelian metaphysics lost their "eternal" reality. But it remained for general semantics to establish those old notions as abstractions which our nervous systems make of complex processes (see Chapters 7, 8, 9, and 10).

The modern non-Aristotelian can (if he is so inclined) call himself a materialist, because he considers modern physics as the discipline that describes reality most effectively. As we have seen, the modern physicist describes the world as composed of events, interactions of matter-energy in space-time. What mystics relegate to "spirit," "will," "Providence," etc., and declare outside of human cognition (or at least outside of systematic cognition), the non-Aristotelian either discards as meaningless or seeks to explain by configurations of events, in principle no different from those which explain the so-called "material" world.

2. *The Semantic Current*

This movement has its roots in the recognition that discourse is not a thing outside of man, like stars or rivers, or butterflies, but something created by man. If discourse has meaning, it is because men have put it there. Discourse may also be meaningless. Discourse has levels. One can talk about things, about talking about things, etc. Communication often fails because these levels are confused.

The Non-Aristotelian Formulation

In England this movement was represented by Viola Welby, Bertrand Russell, C. K. Ogden, I. A. Richards, and others. These people were largely interested in problems of logic and in the theory of meaning and symbols.

In Austria Ernst Mach (1838-1916) analyzed the meaning of some propositions of physics and started the critical movement that finally culminated in the Relativist Revolution. His intellectual progeny formed the famous Vienna Circle of Logical Positivists, to which belonged Rudolf Carnap (now at Chicago), Ludwig Wittgenstein (now at Cambridge) and Otto Neurath (deceased). The criterion of predictability as a measure of truth was most clearly formulated by these people. The Polish mathematician Alfred Tarski is another important exponent of the semantic current.

Two physicists who strongly reflect the logical positivist point of view are P. W. Bridgman (who is largely responsible for the clear-cut formulation of the operational definition) and Philipp Frank.

Henri Poincaré and Albert Einstein, two of the foremost physicists of this century, developed further the critical approach to physics and the linguistic analysis inspired by it. In fact, Frank says in his biography of Einstein, "The theory of relativity was primarily a reform not in metaphysics but in semantics."

3. The Neuro-linguistic Current

The chief exponent of the neuro-linguistic approach is Alfred Korzybski. He examines meaning not merely "logically" but also "psycho-logically." For him *evaluation* and *semantic reaction* are the central points of interest. The term "neuro-linguistic" emphasizes the central problem of general semantics (the discipline formulated in Korzybski's chief work, *Science and Sanity*), namely, the *internalization* of language structure within the structure of

165

the human nervous system, which determines evaluative habits and semantic reactions.

Korzybski's formulation contains a rich and suggestive terminology readily applicable in most situations where evaluative processes are important. Thus the terms "identification, levels of abstraction, elementalism, allness, two-valued orientation, time-binding, self-reflexiveness, map-territory relations," etc., have been either introduced by him or have been used in new ways to describe human behavior. The very term "non-Aristotelian" is due to Korzybski, and the discipline of general semantics is often referred to as a non-Aristotelian system (methodology).

In the past decade or so a number of writers in various fields have acknowledged their intellectual debt to Korzybski: Stuart Chase (social science), Hayakawa (linguistics and literature), Lee (speech), Johnson (psychology and speech pathology), Vogt (ecology), Frohman (psychiatry), Russell Meyers (neurology), Francis P. Chisholm (general semantics), etc. Others like Charles Morris (semiotic), George K. Zipf (biolinguistics), and Brock Chisolm (psychiatry), proceeding along trails other than those indicated by Korzybski, can likewise be considered as contributing to the neuro-linguistic approach.

The writer is indebted not only to Alfred Korzybski, but to all his predecessors and followers, with whose works he is acquainted. There most of the notions presented here have appeared in one way or another.

CHAPTER 17

Are Logical Positivists Idealists?

A book is a one-way road for ideas. The author cannot hear the questions or the objections of his readers. The most he can do is anticipate them.

Objections to the non-Aristotelian formulation may be raised on various grounds. There are, for example, the philosophical objections. "Is not something omitted from knowledge or given up if the only content of truth is predictions? What about the truth of the past? What about the Ultimate Reality, which may be beyond our cognition?"

Then there are the political objections. The rightists call the semanticists leftists, and the leftists call them rightists. Largely this is because semanticists would like to see politics become a part of anthropology or sociology instead of a disreputable branch of religion or demonology, which it is today. They refuse to worship the golden calf of free enterprise and will not sacrifice at the altar of the class struggle.

Third, there are the intuitive objections. "Why all this hair-splitting? Why do semanticists insist on attacking notions whose validity is self-evident? What about Common Sense? Is it not, after all, the best guide to orientation? Are semanticists trying to resurrect the ancient art of sophistry?"

Finally, there are objections on moralistic grounds. "Is not all this emphasis on science misplaced? What good is science without virtue, love, morality, etc.? Can science make us better or happier?"

167

Let us see how our non-Aristotelian, Mr. N, answers these objections.

Is the Past Real?

You say the only criterion of truth is the ability to predict. Would you say, then, that the scientific method is judged entirely for its applicability to predictions?

N: Yes.

Is geology, or is it not, a science? Or let us put it this way. Are the methods of geology scientific?

N: They are.

And yet most of the assertions of geology deal with events of the remote past and not with predictions. And so do the assertions of history.

N: That is a serious objection. But let us take a specific assertion about the past and see what we are doing when we maintain it is true. Choose your assertion.

Woodrow Wilson was inaugurated on March 4, 1913.

N: How do you know?

There are records. I can show you a newspaper of that date describing the inauguration. There are even some eyewitnesses.

N: And if you were to convince anyone that the event did actually take place, how would you proceed?

I would ask him to look at the records and talk to the eyewitnesses.

N: In other words, you would predict what he would find in the records and what he would hear from the witnesses?

Yes, but the events took place *independently* of my predictions. Even if all the records were destroyed, that would not alter the fact that Wilson *was* inaugurated on March 4, 1913. You still have not answered my question about the assertions of geology. Do you or do you not believe that the earth existed before there was anyone to make observations and predictions?

N: I should really ask you what you mean by (1) "believe" and (2) "exist," but that will come later. To let you state your case properly, I will say yes, I believe that the earth existed prior to observers.

Then you believe in the existence of a reality independent of observers and therefore of predictions? Does that not contradict your criterion of predictability?

N: It does not. When I make the assertion "I believe the earth existed before there were any observers" I am aware of the sense in which "believe" and "exist" are used. The meaning of these terms is not self-evident and is not unique. They must be defined operationally in a given context. And the operations that define them will include observations and predictions. In the case of geology, to believe in the long existence of the earth means to organize one's assertions in a certain way, to accept a certain framework of assumptions.

And where are the predictions?

N: If I make use of the framework offered in Genesis or some other mythological formulation, my system will contain more and more contradictions as new observations are made. In fact, the Biblical theory about the age of the earth implies a prediction: no rock formations or deposits will be found which took more than a few thousand years to complete. This contradicts certain conclusions which, on the basis of other observations, we must make about rock formations. The geological theories, on the other hand, enable us to make predictions concerning the correlation of seemingly unrelated phenomena, such as the proportions of

169

radium and lead found in certain rocks and the age of those rocks established by other independent methods. The verification of these predictions is the meaning of my "belief" in the assertions of geology.

In other words, you are unwilling to recognize *any* objective reality independent of an observer. You are an idealist.

N: What's an idealist?

Idealism and materialism are the two irreconcilable camps of philosophy. The struggle between them is as old as philosophy itself. The fundamental assumption of idealism is that mind is primary to matter. Materialism asserts the opposite. Therefore, the point of view of materialism implies the existence of the world independent of observers. Since you always insist on including the observer (that is yourself) into your judgments about reality, you reject the point of view of materialism and must therefore be an idealist. To be consistent, you should in the last analysis deny the existence of everything and everyone but yourself.

Was There a Splash?

N: Before we talk about the existence of the "objective world," let us start on a modest scale. You remember how the ancients argued about the existence of a certain splash?

Certainly. They supposed that somewhere in the wilderness a tree fell into a lake, and there was no one around to hear the splash. Did the splash take place?

N: What do you say?

Of course, it did. And so said the ancient materialists. And it was your prototypes, the idealists, who denied the existence of the splash, because there was no ear to hear it. To them sensations were the primary reality. But the materialists have always recognized the fundamental reality of matter.

N: Would you not say, then, that the observers consist of matter?

They do. Consciousness is only matter organized in a certain way.

N: Do you recognize that matter constantly interacts with other matter, thereby changing its form, that consciousness is nothing but certain kinds of interactions of matter and energy? In other words, do you, as I do, view the world as a configuration of events?

I do.

N: What, then, shall we call a splash?

A portion of such events.

N: How big a portion? Evidently those events must be included which comprise the vibrations of the medium. How about those events which make up the vibrations of the eardrum, the oscillations of the middle ear ossicles, the passage of impulses along the auditory nerves, the activity of the neurons in the temporal lobes of the cortex? Shall *they* be included as parts of that sequence of events, which we designate by a "splash"? It seems to me to be only a matter of choice. We may define as "splash" all those events, including the ones involving the eardrum, etc. Or we may say that the air vibrations alone constitute the "splash"? In the first case, an ear is necessary for the existence of the "splash"; in the second case, no ear is necessary. The argument has been reduced to an argument over a definition, a fruitless argument, since words have no inherent meanings.

If definition is only a matter of choice, why do you always choose to include the observer in your definitions of reality, thus

171

aiding and abetting the idealists? Why do you define the very Truth as *someone's* ability to predict. If the world *is* a configuration of events, as you have just admitted, why cannot Truth be simply defined as that which *is* regardless of whether anyone is looking or trying to predict?

N: Because we never describe events. We describe at best our observations of events and usually high-order inferences from such observations. What we say is always far removed from what "is." Our knowledge depends on the way we abstract, and that depends on the habits we have formed, to a large extent on internalized linguistic habits.

But how about facts? Are not the achievements of science discoveries of facts and of natural laws? Do not those laws *reflect* something real? If they do, then something must be *there*. We may at a given time not have all the facts, but is not the progress of knowledge an approach to *something*? Then that something must be the objective Truth.

N: Allow me to introduce a friend of mine, Don José of Cadiz. Don José has just arrived from the fifteenth century. Don José, I understand you witnessed the return of Columbus' expedition from the Indies. You were quite impressed with the success of the expedition, and now you are an ardent supporter of the doctrine that the earth is a sphere. Is there anything about the doctrine that still remains obscure to you?

Don José: There is. How can the Indians and the Cathayans live upside down? Is it because they are heathen?

N: They don't mind it. In fact, they don't know the difference. They may well believe that it is *they* who are walking right side up.

Don José: The poor deluded souls.

N: But they are not deluded.

Don José: Is it they, then, who are right? Do they walk right side up, and we upside down?

N: Either way you wish. Or neither.

Don José: But which way is *really* up? You twentieth-century scientists have found out so many things. Haven't you found out which way is up?

N: There is nothing to find out.

Don José: Nothing to find out! There is a *truth*, isn't there?

N: You are confused, my friend, because you have taken too seriously the abstractions your ancestors have made of their limited experience. "Up" and "down" are only ways of talking. Sometimes they are useful, as in conversations with elevator operators. Sometimes they are meaningless, as in astronomy. And so it is with all our abstractions. Some are useless; others are of limited usefulness. A few are valid under such general conditions that they are especially valuable in describing the world. Those are generally most difficult to discard.

So far the most useful abstractions have been made by the physicists. But that does not mean that useful abstractions cannot be formed on higher levels of complexity, in biology, psychology, the social sciences. However, the worth of such abstractions must be established before they are labeled "truth." Their worth is in their usefulness for simplifying manipulation of symbols, and the test of their truth value is the amount of prediction they make possible.

This attitude is important if controversies about truth are to be resolved. This attitude points toward a *public* conception of truth instead of innumerable private ones, to general human truths instead of local tribal ones. This public conception of truth is not based on any arbitrary authority masquerading as the voice of God. It imposes no doctrines as an official faith, because it is not aimed at perpetuating itself.

173

The attitude of logical positivism toward truth reconciles unanimity of purpose with the dignity of the individual, while the existing social orders stress the contradictions between these goals. Such unanimity of purpose without sacrificing freedom of inquiry and criticism has actually been achieved in the most developed areas of science. It is worth while to emulate this attitude.

The Dials and Reality

Since you have mentioned the distinction between "general truth" and "local truth," do you not sometimes feel that what you call "general truth" is itself pitifully limited?

N: How so?

You admire the methods of the physicist, and his great ability to predict. But consider *what* he predicts?

N: Eclipses and earthquakes, tides and explosions. If men are able to build machines to perform specific tasks, it is thanks to the predictions of the physicist.

But when the physicist delves into the innermost secrets of matter, all he really predicts is the readings on his dials!

N: These readings are signals from a profound reality. The experimentalist watches the dials, but the theoretician translates their behavior into a fascinating tale.

And there is no way of knowing whether the tale is true except that it enables us to predict further readings. One great physicist tells this wistful allegory: He describes a man on a desert island with a radio receiver. Through this receiver the man gets certain signals, sequences of numbers. Now, the man does not know the "meaning" of the signals he receives. To him they are just sequences of numbers. But he is an intelligent man and a good mathematician. He notes a certain regularity in the signals, and he begins to formulate laws which enable him to *predict* the numbers he is going to hear next. To facilitate his computations, he invents the concepts of "velocity," "direction," "acceleration," etc. Finally, he has learned to predict the signals with great accuracy, and that is the full extent of his knowledge.

N: A sad story. What is the point?

One day two men were shipwrecked on the island. The man with the radio welcomed them cordially. At last he was going to know the truth about the outside. One of the shipwrecked men told him about the oceans and the continents, about the cities, the people, the machines. He told him that the signals he heard were sent out by ships at sea which give their positions to other ships, and that by listening to the signals he could chart the course of every ship sailing the seven seas. He could even hope that someday a ship would come close to his island. He should therefore build a fire to attract attention when the signals tell him a ship is close by.

The other shipwrecked man waited until the first had finished and said simply:

"He is a liar. There are no ships, no cities, no people. There is only one other island just beyond the horizon. A man who lives there, alone like yourself, is sending you those signals. He knew that eventually you would create a 'science' around them, so he keeps up the illusion just to amuse himself. One day he will wreck all your theories by starting an entirely new system of signals or by stopping them altogether."

Now, which of the men is to be believed if there is no way of communicating with the outside world except that same radio which gives out those same signals?

N: What would you say?

I say that the Ultimate Reality is forever hidden from us by the limitations of our observations and of our very intelligence.

175

We have assumed, in the flush of success that nineteenth-century science enjoyed, that we have finally challenged the innermost secrets of nature. But the uncertainties of the new physics have wrecked that faith. Listen to what Max Planck says:

> Formerly it was only religion . . . that was the object of skeptical attack. Then the iconoclast began to shatter the ideals and principles that had hitherto been accepted in the province of art. Now he has invaded the temple of science. There is scarcely a scientific axiom that is not nowadays denied by somebody . . .
>
> In the midst of this confusion, it is natural to ask whether there is any rock of truth left on which we can take our stand and feel sure that it is unassailable and that it will hold against the storm of skepticism raging around it . . .[1]

N: Does Planck eventually find that rock?

Yes. He concludes that the whole structure of physical science rests on these two theorems:

1. There is a real world which exists independently of our act of knowing.

2. The real outer world is not directly knowable.

N: Meaning what?

To quote him again:

> This fact discloses the presence of an irrational or mystic element which adheres to physical science as to every other branch of human knowledge . . . This means that science is never in a position completely and exhaustively to explain the problems it has to face . . . the solution of one problem only unveils the mystery of another.

N: Suppose Planck came face to face with Ultimate Reality, how would he know it? Have you ever asked yourself "What if everything is only a dream?"

[1] Max Planck, *Where Is Science Going?*

Are Logical Positivists Idealists?

Often.

N: What reply do you give to yourself?

None.

N: I suggest you try this. Suppose I woke up and found myself in another world, realizing that the world I had taken to be *the* reality was only a "dream." How could I be sure that the new world was not just another dream, and so on forever, each dream telescoping into the next?

How would that painful fantasy help me dissolve the dilemma?

N: It would help you dissolve it if you were interested in giving your notions operational meaning. Try to give an operational meaning to Ultimate Reality, and you see that it cannot be done. When you admit the possibility of "waking up" to another "reality" at any moment, you are simply admitting the possibility of a particular experience, although you have never had it before and do not know of anyone who has. It is not a bad idea to admit the possibility of any kind of experience, no matter how bizarre. But it is not a good idea to worry about it, because no one has ever computed the probability of its occurrence.

This is about all that can be said about the elusive character of our reality. As for Ultimate Reality, there being no way of recognizing it, even if it happened to come within the realm of our experience, it must be classed with First Causes, Irresistible Forces, Destiny, and other fictions. Recognize Ultimate Reality as just another semantic disturbance, and the "crises" of science will cease to be painful or bewildering. The man who seeks the "rock of truth" thinks a revision of one's way of thinking is something to dread. Physicists of all people should have learned long ago that the periodically recurring "crises" are forerunners of rich harvests of knowledge. Since you have quoted one physicist, I shall quote another:

177

The explanatory crisis which now confronts us in relativity and quantum phenomena is but a repetition of what has occurred many times in the past. A similar crisis confronted Prometheus when he discovered fire, and the first man who observed a straw sticking to a piece of rubbed amber, or suspended lodestone seeking the north star. Every kitten is confronted with such a crisis at the end of nine days.[2]

[2] P. W. Bridgman, *The Logic of Modern Physics.*

CHAPTER 18

Are Semanticists Fascists?

Sometimes you talk like a materialist, but you will not follow the logic of materialism to its inevitable conclusion. In all your views there is a definite taint of idealism. Why don't you come out into the open? Are you an idealist or a materialist?

N: Why is it so important to you to label everything either X-ism or Y-ism? Why do you cling to this two-valued orientation?

Ever since the people of the Western world took up philosophy as a profession or a hobby or a weapon (and you know that philosophy has been used in all those capacities) it was possible to discern two interpretations of reality. One school asserted that reality existed independently of any observer; the other argued that since reality was revealed only through the senses, it could not exist without the senses. To put it vulgarly, it was all in the mind. To this day the struggle between the two ideologies continues. There is a deeper significance to this struggle than a difference of opinion. The materialists have been on the side of science; the idealists, on the side of religion. Thus materialism has been the philosophy of progress, and idealism the apology for reaction.

When Galileo and Bacon ushered in the age of experiment, they were, in a sense, materialists; they recognized that knowledge is obtained by studying the material world. The Church, in opposing experimental science, took the idealist position. It declared truth to be a gift of divine revelation.

179

In the eighteenth century the struggle became even more pronounced. The Newtonian system had been brilliantly successful in explaining the workings of the world by mechanistic laws—in terms of matter interacting with matter. To counter that advance of the materialistic view, the Church sponsored idealist philosophies. Bishop Berkeley wrote:

> It is indeed an opinion strangely prevailing amongst men that houses, mountains, rivers, have an existence, natural or real, distinct from their being perceived by understanding . . . For what are the aforementioned objects but the things we perceive by sense? And what do we perceive beside our own ideas or sensations? And is it not plainly repugnant that any one of these, or any combination of these should exist unperceived?[1]

Don't you see what was happening? When in the seventeenth century the Church was confronted with the evidence of the senses contradicting the teachings of its "science," it contemptuously dismissed the senses as reflecting the temporal rather than the eternal. But when in the eighteenth century it found it could not stem the tide of experimental knowledge, when scientists began to gather this knowledge into mechanistic laws, when a universe began to emerge in which there was no room for the will of God, the Church turned about and declared that, since the material universe was a product of the senses and since so many individuals agreed on what their senses were reporting to them, there must be a superconsciousness (God) responsible for all the individual consciousnesses!

N: Why do you think the Church backed such views?

Bishop Berkeley never concealed his motives. He said clearly enough:

[1] George Berkeley, *Principles of Human Knowledge.*

Matter being once expelled out of nature drags with it so many sceptical and impious notions, such an incredible number of disputes and puzzling questions, which have been thorns in the sides of divines as well as philosophers, and made so much fruitless work for mankind, that if the arguments which we have produced against it are not found equal to demonstration (as to me they evidently seem) yet I am sure all friends of knowledge, peace and religion have reason to wish they were.[2]

In other words, the attention of the people had to be turned at all costs away from the findings of science, since science was undermining the authority of the existing world order. The Church played a prominent part in that order. It supported it and in turn was supported by it. Power resided in the ownership of land. This power could continue only in a certain social structure, where people felt certain obligations because of their social standing, where the duties of the serf to the feudal lord were fixed and hereditary, where the Church exercised its authority in keeping these conditions fixed. The landowning nobility wished to preserve feudalism. They were opposed by the bourgeoisie, who needed science for their voyages of discovery and for their new technology. The bourgeoisie also needed a more fluid social order with a labor market, where a man's obligations were determined by monetary considerations, not by any particular "social standing." The bourgeoisie was inclined to fight the influence of the Church, because it was opposed to the feudal system.

N: Then would you say that the materialist philosophy was the "class weapon" of the bourgeoisie?

In the eighteenth century, yes. And since the bourgeoisie was on the side of progress at that time, it was natural in the eighteenth century for the progressive people, forward-looking people,

---

[2] *Ibid.*

those whose sympathies were with the ideals of the new class, the bourgeoisie, to line up behind an ideology which dealt the hardest blows to the authority of the Church. Once the authority of the church is undermined, many of its doctrines become suspect, such as the divine right of kings, the hereditary obligations of the serf to the feudal lord, etc.

N: All this seems to make good sense. I would describe the "class basis" of an ideological struggle in this way: by an act of identification, a certain view of the world becomes linked with the personality of the man who advocates it; by another identification, the man becomes linked with his class. Is this the way it works?

No, you've got it upside down. It's the other way around. The economic interests of the class determine the ideology of its prophets!

N: Strange that Marx should have come from a family of bankers and Lenin from a family of landowners and that Hitler should have spent his youth as a worker . . . But go on. What happened next?

The bourgeoisie won the struggle in France through the French Revolution. But in Germany there was no German Revolution. The power of the feudal lord remained strong, especially in Prussia, throughout the nineteenth century. Forces attempting to establish some measure of political democracy were severely defeated. In the meantime the French and English bourgeoisies were running their world of "free economy." In that world economic status rather than hereditary birthright became the determining factor of social position, prestige, and security. The manufacture of commodities passed from the hands of skilled craftsmen into large industrial units owned by individuals or corporations and manned by propertyless workers (proletarians), who were hired or fired according to the exigencies of the situation from the point of view of the owners. The profit motive became the primary consideration in practically all human activity, and ideas of morality, individual obligations, and government changed accordingly. Now the proletarians in many countries of Europe began to struggle against the capitalists who grew rich, because they owned the machines to which the workers had to have access in order to earn their living. Questions of wages, working conditions, right of organization, collective bargaining, all the issues in the relations of capital and labor, issues which are still in the foreground of the social and political struggles in capitalist countries today, became of paramount importance.

The bourgeoisie, instead of being representative of advanced, progressive ideas, as they had been when they carried on their struggle against the nobility and the Church, now found themselves on the conservative side of the fence. They held the reins of power. Even when they had to share that power with the remnants of the nobility, as in Germany, they felt that the *dynamics* of the situation was such that their power would keep increasing. Therefore, they were interested in opposing social change, especially social changes advocated by the workers (increase of political democracy, demands for social security, extension of education). To be sure, in some countries the bourgeoisie were, as a whole, more conservative (or liberal) than in others, and within the ranks of the bourgeois classes there was a spectrum of political thought. Some sections of the bourgeoisie even fostered "radical" reforms along socialist lines (as, for example, Robert Owen). On the whole, however, the capitalists and the people who were in direct social contact with them, that is, shared their aspirations, lined up in the conservative camp, while the workers and the intellectuals who sympathized with them organized the various labor and socialist parties of Europe.

183

N: What became of the struggle between materialist and idealist philosophies?

I am coming to that. The most important event of the nineteenth century was the publication of the Communist Manifesto by Marx and Engels in 1848. In this pamphlet, the lines between the opposing camps, the bourgeoisie and the proletariat, were sharply drawn. The victory of the proletariat in the coming struggle was declared inevitable. Just as the bourgeoisie had wrested the power from the aristocracy, so the proletariat were going to seize power and reorganize society in such a way that economic classes would be abolished and the war between them that had gone on ever since the dawn of history would finally cease.

The working classes needed a philosophy upon which to found their ideology. This philosophy appeared.

N: Dialectical materialism?

Exactly. The materialism of the natural sciences, which so well served the bourgeoisie in their struggle against feudalism, was extended by Marx and Engels to the social sciences. History then appeared not as a record of God's whims, nor as a narrative of the exploits of kings and warriors, but as an evolution of society. Just as previously natural laws were discovered that explained the working of the universe and at the same time gave man control over nature, so by means of dialectical materialism, laws of human society were discovered which explained the working of history and at the same time promised to give man control over his own destiny. By discovering the laws of social evolution, the workers acquired power to build a social order of their own choosing.

N: And did they?

Ruling classes never relinquish their power voluntarily. In Russia the workers were victorious. Elsewhere the struggle is still going on. What side are you on?

Are Semanticists Fascists?

N: Is this a rhetorical question? It seems to me you have decided long ago what side I was on. In 1942 you wrote about semanticists:

Their intentions may be of the best, but their leadership is dangerous. They are most effective in pointing out to us how little we understand one another. But their cry is, "Don't despair, boys; cheer up. All we need is to get together and define our terms! Semantics—that's what we need!" A sober onlooker in the Vanity Fair of 1942, threatening our very existence, will be reminded of the cheerful cries of a hawker vending panaceas at a circus.[3]

In 1946 you wrote:

Whenever a man or a movement exhibits all or most of the usual fascist ideas and is named accordingly, some semanticist is sure to arise and pronounce the naming meaningless. The left wing has its labels, he will say, no less than the right; and both sets of labels lack content. Such "impartiality" is mere show. In reality it protects fascists by enabling them to escape public identification, and it injures anti-fascists by an accusation of word-mongering. It is now scarcely possible to gather men together on behalf of human welfare, without some one's blocking the whole program by a complaint of "semantic confusion." If we were to apply to the semantic philosophy one of its own favorite tests, the operational, we should find that its real meaning, abundantly demonstrated in practice, is defense of things as they are.[4]

In 1947 you wrote:

Semantic idealism, like all the other teachings of modern idealist philosophy, is the product of the decay and the cultural decadence of the capitalist society. Like all the currents of modern idealist philosophy, semantic idealism is a spiritual weapon of imperialism in its struggle against the progressive ideas of our time. Poisoning the consciousness of the intellectuals with the poison of scepticism, nihilism, and ag-

[3] Margaret Schlauch, "Semantics as Social Evasion."
[4] Barrows Dunham, *Man Against Myth.*

nosticism—scientific, moral, political, the semanticists are the most vicious enemies of progressive ideas.[5]

Well, *are* you a Fascist? Or perhaps you insist that, since fascism is "only an abstraction," it doesn't exist?

N: Such views have often been attributed to me. Yet all that follows from the theory of abstraction levels is that fascism does not exist *in the same way* as its extensional manifestations—concentration camps, book burnings, "labor fronts," and notions of racial or national superiority. Similarly, the existence of capitalism is different from that of corporations, holding companies, and stock markets, which show optimism when the probability of war increases and pessimism when a "peace scare" occurs.

But capitalism *exists*, doesn't it? Yet one of your writers said, "There is no such beast as Capitalism."[6]

N: That is true. There is no such beast. I mean it literally. You will not find him in any zoo, nor roaming the jungle.

Please keep the discussion serious.

N: I am dead earnest. It is important to know that capitalism is not a beast. Nor is socialism a bear, for that matter. Yet orators often describe them as such, and cartoonists of both East and West actually picture them so with long fangs and dripping saliva. By this promiscuous and irresponsible use of metaphor they perpetuate a confusion of abstraction levels, allness reactions, elementalism. When such orientations are established, it is easy to manipulate large masses of people, and I think you will agree that in many instances the results of this manipulation are deplorable.

Once you've got "socialism" identified with a beast, you can often block public works, free education, organized health service. If you speak vaguely of capitalism, you can attack enterprises like

[5] B. Bykhovsky, "The Morass of Modern Bourgeois Philosophy."
[6] Stuart Chase, *Tyranny of Words.*

the consumers' co-operatives if they happen to flourish in a "capi-talist" country. The Great Soviet Encyclopedia, for example, has this to say about consumers' co-operatives.

At present in the era of monopolist capitalism and fierce class struggle, the "Rochdale Principles" have become particularly injurious and reactionary. . . . The majority of consumers' cooperatives which supply the workers are headed by reformists . . . The object of these petty-bourgeois-Utopian theories is to weaken the revolutionary determination of the proletariat, and they are harmful to its struggle for liberation. The revolutionary cooperatives (those controlled by Communists) are vigorously combatting these cooperative illusions, struggling for revolutionary methods of cooperative work along with the revolutionary organizations of the proletariat. The opportunist leaders of cooperation stubbornly defend their positions and their commanding role, resorting to every possible method, including the elimination of the supporters of revolutionary methods.

On the other hand, Mr. Elmer E. Harter, speaking before the Committee on Ways and Means in the House of Representatives in connection with proposed revisions of the internal revenue code, does not seem to think that consumers' co-operatives are instrumental in "weakening revolutionary determination." Says Mr. Harter:

It is our Nation which has been called upon in the last two World Wars to save democracy . . . It is our Nation which protects the minority in its fundamental rights against the action of the majority. It is our Nation which guarantees freedoms of religion, speech, and the press. . . . To borrow any alien concepts of government or taxation from other governments in the world would be a betrayal of our forefathers and of our fundamental freedoms. . . . To guarantee them [consumers' co-operatives] the right to go into this business [milk distribution] and at the same time to make them immune from the same type of taxation that corporations . . . are subject to, is not democratic gov-

187

ernment. . . . Such government is foreign to our way of life and has always resulted in . . . dictatorship and revolution.[7]

So long as you stay in the rarefied atmosphere of "imperialism" and "class struggle," "democracy," and "fundamental freedoms" you can easily prove that any movement is an "imperialist tool" or the "spearhead of communism." But if one examines the actual working of these movements instead of their pedigree, one gets an altogether different picture. However, once you have committed yourself to an interpretation of history as a sequence of life-and-death struggles between classes in which "ideologies," "philosophies," etc., inevitably choose up sides, you are reluctant to view history in any other way. Thus everything is either fitted into the picture or else "explained away" or ignored. Soon analysis of events degenerates into label-sticking and name-calling. One side labels the distribution of land among those who work it "robbery." The other side calls unrestricted expression of opinion and academic freedom "bourgeois decadence." One side equates planned economy with serfdom; the other side brands a *communist* government traitor to the "Marxist-Leninist" cause, because it has not brought about an immediate collectivization of agriculture. Under such circumstances communication breaks down.

Is the Class Struggle "Real"?

This emphasis of yours on communication often beclouds the issues. Class struggles are not a result of misunderstandings. It is quite possible for oppressors and the oppressed to "understand" each other. The oppressors say in effect, "We shall continue to rule and to exploit your labor." The oppressed say, "No, you shall not." There is no mistaking each other's meaning, but the struggle of diametrically opposed interests grows ever sharper.

[7] *Hearings before the Committee on Ways and Means House of Representatives Eightieth Congress on Proposed Revisions of the Internal Revenue Code*, Part 4, p. 2812.

Are Semanticists Fascists?

And still the semanticists insist on providing cure-alls for the ills of the world by crying for bigger and better dictionaries.

N: One could, perhaps, reiterate at every opportunity that semanticists do *not* believe dictionaries to be useful sources of knowledge; not even useful sources of "definitions" except in special cases. But evidently it is as futile to do so as it was for the Jews to maintain for centuries that they did *not* approve of ritual murder or for the Communists that they were *not* in favor of nationalizing women. At your leisure, please read Chapter 7 of this book or any of the books on semantics cited here.

What you say about conflict is important but not too accurate. Except in cartoons, hardly anyone today says, "We shall continue to rule and to exploit your labor." The literature put out by the National Association of Manufacturers proclaims that only in a capitalist society do people "rule themselves." Editorials in Soviet publications, on the other hand, argue that capitalist "democracy" is an illusion invented to mask the "fact" of the class struggle, that only a socialist society can be really democratic, and that only the Soviet society is really socialist.

Which is true?

N: To me, as you know, truth means the ability to predict. Predictions can be made only about operationally definable and experimentally verifiable events. Try to define "rule themselves," "class struggle," or even "socialism" not by words but by events to which they refer and see how difficult it becomes to make the glib statements that fill the press.

Do you or don't you believe that there is a class struggle in the United States?

N: It is certainly possible to list events which could be collectively referred to as "class struggle." A strike, antistrike legislation sponsored by a lobby of manufacturers, the organization of a

189

tenant farmers' union, the intimidation of its members by land-lords, can be meaningfully referred to as instances of "class struggle." On the other hand, you have labor leaders eulogizing free enterprise, joint labor-management committees, and political parties in which both "workers" and "capitalists" are active. Why is one set of events more "real" than the other?

Class collaboration is a myth invented by the capitalists and renegades to camouflage the basic fact of history, the class struggle.

N: Perhaps you are right. But how do you refute the Nazis, who have maintained that the class struggle is a myth invented by Marxists and Jews to divert the attention of Germans away from the basic fact of history, the struggle of races for supremacy?

The racist theories don't stand up under scientific analysis.

N: They certainly don't. And I agree with you that scientific analysis should be applied to all questions of "reality" and "truth." Since the dialectical materialists are extending scientific analysis to the development of human society, they should bring scientific analysis into that field.

They have.

N: The theory of class struggle developed by Marx, Engels, and their successors was a brave attempt. A physicist calls such attempts "first approximations." As any other scientific theory, it was an abstraction made by the observers of their observations. What they observed were records, in themselves high-order abstractions of events, mostly European and mostly of the past three or four centuries. They found that in talking about those events it was useful to speak of "classes," "class interests," and the "class struggle." These proved to be *useful* abstractions, more useful for integrating historical patterns than "the will of God" or the ambitions of kings, which were formerly supposed to be the chief levers of history.

Are Semanticists Fascists?

Now you talk like a pragmatist.

N: Perhaps. The physicist, when he calls the concepts he works with "useful" instead of "true" is being modest and is ensuring himself against semantic disturbances he would otherwise suffer when in time he had to recognize the limited validity of these concepts. Thus the modern (non-Aristotelian) physicist will call "force," "velocity," "temperature" simply *useful* concepts; the modern biologist will apply the same label to "gene," "mutation," "species," etc. They are simply linguistic tools and there is nothing eternal in their usefulness. The road of science is cluttered with discarded notions which have outlived their usefulness, the "phlogiston" of the eighteenth-century chemist, the "ether" of the nineteenth-century physicist, etc., etc.

The first commandment of scientific rigor is "Fear not to discard obsolete notions."

Then you maintain that the class struggle is an obsolete notion?

N: I maintain nothing of the sort. I say that its usefulness should be constantly gauged by the integrations and predictions one is able to make by means of it of events on lower orders of abstraction.

At least two distinct paths to the understanding of human behavior have been opened since the time of Marx. One is based on the culture concept of modern anthropology. The other stems from the theory of motivations initiated by Freud. There is no need to set Freud *against* Marx or the theory of cultural integration *against* the theory of economic determinism, although people committed to rigid two-valued orientations insist on doing so. None of those theories can yet claim any validity even distantly approaching that achieved by the physical sciences. All of them are attempts to systematize abstractions of the events of history along different lines. Each system of abstractions may be an equally valid "cross section" of history.

Where do you come in?

N: I am trying to provide an even more general theory of behavior based on evaluative processes. The understanding of these processes is indispensable for *all three* schools of thought relating to human behavior. Whatever the value of each interpretation is, it cannot but be enhanced by the inclusion of the evaluative process. No matter how Marxist you are, it is more meaningful to say "These people behave as they do because they *evaluate* events as capitalists" instead of "They behave as they do because they *are* capitalists." Not only does this reformulation enable you to rationalize innumerable instances of noncapitalists behaving like capitalists and vice versa, but it also directs your attention to those devices by means of which people are made to act contrary to what, according to your theory, should be their "class interests." Similarly, the anthropologist will gain by examining the evaluative patterns set by a given culture complex. The Freudian will attempt to link his "basic biologic drives" with the notion of culture that is supposed to direct those drives along certain channels.

In a way, considerations of culture as an important factor in behavior and social structure are already found in Marx and Engels. But they insisted on calling the economic structure of society "primary" and everything else "secondary," a "superstructure." It was understandable that they should think so, since they were chiefly responsible for developing the theory of the economic component of motivation. The dialectical materialists who followed them made a fetish of this "priority" as they did of the "priority" of "matter" over "mind" without bothering to give their formulation any operational meaning.

In a systematic development of motivation theory, the Marxist theory of economic determinism will probably be considered an important contribution. But the discovery of an important component should not have prevented the exploration of other factors in motivation. Perhaps further study of the subconscious will point out the origins of powerful aggressive drives, for which the possibilities of economic exploitation and competition are just one possible channel. Perhaps if the channels of economic exploitation are shut off as they were in the Soviet Union, these tendencies to dominate, to manipulate the behavior of large masses of people, seek other channels—and find them. But Marxist dogma refuses recognition to any but the orthodox means of "exploitation": chattel right, land rent, and surplus value. Perhaps the irritation in the Soviet Union toward psychiatric and anthropological theories originating in the West stems from the way these theories remind them of the necessity of eventually abandoning comfortable dogmas.

"Don't look," said the worthies of Pisa, when the light and the heavy balls fell together.

You still have not told me how you stand politically.

N: You mean how do I vote?

Well, yes, whom do you vote for?

N: You forget, my friend, that I am a composite outlook, not a citizen. Many citizens have absorbed with varying degrees of thoroughness some of my ideas, but this does not necessarily give them uniform political convictions. If one were to use scientific method in choosing public servants, perhaps elections would become unnecessary.

There! I have always suspected that you were a Fascist.

CHAPTER 19

How Evident Is Self-evident?

Do You doubt everything?
N: Explain.

Is there nothing that you believe wholeheartedly and without reservation? Don't you find it a torment to go through life qualifying everything you say by "ifs" and "almosts"? How can you expect many people to adopt your outlook? Don't you feel that security is a basic need; and isn't security attained by a faith? Even mathematics rests on the intuitively recognized truth of self-evident assertions.
N: Name one.

Twice two is four. A straight line is the shortest path between two points.
N: Let us take the first one. Why do you say it is self-evident?

Do you mean that you do not believe that twice two is four?
N: That assertion can be made in several contexts. Operationally it may mean this: "Take an aggregate of cats, which when counted is denoted by 'two.' Take another similar aggregate. This combined aggregate, when counted will be denoted by 'four.' And similarly for oranges, church steeples, and many other things."

All this talk just to say, "Twice two makes four?"
N: It is necessary in order to know what one is talking about. One must establish a bridge between assertions and experience.

194

How Evident Is Self-evident?

Have you ever had an experience when twice two did *not* make four?

N: Yes. Mix two gallons of water with two gallons of alcohol. The resulting mixture will not measure four gallons.

So what? There must have been a chemical reaction there or something.

N: Very likely. Yet this is a situation in which "twice two makes four" does not apply.

But can't you divorce numbers from cats, oranges, and gallons? Isn't that done in mathematics? Isn't it true that when you speak of pure numbers, twice two is always four?

N: As an assertion of pure mathematics, "Twice two is four" assumes yet another meaning. In that context it is not an assertion about things at all, but an assertion about assertions. It follows from the rules that you have set up for counting. When you are setting up such rules, you are setting up a *logic*.

Well, then, in logic, if you insist, isn't twice two always four?

N: That depends on what arithmetic you use, on the rules you have set up for counting.

Is there more than one set of such rules?

N: Certainly. I am sure that you yourself have used at least two kinds of arithmetic. One is the ordinary kind, where you never count the same thing twice, as in counting cows in a herd or your sons and daughters. Another kind is the "circular" arithmetic you use in reckoning the time of day.

Suppose it is seven o'clock, and you want to know what time it will be fourteen hours later. You make a rapid calculation using the "circular" arithmetic. In that system, seven and fourteen make nine. The answer is nine o'clock.

Then you would say that "Seven and fourteen make nine" is a true assertion?

N: *In that context, yes.* It is not strange if one keeps in mind that assertions must refer to certain experiences. Here the numbers refer to the hours of the day, and addition to the movement of the hour hand in the clockwise direction (in the direction "later"). The arithmetic used here has its own consistent rules. They seem strange only if one is convinced that the rules of "ordinary" arithmetic are the only possible ones. But they are no more strange than any other rules. Here they are:

$1 + 1 = 2$

$2 + 1 = 3$

etc., as in ordinary arithmetic up to

$11 + 1 = 12$

But $12 + 1 = 1$, not 13, and in general any number remains unaltered by the addition or subtraction of any multiple of 12. The number 12 is the "zero" of this arithmetic.

Isn't this rather artificial? Aren't you just pretending that $12 + 1 = 1$ just for the purpose of telling time? Isn't $12 + 1$ *really* 13, no matter what we call it?

N: I knew a lady once who went traveling. She was convinced that Paris and Rome were populated by "foreigners." She probably would not admit it, but she had such a "feeling" deep down inside. She learned to speak French, but when she spoke it, she thought that she was only "pretending" to speak, making all those strange sounds just to make the "foreigners" understand. She always retained the feeling that the *real* names for things were the English ones.[1] What do you think of her attitude?

Provincial.

[1] See also the excerpt from *Huckleberry Finn* in Hayakawa's *Language in Action.*

N: With overtones of intolerance and rudeness. Now the attitude of disbelief toward the "strange" arithmetic, where $12 + 1 = 1$, has no such overtones, of course, because no evaluation of culture is involved. It is just the result of a lack of experience in thinking about symbolic systems and symbol manipulation. But so is the narrow-minded attitude toward the French language the result of such a lack. I have taken this example to show that such lack of experience can have socially significant consequences.

Mathematics is an excellent aid to achieving a cosmopolitan attitude. Do you play golf?

I do.

N: In the course of your game, you take several walks between the shots. Suppose you walked 300 feet in the first walk and 400 feet in your second walk. How far would you be from your starting point?

That depends on the directions in which I walked, doesn't it?

N: I am glad to see that you too are beginning to qualify your assertions. Well, suppose you walked 300 feet north and then 400 east.

If I remember my high school geometry, then I will be 500 feet from the starting point.

N: You remember the theorem of Pythagoras very well. But suppose you walked both times in the same direction?

Then I would be 700 feet from the start.

N: And if you went in opposite directions?

I would be 100 feet from the start.

N: Excellent. You see that it is not enough to know the lengths of the walks. One must also know the directions. There is a special kind of mathematics that deals with such problems called "vector algebra." The numbers in this algebra are called "vectors," and one can "add" them. The addition of vectors has many of the properties of ordinary addition, but *not all*. It is not true, for example, that the length of the sum of two vectors necessarily equals the sum of their lengths. If a vector of length 3 is added to one of length 4, the length of the sum may be anywhere from 1 to 7, depending on the directions of the vectors.

If, instead of a golf course, you take your walks up and down a road, then you have a simpler mathematics, the arithmetic of positive and negative numbers. In this case, a walk of 300 feet added to one of 400 feet will get you either 100 or 700 feet from your starting point.

If you restrict your walks still further and demand that they be always in the same direction, the mathematics is still further simplified. It then reduces to ordinary arithmetic taught in the grade schools. Here $3+4$ is always 7.

Different things may be represented by "numbers," and operations on them may have different meanings in different contexts. There are no "real" meanings of numbers any more than there are "real" meanings of words. People who think there are usually signify by the distinction "real" the meaning to which they are accustomed because of early linguistic habits.

I suppose you can also show that the straight line is not necessarily the shortest path between two points.

N: The assignment of operational meaning to this postulate presents formidable epistemological difficulties. Let us take an easier one, the famous Parallel Postulate of Euclid. It can be stated in a variety of equivalent ways, but it seems particularly "self-evident" in this form:

"Given a line and a point not on it, one and only one line can be drawn through the point which fails to meet the given line, no matter how far it is produced in either direction."

Isn't this exceptional line the line parallel to the given one?

N: Call it that. But be careful of the little word "the." By it you are already implying that there is one and only one such line. In other words, when you say "*the* line parallel to the given line" you are already accepting the truth of the postulate.

What's wrong with that?

N: Nothing. It is a good postulate. But it is not the only possible one. One could assume with equal success that a great many lines can be drawn through a point exterior to a given line, all failing to meet it.

Oh, yes. In different planes.

N: No, in a single plane.

How can that be? Suppose on one side of the point the second line recedes from the first; then it must approach it on the other side. So if we allow it to be produced to any desired length, it must meet the first line eventually.

N: Why must it? Suppose the point is one foot from the given line. Suppose in the first 10 feet of length the second line approached the first by half that distance, in the next 10 feet by half the remaining distance, etc. At this rate, the second line will never reach the first, even though it is always approaching it.

I see you are using the same sort of argument that B used in Case 8 of Chapter 1. But do straight lines behave that way? If the second line approached the first by half a foot in the first 10 feet, will it not also approach by a half foot in the second 10 feet and thus meet the first line at 20 feet?

N: The trouble with that argument is this: in order to prove that straight lines behave as you describe, you must assume the Parallel Postulate to be true, and its truth is what you are trying to establish. Without realizing it, you are using a circular argument, such as often is used by people attempting to "prove" religious or political dogmas.

Is it impossible, then, to prove the Parallel Postulate?

N: It is impossible to prove it without assuming something, which, in effect, is equivalent to it.

Then how can one be sure it is true?

N: The preoccupation with this question revealed two different senses in which "true" was used. Failure to realize this was responsible for quite an amount of confusion.

One sense is the usual one: an assertion is true if it is in harmony with experience, such as "grass is green" and "sugar is sweet." The most esoteric assertions of physics stated in mathematical language also belong to this category of truth, since the ultimate judge is experience, the verification of predictions implied in the assertion. But there is another sense in which "true" is used. An assertion is considered "true" if it follows logically from other assertions known or assumed to be "true." Often the word "valid" is used for such assertions.

In mathematics assertions are proved to be *valid*, not true in the first sense. They are deduced from certain basic assertions (postulates) assumed "true." There is no way of proving them true in the physical sense, because they do not assert anything about the world and therefore cannot be tested. For example, the postulates of geometry cannot possibly say anything about the world, because there are no such things in the world as "points," "lines," or "planes." These are only abstractions which we make of our experiences in the attempt to map them on language.

It remained for Bolyai and Lobachevski (and later Riemann) to show that equally consistent geometries could be constructed on sets of postulates different from those of Euclidean geometry.

But which geometry is true?

N: Presumably by this question you mean which geometry can be best applied to the physical world?

Yes.

N: The question is meaningful, but please realize that you are asking a question in *physics*, not in geometry. For the purposes of terrestrial measurements, the old Euclidean geometry is adequate. In matters dealing with cosmic distances, another geometry (one of Riemann's) has proved useful.

Useful! Useful! I want to know what is *true*, not what is "useful."

N: Then why ask me? I don't derive my authority from divine sources. All I know to be true is what I can compare with experience. Such comparisons are only a matter of getting the best fit. One can depreciate the pragmatic approach to truth by dubbing it "opportunistic." Of course, one does not serve truth if one accepts something as true only because it serves to gain some end having nothing to do with the search for truth. Thus people who do not believe some of the assertions of religion but maintain that they are true, because they keep people out of mischief, may be called "pragmatic" in the vulgar sense. But if one's ends are simply better maps, then the most useful maps are the truest.

Why, then, did philosophers and mathematicians try to prove the Parallel Postulate for two thousand years?

N: There are various reasons. In the first place, looking upon the postulates of geometry as arbitrary assumptions, rules of the game, is a comparatively new attitude. At first they were thought of as "self-evident" truths. Somehow the Parallel Postulate did not seem quite so self-evident as the others, probably because it contained the notion "never." One naturally feels uneasy when one says that something will *never* happen. So the geometricians thought they might find a proof for this assertion instead of taking it on faith.

Secondly, many felt the power and the grandeur of formal logic as a tool for discovering new truths (new truths in mathematics are discovered exclusively by formal logic). This method seems the more elegant the fewer things one must take on faith. So it appeared desirable to cut the number of postulates to the absolute minimum.

Logical edifices are not confined to geometry. The magnificent attempt of Thomas Aquinas to derive the entire Catholic system of beliefs by formal reasoning from only a few assertions is another example of the high esteem in which deductive reasoning was held. From the point of view of resolving controversies, the less things you ask people to take your word for the easier it is for them to believe you. If it were possible to agree on a few basic "truths," and if everyone used the same logic, then there would be no unresolved controversy at least as to what was true. If it were possible to find a few basic values to which everyone would subscribe, and if it were possible, by means of logic, to decide in each case whether a given course of action was in accord or in conflict with those values, one could also achieve agreement in all questions of ethics. Thus the attempts of Aquinas and the scholasticists were praiseworthy. It should be noted that they were inspired by the example of geometry as a "self-consistent" system. Euclidean geometry gave rise to a whole ideology.

What happened to it?

N: Oh, it still persists among people who believe that the synthesis of Thomas Aquinas is a most useful guide to orientation even today.

You do not think it is?

N: No. Its method has all the shortcomings of the Aristotelian outlook. It tacitly assumes the sufficiency of definition by classification. It usually does not differentiate between levels of abstraction, and when it does, it assigns a "higher" reality to "universals" than to particulars, assuming that Man as such has certain properties "natural" to him, no matter what may be observed in Smith, Jones, and Kelly, today, tomorrow, or next year. Thomas Aquinas had no inkling of a notion about how the human nervous system functions, of how our knowledge of the world is filtered through our linguistic habits. He was entirely ignorant of the structure of the universe, believing, as his contemporaries did, that our little planet is a magnificent stage upon which the most important events of eternity, the Fall and Salvation of Man, are unfolding. He believed the total span of existence to be a few thousand years.

But what makes the system most useless and even misleading is its utter failure to rely on carefully checked observations. It is a model, complete in itself, like Euclid's geometry which inspired it, requiring no confirmation, no correction, no modification in the light of new knowledge, constructed as it was, of "self-evident truths" and a superstructure derived from them by "pure reason."

The various philosophical systems that have emerged from centuries of European thought resemble this model. European learning was burdened by its Aristotelian heritage. Each new generation of philosophers inherited from their teachers the same old categories, "soul," "mind," "the Deity," "spirit," "free will," "substance," etc., etc., all words, words, words. In their indiscriminate use of these words the systems were much alike. Nevertheless, hardly two of them spoke the same language or agreed on anything important.

Was philosophy, then, a waste of time?

N: Is the babbling of a child, learning to speak, a waste of time?

No, but the child eventually learns to speak.

N: Some philosophers have also learned to speak. They are now referred to as scientists.

Is there no more room for philosophy?

N: There is ample room for philosophy. The philosopher of today can still become respectable by rendering unto the scientist what is the scientist's—the business of answering questions about the world. The philosopher should realize once for all that he has no equipment for answering questions about the world. This does not mean that a philosopher cannot at the same time be a scientist too. In fact, such a combination is highly desirable and should be encouraged. Some of our greatest modern philosophers are scientists of the first magnitude. But it should be admitted by philosophy that questions about the world are answered by the methods of science, that is, by observation, calculation, inference, experimentation, etc. *There are no other effective or reliable methods.* And most important, the philosopher should rid himself of the delusion that he still harbors sometimes, that his job is to provide answers to questions which "science cannot answer." The philosopher's job is first of all to be a vigilant and severe critic of science.

But how can he? If he can't answer any questions about the world, how can he decide whether the answers science gives are true?

N: Not true but *valid*. The validity of the conclusions of science are a legitimate realm of the philosopher. Besides, there are not only "right" and "wrong" answers. There are also meaningful and meaningless answers, and what is even more important, there are also meaningful and meaningless questions. It is by no means always easy to decide whether a given question about the world has any meaning. On the other hand, sometimes answers are given to the same question which seem entirely different, even con-

204

tradictory. It sometimes turns out that, nevertheless, the two answers mean the same thing. It is important to know this when it happens. Such matters are decided by semantic analysis. Semantics, then, is a legitimate branch of philosophy. Logic is another. In fact, wherever it is necessary to make *assertions about assertions* the philosopher can safely take over.

We have already seen that pure arithmetic consists of assertions about assertions, and so does pure geometry. This is true of all mathematics, since mathematics makes no assertions about things at all. Thus that vast empire of knowledge falls legitimately into the realm of philosophy. It does not seem as if the philosopher is being robbed of his function!

It is not the business of the philosopher to answer questions about the world, but it *is* his business to ask them, that is, to *invent* new questions. Armed with his epistemological tools, logic, semantics, and mathematics, the philosopher should, of course, screen the questions that force themselves into his consciousness so as to dismiss the meaningless ones based on semantic disturbances. However, he should not be too timid, prudish, or pedantic about it. Often it will not be immediately apparent whether operational meaning can be assigned to a question. The philosopher should not hesitate to play with such questions, but his task does not stop there. He should seek ways to assign operational meanings to such questions, so that new scientific procedures may suggest themselves. The time-honored pastime of "philosophizing" is therefore still open to philosophers. They should realize, however, that the products of this activity are only raw materials of thought, to be refined, sharpened, brought into focus by semantic tools, until they become meaningful questions about the world, real problems to be solved. Then they can be passed on to the scientist.

CHAPTER 20

How Certain Is Certain?

You seem to take delight in demolishing the old comfortable certainties of common sense and in scoffing at the "eternal" truths of the philosophers. Your iconoclasm does not go far, since in their stead you are establishing the "certainties" of science.

N: These are safe, because they are not sacred.

Then they are not certainties.

N: You are right; they are not. But it is you who called them certainties, not I.

Then how are they to be believed?

N: They are the best we have.

Then there is no certainty?

N: How certain do you want your certainties? If you send a letter to one of the 140,000,000 inhabitants of the United States addressed properly, are you certain it will reach its destination?

Reasonably so.

N: But suppose you are trying to find someone in a crowded baseball park?

Not much chance.

N: What's the difference?

How Certain Is Certain?

The letter does not go to the addressee directly. It goes to a particular post office; from there to a particular branch; then to a particular mailman, who brings it to a particular house.

N: The U.S. mail is an *organized* enterprise. Let's take another example. If you know a person's name and address, you can find his telephone number easily, even though the book contains hundreds of thousands of names. But try to find to whom a given telephone number belongs, and you may hunt through the same book for weeks without success. The telephone book is *ordered* according to names but not according to telephone numbers. Organization implies order (or structure). When the structure of some organized area is known to us, we can orient ourselves in it.

The absence of order we call chaos. The telephone numbers, as they appear in the telephone book or the license numbers of cars passing a certain corner are in no particular order and constitute a chaos. Can we say something about a situation where there is no apparent order, where chaos rules? Sometimes we can.

If you are willing to do something tedious for a few minutes in the interest of this discussion, open the telephone book at random and count the number of 2's you see among all the telephone numbers on the page. Do the same for 5's, 0's, etc. See how nearly equally distributed are the numbers of times each digit occurs on a page. If you have the patience to do this over ten pages, you will note even greater uniformity.

As I start out of the city for a long Fourth of July weekend, I have no way of knowing whether I will come back alive. Nor does anyone else of the millions of people who start out with me. But an agency which keeps statistics of accidents predicts that so many are going to be killed and even gives a breakdown of the figures according to traffic deaths, drownings, etc. Their guesses are usually good.

It seems chaos too has its laws, its "order." Accurate predictions can be made both on the basis of order and on the basis of chaos. Insurance companies and gambling houses, advertising agencies and physicists are able to conduct their business by computing *probabilities of events*.

The notion of probability illustrates in a fascinating way the application of the non-Aristotelian formulation to the theory of knowledge. The Aristotelian evaluation of assertions assigns to each just one of two truth values, "true" or "false." If we represent these values sybolically by "1" and "0," then, according to Aristotelian logic, an assertion either has a full measure of truth (value "1") or no truth at all (value "0"). The notion of probability enables us to give partial (fractional) truth values to assertions. Sometimes we are even able to calculate these values.

Consider these two assertions:

1. If a coin is thrown, and I get a dollar for every heads and pay a penny for every tails, I shall have a net gain at the end of ten throws.

2. If I get a penny for every tails and pay a dollar for every heads, I shall have a net gain at the end of ten throws.

Which assertion seems "truer"? Obviously the first. But can you be absolutely sure that the first is true and the second false? Can it not happen that ten tails are thrown in a row? If it happens, then the first assertion is false, and the second true!

What has this to do with "partial" truth? After all the *complete* truth of one or the other assertion is established once the "die is cast" or, in this case, the coin thrown.

N: That is so, but quite often we must act *before* the outcome of a situation is determined. If you have your choice to play the game, would you rather play under the conditions of the first or of the second assertion? Yet even if you choose the first, there is a chance that you may lose.

208

Still considerations of probability are the best guide for action that we have.

Even in deductive reasoning, where we still seem to employ Aristotelian syllogisms, we are really guided by probability considerations. If you happen to be in an Asiatic city during a cholera epidemic, it is a good idea to pour boiling water on fresh vegetables before serving them. A syllogistic chain of reasoning in support of this procedure would go something like this.

All fresh vegetables are covered with cholera bacilli.
These are fresh vegetables.
Therefore, these vegetables are covered with cholera bacilli.

. . . .

All people who ingest cholera bacilli contract cholera.

. . . .

All cholera bacilli which come in contact with boiling water die.
Etc., etc.

These chains enable one to come to the conclusion:
Therefore, if I pour boiling water on these vegetables, I will not contract cholera; otherwise I will.

Actually every one of the "all-statements" in the chain of reasoning is *false*, according to Aristotelian standards. The most one can say is
Some fresh vegetables are covered with cholera bacilli.
Some people who ingest cholera bacilli contract cholera, etc.

As we have seen in Chapter 12, a syllogism cannot be constructed from "some-statements" alone. *If we adhered strictly to Aristotelian logic, we could never come to any conclusion on how we should act.* By relinquishing the extreme values (true and false) of assertions, and estimating their intermediate probability values instead, we can restore our ability to guide our actions by reasonable considerations. Moreover, by rejecting "absolute truth" and "absolute falsehood" of empirical judgments, we are prepared for any possible surprises.

You take chances every day. You have a choice of getting to the street from your third-floor apartment either by walking downstairs or by jumping out the window. If you are like most people, you choose to walk. It is quicker out the window but "safer" down the stairs. What does "safer" mean in this case? Does it mean that the assertion "I will be unhurt if I walk downstairs" is 100 per cent true, and the assertion "I will be unhurt if I jump out the window" 100 per cent false? It does not, because there have been cases where people were unhurt after having jumped from third-story windows and also cases where people were killed falling downstairs; and one or the other may happen to you. Yet you choose the stairs and are, of course, right in doing so, if you want to be reasonably sure that you will not be hurt.

The truth of any assertion depends on how reliable are the predictions implied in it. The question "Are there any absolutely true assertions about things?" then reduces to the question "Are there any absolutely reliable predictions?" Practically speaking, there are; theoretically speaking, there are not.

Suppose you hold a ball and say, "If I release the ball, it will fall." For all practical purposes, this is an absolutely true prediction, that is, the probability of the ball's falling is practically "1." You may give any odds on a bet that it will fall. Yet there is a chance that it will not, a chance so remote that its value if written out as a decimal would take enough paper to fill a universe because of the zeros following the decimal. The fact is that the air surrounding the ball is not a "continuous" substance, as Aristotle supposed, but consists of exceedingly minute particles (molecules) in constant motion. The motion is random (chaotic), so that at any moment there are about as many molecules striking up at the bottom of the ball as are raining down on it from the top. The impacts of these molecules are what we call the air pressure on the ball. There is quite a bit of it, about fifteen pounds per square inch. But since it is the same all over, the net effect of the force on the ball is zero. Thus the force of gravity will accelerate the unsupported ball toward the ground.

But it *might* happen that just before you release the ball so many more molecules happen to accumulate below the ball (or there might not be enough above the ball) that the air pressure below would exceed that above sufficiently to counteract gravity or even to send the ball shooting upward!

Of course, it is useless to put such a "theory" to a test. The molecules have no way of knowing that we are performing an experiment, and even if they did, it is doubtful whether they would oblige us with a demonstration. The point of the matter is not physics but logic. There is no *logical* necessity about any prediction we make about things. Logical necessity is confined to assertions about assertions, as in mathematics. But once that last step is made, once language is linked to experience, we pass from the world of logical implication to the world of probabilities. No amount of "iron logic" or "common sense" can prove anything about the world. The "certainties" of science are only high probabilities. Some are so high that you can be quite sure you can depend on them. Others are not so high but still may be extremely useful. But the ultimate authority for any scientific assertion is verification of specific predictions. There are no shibboleths of truth.

The most accurate scientific predictions are made in physics. And there are two branches of physics where predictions based on a few simple assumptions are especially successful. One is celestial mechanics, the other the kinetic theory of gases. In the first, we deal with a small number of "bodies" so far from each other that their interactions can be considered separately. It is thus possible to describe rather completely the *structure* of the system. Thus celes-

211

tial mechanics emphasizes *order*. On the contrary, the kinetic theory of gases deals with vast numbers of rapidly moving and colliding particles. There is practically no way of tracing any individual particle or even recognizing it among its fellows. Such a state of affairs is an excellent example of *chaos*. Yet, paradoxically, prediction becomes as easy in chaos as in order. This is because the laws of probability when applied to vast numbers of similar objects become almost exact. Rigorous mathematical reasoning becomes possible. Predictions made on the basis of that reasoning are as reliable as can be desired, but they are never free from a trace of uncertainty, because what we describe is never reality but an abstraction of reality with characteristics left out.

Suppose it were possible to know everything at once at some instant. Could one then predict everything?

N: Confronted with such a question, a non-Aristotelian philosopher would first inquire into its meaning, that is, its operational meaning. Even if he took "to know" as an undefinable "primitive" term, he would still have to describe "everything at some instant" in operational terms. His knowledge of the implications of the relativity theory and of quantum mechanics would then force him to the conclusion that "everything at one instant" has no operational meaning at least in terms of those operations which we must perform in order to "know" reality.

However, for the mechanistic philosopher in the golden age of celestial mechanics there were no such difficulties. Believing, as he did, in the existence of an absolute framework of Space and in a Time which flowed regularly and independently of any events or measurement, the mechanistic philosopher could imagine a Supreme Intelligence, who could know "everything at one instant." His God still retained his omniscience, although he had to yield his omnipotence to the relentless sequence of causes and effects.

212

How Certain Is Certain?

The mechanistic philosopher interpreted the magnificent outlines of the edifice of scientific knowledge, which began to emerge in the eighteenth and nineteenth centuries, as a revelation of complete determinism. Laplace, the great mathematician-astronomer, put it this way:

> Nous devons donc envisager l'état présent de l'univers comme l'effet de son état antérieur, et comme la cause de celui qui va suivre. Une intelligence qui, pour un instant donné connaîtrait toutes les forces dont la nature est animée, et la situation respective des êtres qui la composent, si d'ailleurs elle était assez vaste pour soumettre ces données à l'analyse, embrasserait dans la même formule les mouvement del plus grand corps de l'univers et ceux de plus léger atome: rien ne serait incertain pour elle, et l'avenir comme le passé serait présent a ses yeux. L'esprit humain offre dans la perfection qu'il a su donner à l'astronomie un faible esquisse de cette intelligence.[1]

[1] We should therefore view the present state of the universe as an effect of its preceding state and as a cause of the one to follow. An intelligence which could know at a given instant all the forces impressed upon the world and the respective positions of all the particles which compose the world, could, if it were vast enough to analyze these data, summarize in a single formula the motions of both the heaviest bodies of the universe and of the lightest atoms. Nothing would remain unknown to it—the future like the past would be revealed to its eyes. The human mind, in its achievements in astronomy has given a feeble imitation of such an intelligence.—P. S. Laplace, *Théorie Analytique des Probabilités*. [My translation—A. R.]

CHAPTER 21

Is Science Enough?

The universe a swarm of particles? The world a machine! Is this the final pronouncement of science? Are you trying to drive the spiritual forever from the scheme of things? Where are the intangibles? Where is genius? When love awakens, when a symphony is composed, is nothing happening but a recombination of "particles"? Where is freedom? Is there nothing to strive for, since the course of the universe has been predetermined from its very beginning?

Will not the human element forever remain unpredictable?

Is not science itself just one of many possible ways of looking at the world, and is not intuitive, unverbalizable knowledge and poetic truth entitled to at least an equal position as guides for orientation?

In other words, are you not, N, deeply intolerant when you make your solemn pronouncement "There are no other effective or reliable methods of acquiring knowledge than the methods of science"?

N: I try to do two things: to be aware of the difference between words and things and to check my judgments based on one kind of experience by other kinds of experience. Actually everyone who is not completely insane does these things in some measure. If one does this consistently enough and pursues the implications far enough, one arrives at a scientific, non-Aristotelian orientation.

What you are asking, I presume, is whether it is advisable to pursue the implications far enough. The answer to the question depends on one's orientation. If one values the ability to predict and to manipulate one's environment (including one's self), the answer is yes, because as far as we know the method of science is the only method we have for making the world systematically more predictable and manipulable. This method consists of creating symbolic maps whose structure resembles as closely as possible the structure of reality.

True, symbolic behavior may have another function besides those of communication and heuristics—the expressive function. As a vehicle for this function, language need not give information or solve problems. Its purpose becomes rather to "call to mind," as Susanne Langer put it,[1] or to engage in flights of fancy, unhampered by logic. Indeed, there may even be a common ground between imaginative art and philosophy. Once freed by science from the task of contemplating the known world, philosophy may well construct "possible worlds." The genius of imaginative experimentation can be transferred to the realm of ideas, and the philosopher's chair may then become a "laboratory."

Yet art and philosophy are ways of human behavior and as such a part of the real world, a legitimate field of exploration for science. A composer may not know and may not care what happens in his nervous system when he is composing a symphony, but it is the business of the psychologist to find out and to describe his findings in a language based on communicative and heuristic principles rather than expressive ones. Who will proclaim these matters taboo?

To be sure, some people fear analysis and would like to exclude scientific attitudes from their outlook at least in certain areas. Some may wish to regard their feelings of "free will" as inviolable. They will refuse to accept any evidence of the influence which

---

[1] Susanne Langer, *Philosophy in a New Key.*

their genes, their glandular secretions, or their semantic environment may have on their motivations and drives. Some have associated the sexual functions with awe, dread, or shame. They incline to view investigations in this field with alarm, either frankly prudish or masked by a romantic fear of "disillusion." Others have taboo areas of religion, race, social order. Still others simply resent mental effort of any kind and rationalize their resentment by proclaiming scientific analysis "cold," "dry," or "brutal." They often declare that they get along "successfully" without it, relying on "common sense," "intuition," or "divine guidance" in the solution of their problems. Certain psychiatrists point out that in fact the predominant motivations of people are based on the Irrational rather than on the Rational.

Still it is one thing to *recognize* the importance of the so-called irrational in human behavior, as modern psychiatry does, and as Susanne Langer says should be done in modern philosophy, and quite another to declare those motivations forever outside the scope of rational analysis as some authorities in psychiatry and in social science do. If we may generalize from our experience of the past, and if science is allowed to continue its quests, no phenomenon will ever escape from the scrutiny of the scientist and from being fitted into the over-all scheme of things. The only thing that can be said to the timid ones is "Don't look, if you don't like the conclusions."

One example will suffice to illustrate how the hard-boiled physiological psychologists go about delving into the "mysteries" of human behavior.

The subject faces several light bulbs of different colors, which light up one at a time. He is told to keep a finger on a buzzer and to signal every time the *red* bulb lights up but at no other time. After a few trials, the subject's reaction becomes quite prompt. However, in the course of the experiment the subject makes several mistakes, ringing the buzzer at the appearance of lights other than red. When asked why he made the mistakes, the answer is usually, "Oh, somehow I had the feeling that the red bulb was going to light up."

The subject does not know why his "intuition" led him astray, but the psychologist does. During the first few trials, when the subject reacted correctly, the appearance of the red light was preceded by a faint clicking sound, *which did not penetrate into the subject's consciousness* (since he never became aware of it). Yet the subject unconsciously associated the sound with the imminent appearance of the red light. The mistakes occurred when the psychologist let the clicking sound precede the lighting up of bulbs other than red!

How much "intuitive" behavior may be based on such "subliminal cues"? How many hunches are nothing but unconscious associations, and are dramatically remembered when they result in a correct decision and conveniently forgotten otherwise?

How much do our "tastes" in food, dress, music, painting, personalities have to do with such subliminal cues, and what a world of discovery is promised in them! There lies the road to the solution of scores of "enigmas," "culture personalities," "culture souls," and "culture genius," with all due respect to the insight of the speculative philosophers (à la Spengler) who have brought these notions to our attention.

Similar should be our attitude to the so-called "poetic truth," an instrument of expression to the poet but a subject of inquiry to the scientist.

Now let us turn to the mechanistic conception of the world as a "machine." Laplace (see the end of the preceding chapter) tacitly assumed

(1) the existence of fundamental particles of which the universe consists and which have no further structure,

217

(2) the sole "causative" framework in the universe to be the laws of mechanics as postulated by Newton or their analogues, and

(3) the meaningfulness of the notion "the state of the universe at a given moment."

In the light of the discoveries of modern physics and the logical analysis that it inspired, all three assumptions are inadequate. Hence Laplace's picture is untenable. Yet the metaphysical difficulty usually called the "free will vs. determinism dilemma," which invariably emerges in discussions dealing with the role of science in human affairs, is not thereby resolved. The dilemma has deeper implications than Laplace's world-machine. All scientific investigation is directed toward the discovery of more or less determinist aspects of nature, the more determinist the better from the point of view of science. In this way, mechanics was most successful in describing nature (in astronomy, for instance); complete determinism was discovered or at least a state of affairs nearly approaching complete determinism.

Astronomers observe initial positions and velocities of planets and predict with wonderful precision their positions a long time ahead. Laplace's description assumes that just these methods can be extended to all events: the present completely determines the future. Even though unrealizable, this seems to be the ideal goal of science.

Yet scientific inquiry is declared to be a road to *freedom*. Indeed, it is pointed out that knowledge of the forces of nature enables us to harness them for our use, and we cannot help feeling that this somehow makes us "free," for instance makes us more independent of the whims of natural catastrophes, the ravages of disease, etc. But how can that be if the goal of science is to declare more and more processes to be subject to more and more determinist laws? Eventually our so-called "acts of will" and "choices" will be discovered to be necessary consequences of our previous state.

Is Science Enough?

What will happen to "freedom" then? Is the final result of the search for freedom the discovery that there is no freedom?

A semantic analysis of this question is instructive. First let us recognize that the notion of "freedom" is not without emotional connotations. True, it could conceivably be divorced from such connotations for the purposes of analysis. Still it is important to note that the very origin of the notion must have sprung from an attitude that "freedom" is something desirable. That is not to say that "freedom" is a universal value. All we say is that where the notion of "freedom" *does* arise, it is supposed to stand for something desirable. One could state this in another way, namely, that constraint (the opposite of freedom) is something undesirable.

People who show a distaste for or a horror of "determinism" usually confuse it with constraint. To see this, suppose someone tells you that you are not a free agent, because you are not able to commit suicide. Your protestations to the effect that you could commit suicide if you "chose" are of no avail, because you are told that you are not free to *choose* to commit suicide. The only way you can prove that you are free to do so is *to do so*, and that would be pointless. So you must admit that you are not free to choose certain things. Generalized, this observation becomes identical with Schopenhauer's remark: "Man can do what he will, but he cannot *will* what he will."

Is this inability to choose self-destruction disturbing? It may be to some people but probably because they fail to extensionalize. Instead of realizing that their "lack of freedom" in this particular case merely protects them from blowing their brains out, they react to the words "lack of freedom" in whatever context it is used as they would to a jail sentence. On the other hand, an extensional evaluation of "lack of freedom" at once tells us that it becomes important only if an element of frustration is involved: we wish to do something and cannot because of a constraint, or (and this is

219

usually much worse) we do *not* wish to do something and *must* because of a compulsion.

The latter situation had been exploited as subject matter of tragedy long before a scientific basis was developed for describing it. The Destiny of Greek tragedy, the "fatal" character trait of Shakespearean heroes, and the more sophisticated compulsions of Dostoevski's characters are all based on observations of human behavior.

In its most dramatic form, the tragedy of determinism involves a prediction made to the hero of his fate. In spite of the fact that this knowledge seems to the hero to give him an opportunity of avoiding it, he is nevertheless driven to it by the "predetermined" course of events (see Oedipus, Macbeth, etc.). The Aristotelian standards of "pity and fear" are attained in such tragedies by the fact that the audience too shares the conviction of the hero that the knowledge of what is to come *ought* to enable him to forestall the catastrophe. Yet as the action unfolds, one gets the horrible realization that it cannot be forestalled. Here is "lack of freedom" at its worst.

Experience seems to indicate, however, that knowledge of a situation *does* enable us to forestall the undesirable. Therefore, in the light of experience, there seems to be nothing wrong in assuming that additional knowledge is equivalent to additional freedom. Such freedom can be easily described in operational terms, as the following example shows.

A holds a dime in one hand and holds both hands behind his back. B tries to guess the hand with the coin. No matter how much B would like to guess right each time, he is *bound* to guess wrong approximately 50 per cent of the time if the game is played long enough. Moreover, A can *predict* that B will guess wrong about half the time. B's "fate" is thus to a certain extent "determined" and predictable, and in that sense he is not a "free agent."

But now suppose B can read A's mind. Then, of course, B can

guess 100 per cent of the time and will appear to A as a free agent. On the other hand, if A can read B's mind, he can switch the coin just as B is about to make a right guess and have B guess wrong all the time. (The game is played honestly: the coin can be switched at any time prior to B's declared guess but not after.) An interesting situation will occur if both A and B can read each other's mind. The one who can get his guess in *last*, that is, in the interval of time between the "decision" and the "act," will be the free agent.

Suppose A holds the dime in the left hand. B reads his mind and "decides" to guess "left hand." A reads B's mind and switches the coin; B reads A's mind and switches his guess, etc. Eventually a time will come when the switch can no longer be made. The one who got his guess in last will win. In other words, from a certain moment on, events are determined.

A similar situation was dramatically depicted in a Russian film about the battle of Stalingrad. The Russian commander had only a limited supply of artillery ammunition. He knew the Germans were preparing an all-out attack on his positions. If he economized the ammunition, his fire would not be sufficient to hold off the attack. On the other hand, if he shelled the German positions heavily, he would spend his ammunition. The Germans would then have leisure to re-form their lines and attack later with no artillery fire opposing them. The situation was completely changed when the Russian commander was informed by his intelligence agents of the *precise time* of the attack. He started shelling the German lines just one hour before the attack was scheduled to begin. His guess was that the Germans could not communicate a complete change of plan within an hour; so that the attack would start as originally scheduled. Since the German lines were disorganized by the heavy artillery fire, the attack was beaten off, even though the Russians shot away all their ammunition in a half hour. The Russian got in the last guess.

221

Stated in operational terms, the "free will vs. determinism" question ceases to be a dilemma. On the other hand, a metaphysical approach to the problem, whether one takes the side of determinism or of free will, is likely to discourage attempts to learn as much as possible about the universe. The "free-willer" is likely to declare that there are areas forever closed to scientific knowledge, such as certain aspects of human behavior. The consistent "determinist" cannot without abandoning at least a portion of his outlook undertake any act whatsoever, because an act involves a choice, and a choice involves an assertion in the form "If I did *not* do this, such-and-such would happen." But the word "if" should be meaningless for the consistent determinist, because it implies the possibility of choice!

Neither "free will" nor "determinism" describes nature objectively, that is, by operational terms used in certain contexts. In actual situations, there are always the observers and the observed. It is knowledge available to the former and unavailable to the latter that makes meaningful the expressions "freedom" and "fate." Thus, when we study nature, we are the "free agents" and nature is "determined." When we study ourselves, we are both "free" and "determined," but as a result of our study, by learning under what conditions our behavior is determined and how, we *become* more free. One of the objects of psychiatry is to make available to the patient knowledge about himself which will enable him to "choose" where he was not free to choose. Collectively speaking, social science should perform a similar function, where the "patient" is society. Schopenhauer's remark is truer if qualified thus:

"Man can do what he will, but his ability to will$_2$ what he will$_1$ is limited by the extent of his ignorance."

The subscripts indicate that the two "wills" are not on the same level of abstraction.

222

Is Science Enough?

POLITICAL FREEDOM

Freedom of choice means little if the consequences of choice are not known. In the "Button, button, who's got the button" game described above, B has freedom of choice in his guesses, but this freedom does not have much significance if he does not know in which hand A holds the coin.

The people of Plutonia are "free" to choose their leaders. But they do not know the consequences of their choice. They do not know, for example, that the orientation of their chosen leaders makes war almost inevitable. They don't want war; yet they are not free to prevent it.

The people of Neptunia can "read what they will." But their "will" is conditioned by a powerful propaganda machine. They are not free to will$_2$ what they will$_1$ to read. Hence they are no more free in their choice of reading matter than if they had a strict censorship.

It seems futile to define "freedom" as simply the ability to perform "acts of volition." What may seem "freedom" from the inside, an act of volition, may well be the anticipated response to someone's well-planned stimulus calculated to destroy the freedom of the responder in future matters. When Neptunians and Plutonians in free elections choose military-minded leaders, they are performing acts of volition. So does the alcoholic and the drug addict, when he indulges. So does the compulsive psychotic and the suicide.

Freedom means the ability to perform acts of volition *on the basis of predictable consequences.*

Hence to deprive large numbers of people of freedom does not necessitate "physical" constraints. All that is required is to keep them in ignorance concerning the consequences of their choices and to foster in them semantic reactions of stereotyped predictable, easily manipulable design.

CHAPTER 22

Is Science Moral?

A fundamental value in the scientific outlook is concern with the best available map of reality. The scientist will always seek a description of events which enables him to predict most by assuming least. He thus already prefers a particular form of behavior. If moralities are systems of preferences, here is at least one point at which science cannot be said to be *completely* without preferences. Science *prefers* good maps.

This preference has profound consequences. There are certain recognized obstacles to the search for truth. Therefore, if the recognition of truth is taken as a primary value, these obstacles must be removed. In this necessity for removing the obstacles, a general direction for the establishment of an ethics is implied.

A set of evaluative habits, an orientation, a social structure, a culture pattern which tends to facilitate the search for better maps will be considered by the scientist as "good"; that which hinders this search will be considered "bad." Of course, no actual social structure or culture pattern can either completely promote or completely inhibit the search for truth and therefore cannot be either entirely good or entirely bad. Further analysis breaks the high-order abstractions (social structure, culture pattern) into lower order components (church, state, educational system) which can be separately evaluated.

The measure of the sanity of an individual, as Korzybski and others have repeatedly pointed out, is the correspondence between reality and the map the individual makes of reality. The sanity of individuals is the concern of physicians.

Similarly, the measure of sanity of a society may be defined in terms of the opportunities provided by its institutions to its members for the achievement of greater sanity. The sanity of society should be the concern of social scientists.

Let us pursue this analogy between social science and medicine a step further. In medicine the case is clear cut. The pathologist studying a disease by examining slides in the laboratory need not and indeed should not consider the disease "evil." The specificity of his behavior demands that he not let wishful thinking, fear, or compassion interfere with his inquiries and analysis. But medicine *as a whole* cannot be impartial in the general struggle between man and the parasites that plague him. The operational definition of *social* sanity makes the goal of social science clear cut and thus sets a limit to its "impartiality." The *study* of a social structure or a culture pattern can and should be conducted without moralistic bias, but the *evaluation* of a society or a culture can and should be made in terms of the values dictated by the preference for sanity. Since the values are not arbitrarily chosen but flow out of scientific practice itself, the scientist cannot discard them without becoming inconsistent, that is, without negating his own activity. Let us examine some of these values more closely.

FREEDOM OF INQUIRY

The cherishing of freedom of inquiry excludes for the scientist innumerable religions in which "taboo topics" play a prominent part. In fact, legends persist in some religions which depict man as a carrier of an "original sin" for *daring to inquire*. The story of Prometheus is one such legend, but there are others. If in the scientist specific forms of behavior prevail (see Chapter 14), that is, if his "emotional drives" are geared to his intellectual pursuits, such views of man should be not only logically unacceptable to him but also morally repugnant.

Freedom of inquiry implies a critical attitude toward all formulations of knowledge. The scientist recognizes the relative character of such formulations. He knows that there is "no last word but only the latest."[1] Therefore, for the scientist there can be no oracles, no authority *as such.*

DEMOCRATIZATION OF KNOWLEDGE

Direct evidence takes precedence over any authority. No assertion is meaningful unless it is verifiable. No experimental fact is established unless it can be observed by *anybody* using similar techniques of observation. Therefore, *anybody* is a potential scientist. In principle there is nothing to prevent a bright high school youngster from upsetting the most "established" scientific theory.

The scientist should consider desirable the extension of scientific knowledge to *all* people. In his inquiries about human behavior he may well discover deterministic factors which may mean the ultimate destruction or degradation of humanity. If knowledge of these factors is confined to a few workers in the field like himself, they may indeed remain "deterministic," so that the scientist's reward for having labored would be a dubious one—the knowledge of the impending catastrophe, which will, of course, engulf himself. If, however, such knowledge can be widely and quickly spread, the "determinism" may dissipate itself. As we have pointed out, determinism is a property of the observed and a function of the ignorance of the observed relative to the observer. A social scientist who predicts a race riot in a given community may, by getting the news to enough people, prevent its occurrence.

STATUS OF THE SCIENTIST

The scientist, like any other individual, cannot be indifferent to the status he occupies in his society. Since this status is in a large sense dependent on the structure of the society and on the culture

[1] Quoted from Wendell Johnson's *People in Quandaries.*

pattern, the scientist cannot be indifferent to these no matter how far removed from "social and political questions" his particular investigations may be.

Consider a physiologist working in one of the "nonpolitical" areas, say investigating the permeability of cellular membranes. If he is to solve his problem, the following conditions may have to be fulfilled:

1. He may have to perform accurate measurements. Therefore, he requires certain kinds of equipment, which he may not have the skill, the facilities, or the time to make. It must be built by other people and made available to him.

2. He must have access to information concerning the work others have done on his problem and on related subjects. This implies not only the existence of accessible libraries but also the opportunity to correspond freely with men in Neptunia, Plutonia, or any other country where similar work is carried out. In other words, a scientist must be free to exchange information with other scientists.

3. He himself must be fed, clothed, and sheltered. This implies that his community should consider the problems on which he is working of sufficient importance to assign a certain part of its income to support him and others like him.

4. He must be free of excessive psychological tensions, such as fear. For example, he should be reasonably sure that the security of his position depends upon his competence as a scientist *only*; that his dependents are secure from privations and from persecution; that other scientists, upon whose work his own progress depends, are likewise secure from privations and persecution.

In other words, to solve his problem *most effectively*, the scientist must live in a culture in which scientific behavior is encouraged. No matter how remote from so-called "reality" a specific scientific problem may be, its effective solution is intimately connected with

227

the structure of society not only of a particular community but of the entire world. Any attempt, therefore, to consider scientific behavior apart from its social implications splits the unsplittable and is elementalistic. The scientist *as a scientist* should be profoundly interested in the goals pursued by or inherent in various forms of social organization, since they determine his effectiveness and his status.

STATUS OF THE INDIVIDUAL

Since the principle of the democratization of knowledge implies that *any* individual should be considered a potential scientist, it follows that the scientist is concerned with the status of any individual. The scientist is fundamentally a democrat. However, the democratic principles mean little to him unless they are extensionalized. Not merely the formal right to participate equally in the business of being human but *actual participation* should be extended to everyone. This implies the existence not only of constitutions, laws, and other "maps" but of the actual territory: effective means of production and equitable distribution of necessities and, above all, freedom from fear.

To be sane means to be able to inquire about reality, to examine reality, and to construct an adequate map of reality. This is impossible under the stress of fear and rage. The scientist as scientist will always act in such a way as to minimize the amount of fear and rage among men. This in itself implies a great deal of what some older ethical systems proclaimed "right" and "just." Dr. S need not have worried how he could justify his profound urge to "love his neighbor" on scientific grounds alone. It is justified, because "love" is conducive to co-operation, and co-operation allays fear, reduces the probability of conflict, and is therefore a factor in eliminating rage. On the other hand, many other "values" of some old ethical systems could probably not be derived from the fundamental rules of sanity. Among such "values" are "national honor," "faith," "chastity," "necessity of baptism," and refraining from pronouncing the name of one's mother-in-law. If they cannot be derived from the fundamental postulates of sanity, no one should be obliged to accept them. They should be viewed as unnecessary restrictions of freedom, conducive to conflict and its inevitable by-products, fear and rage. It will be noted that in almost all instances prompt fear reactions and prompt rage reactions against violators must be cultivated in people if various "local" moral codes are to be preserved.

ORIENTATION TOWARD THE FUTURE

The scientist, by the very nature of his attitude toward knowledge (prediction), is thoroughly oriented toward the future. For him the past is interesting only inasmuch as it helps to understand the present and hence to predict, and to some measure control, the future. This too has far-reaching ethical implications. All acts whose motivations arise only from the considerations of past events lose their justification. "Precedents" become unacceptable as guides for action. Moreover, the whole notion of "justice" is profoundly modified. "Revenge," an exceedingly important component in many ethical systems, becomes as senseless as beating a piece of furniture one has bumped into. So does the punishment of crime. Although for the scientist the ability to choose, once the consequences of choice are known, implies a *relative* "freedom of will," yet the scientist by his study of the world constantly strives to make it appear more "predetermined" by making it more predictable. The "criminal," therefore, appears to the scientist *not* free, inasmuch as he can be made the object of study. It becomes meaningless, therefore, for the scientist to separate aberrations of "physiological" functions, commonly recognized as disease, from those "psychological" aberrations which are still labeled in our prescientific legal language as "crime." There is no room in the ethical system of the scientist for such concepts as "paying the debt to society," "redemption of sin," "retribution," etc., and for all the morbid aspects of religious ethics that are commonly associated with those concepts.

THE SCIENTIST'S EVALUATION OF SOCIAL ORDER AND CULTURE

In terms of the values described above, social orders and cultures can be evaluated by the scientist. Those values are not arbitrary. They must be used by the scientist if he is to behave consistently as a scientist. We cannot, therefore, be altogether in accord with the view of George A. Lundberg, who says:

"Can science tell man in what *direction* he should go? Yes, if man will tell scientists where he wants to go."[2]

The fact is that different men want to go in different directions, *and some of these directions are incompatible with the direction inherent in science itself.* Moreover, the men who are now (1949) in the position of actually guiding our society have already chosen directions away from the goals implicit in scientific behavior. To be sure, Mr. Lundberg points out that scientists, in furnishing the rulers the information they require, should also make known the "costs and consequences" of different possible courses of action. Unfortunately, however, the farsightedness of the rulers cannot be depended upon. The ruler of Neptunia may well ask a scientist, "How can I destroy Plutonia?" and obtain a reply, "You can destroy Plutonia so-and-so, but beware, because the destruction of Plutonia will eventually lead to the ruin of Neptunia." We have no assurance that the ruler of Neptunia will take note of that part of the reply which follows the "but." He may gleefully scamper off on his idiotic mission immediately after getting the information he is primarily interested in.

[2] George A. Lundberg, *Can Science Save Us?*

In answering questions on "how to get there" the scientist must well consider *who* asks them. We do share the hope expressed by Mr. Lundberg that once "reliable estimates of the near and remote consequences of alternative courses of action" are available to men, their choice of values will be conditioned in such a way as to liberate them from the "absurd and fantastic notions" that now pervade practically all mores and institutions. But we must ask for the meaning of the term "available." The *Bulletin of Atomic Scientists*, in which "consequences" are often discussed, is "available" at 50 cents a copy. However, for each person reading this publication, there must be tens of thousands who imbibe the ethical pronouncements of Daddy Warbucks.

There are some things in which the scientist *cannot* be impartial. He cannot be impartial in the choice between a procedure based on misevaluation and superstition and one based on accurate observation, critical attitude, and carefully weighed arguments. Similarly, he cannot be impartial in his judgments about forms of social organization or about patterns of culture, if it is clear that one form tends to encourage scientific behavior and another to inhibit it.

It is quite another thing when the scientist is asked to give definitive answers on the merits of existing social orders or moral codes. Because the scientist is convinced of the relativity of knowledge, because he must be ready to cope with new evidence, because he must keep his orientation flexible, there are a great many questions to which the scientist must say, "I don't know." And certainly social science is still too young, its techniques still too undeveloped, its observations too scanty, its opportunities for controlled experiment too rare to enable it to make unequivocal pronouncements on the superiority of this or that existing or proposed social order, especially since the questions are usually asked in such a way as to imply a superiority *in every respect*. A scientist

231

knows nothing without sufficient opportunity to observe and to experiment. Such opportunity has not been given to him in any of the existing social orders.

Most rulers in our day of conflicting "social philosophies" expect *loyalty* from the social scientist. And many social scientists abandon the principles of scientific behavior and declare their loyalty (consciously or unconsciously) to the National Association of Manufacturers or to the Politburo. Compared with this sort of "social science" the position of the relativists is certainly a step forward. Dr. S', like Mr. Lundberg, implicitly disavows loyalty to any of the existing social orders or moralities *in principle*. He is quite right in doing so. But he should realize that such emancipation carries with it a new loyalty, namely, to a morality and a social order which do not demand loyalty *a priori*, in which investigation, criticism, intellectual cross-fertilization, and intellectual revolution are always possible and always welcome. That is scientific morality and scientific social order. These demand that we discard the notions of the world and of ourselves acquired through prescientific metaphysics and perpetuated through prescientific language habits.

The moral outlook inherent in science is not bound to this or that culture, even though it has borrowed standards from many cultures. True, the scientific view of the nonhuman world is largely a product of the West; but the most characteristic by-products of Western morality, laissez faire, individualism, racism, nationalism, are anything but scientific. The great religions of the East (one of which has been adopted in a monstrously distorted form by Western peoples, who had never had a moralistic religion) have developed views on man which more closely approach the scientific outlook than the current Western notions.

So it is incorrect to say that the scientific outlook is simply a by-product of a particular culture. It is rather the essence of a culture which has not yet been established—a *culture-studying* culture. Ironically, the anthropologists, who often are most emphatic in stating that no noncultural standards of evaluation exist, are among the most active builders of this new culture-studying culture, whose standards transcend those of the cultures which the anthropologists study and thus give them an opportunity to emancipate themselves from the limitations of the local standards. The anthropologst can remain the anthropologist both in New Guinea and in Middletown, in spite of the fact that he may have been born in Middletown or in New Guinea.

The moral attitudes contained in the scientific outlook have a different genesis from those contained in ordinary "unconscious" cultures. They are a result of a "freer choice," because they involve a deeper insight into the consequences of the choice.

EPILOGUE

In the Office of Dr. S.

The winter afternoon was fading. Dr. S, the physicist, silhouetted against the window, was absent-mindedly tracing a formula with his fingernail on the perspiring glass, and through the silence came the naïve melody of the campus clock chiming four.

And suddenly someone flipped the lights on, and the magic of twilight was gone. There were no more personified ideologies in the room, just people. One could recognize neither the dialectical materialist, nor the Thomist, nor the humanist, nor the non-Aristotelian among the youngish, maturish, and elderly men and women who had gathered for a chat, as was their custom on Saturday afternoons, in the office of Dr. S. Now they resembled each other to a remarkable degree. One could recognize in their clothes, in the tones, in their gait the *Homo academicus*. At any rate, that was a standing quip with Dr. S'.

Dr. S', the anthropologist, was silent now, paying homage to the somber mood that descended on the gathering, but those who knew him well could hear him think:

"The *Homo academicus* views the history of the world as a history of ideas. And all too often he gets the notion that mankind needs an 'integrated' idea of the world. As a rule, the *Homo academicus* does not have at his disposal armies and torture chambers, which is just as well. If he did, he would probably use them in the same way as the conquerors of Mexico and the agents of the East India Company used them, and all the rest of the gentry

234

who believed that mankind had to be 'saved,' 'organized,' 'unified,' or *'gleichgeschaltet.'* "

We were breaking up. Someone gathered up the beakers from which we had been drinking our tea and carried them back to the chemistry lab down the hall. One was aware of overcoats and rubbers and ordinary remarks about ordinary affairs.

Outside I lingered awhile to admire the snow-covered campus fading in the twilight and to wonder that here in these laboratories transgalaxium was born. The *Homo academicus* had been the father: his was the germ of the idea; he had been the mother: his was the labor of bringing it into the world; and he had abandoned it, had given it to the statesmen and the generals to make a soldier of it or a monster or anything they pleased.

"And if the *Homo a.* kept the power instead of relinquishing it to professional power wielders, would he have become a professional power wielder himself, as Dr. S' says?" I thought. "The curse of the Nibelung's ring . . ."

"Going my way?" said the non-Aristotelian. But now he was Dr. N, professor of neurophysiology, kindly, bearded, and lonely. His discoveries were not spectacular like those of Dr. S, and journalists had never found his theories interesting enough to garble on front pages. A "profile" reporter had written him up once with sympathy and understanding and had given a surprisingly good popular account of his ideas.

"Yes, indeed, Dr. N," I said. "I should very much like to go your way."

And we walked together across the campus and then along the main thoroughfare of the community between brightly lit stores and the row of parked cars. I wanted to hear more, and I felt that he was going to tell me more and was regathering his thoughts after the stormy afternoon session. At last he said:

"Medieval obscurantism died when celestial mechanics was

235

born. No longer could people talk about the nine circles of hell, about stones 'wanting' to seek the center of the earth, or planets executing 'eternally perfect' movements. The deathblow to current obscurantism about the human mind and soul and conscience and character and good and evil will come by way of the physiology of the human nervous system. It took a long time to expel organismic gremlins from astronomy. Perhaps it will take even longer to chase the gremlins out of accounts of human behavior. Nevertheless, the days of organismic interpretations of human behavior are numbered."

"Are we machines?" I asked.

"A particular kind of machines. Do you know what servo-mechanisms are? This is a term used by electrical and communication engineers to describe devices which transform a given input pattern of signals into a desired output pattern of signals. The energy for the output is not furnished directly by the input; it is provided by an internal source. With us the input is the stimuli of the external world; the output is our behavior. But there are many complex intermediate steps. And, most important, we are potentially able to evaluate our own performance. We are *self-studying* servo-mechanisms."

"But mechanisms nevertheless?"

"Yes. I know that when I say yes I arouse all the ire of the traditionally minded sentimentalists who, not knowing what we can mean by 'mechanisms' nowadays, will immediately retort, 'Man is *not* a machine!' The key term is 'self-studying.' A *self-studying* servo-mechanism is *not of the same order* as those mechanisms such as lathes, presses, and turbines which most people mean by 'machine.'"

"Mechanisms, like abstractions, have order?"

"Years ago Bertrand Russell published his paper on the theory of types in the *American Journal of Mathematics*. As one starts

236

to read it, one is surprised that it was published in a mathematical journal. One might say that it starts out with some old jokes. At any rate, some of these so-called 'paradoxes' are often told as amusing riddles. They had been invented by the Greek Sophists. Today sophistry has acquired a meaning close to quackery, and many people think that the original Sophists made their jokes in order to confuse or deceive honest, common-sense loving people. Yet these paradoxes contain a profound problem which could not be posed except by people deeply concerned with truth.

"As a simplest example of such a logical paradox Russell takes the assertion of the man who says, 'I am lying.' Is this assertion true? It appears that if the assertion is true, then it is false, because the man is lying; but if it is false, then it is true, because he *is* lying!

"The importance of such paradoxes is that in subtly hidden form they crop up in mathematics and present serious difficulties.

"In attempting to get around these difficulties, Russell proposed this rule: 'Whatever involves *all* of a collection must not be one of the collection.' According to this rule, 'the class of all classes' is not itself a class in the sense of its member classes; an assertion about all assertions is not itself an assertion of the same kind. This leads to the theory of types. Russell considers the 'individual' (something devoid of complexity) as the first logical type; elementary propositions about individuals as the second logical type; second order propositions (about first order propositions) as the next, etc. Thus a man can say 'All first-order propositions affirmed by me are false' and still make a true (second-order) proposition. He is then a first order liar, but not necessarily a second-order liar.

"To a certain extent we can see the analogy of the theory of types in the levels of organization of organisms. An animal which 'adjusts' to its immediate environment has certain potentialities of survival. An animal able to 'adjust$_2$ its adjustment$_1$' (to learn) has more potentialities. An organism cognizant of the *learning process* has still more. We are organisms (or mechanisms) not merely endowed with a nervous system but with a nervous system which can *study itself.* Therein lie our potentialities of survival."

We had gone a half mile, and the cold began to make itself felt. A tavern seemed cozy and inviting, and the idea of a glass of Pilsner before dinner equally welcome.

"The ultrarelativists have not really learned the lesson of Relativity too well," said Dr. N over the Pilsner. "There are two great lessons in the Theory of Relativity, a negative lesson and a positive one. The negative lesson destroys faith in existing 'invariants.' The rock of faith on which nineteenth-century physics was built was the faith in the invariance, in the objective validity, of 'distance,' 'time interval,' 'mass' with respect to all observers. The Theory of Relativity destroyed that faith.

"But there is also a positive lesson, which people who learn about Relativity from the Sunday supplements and even some people who get their information from much more authoritative sources have never learned. In demolishing the old absolutes, the theory established a higher type of invariant, the 'space-time interval,' on which all observers could agree even if they agreed to disagree about the special projections of the space-time interval.

"The relativist anthropologists, it seems to me, are among those who have only half learned the lessons of Relativity. They've learned the negative lesson all right. In examining the existing cultures of the Kwakiutl, the Athabascan, the Chinese, or the residents of Middletown, the relativists show how human needs are culturally conditioned, and how the needs most emphasized by a given culture are those most acutely felt. Thus the relativity of specific cultures is established, and such culturally determined values as private property, monogamy, head-hunting, and the

238

communal ownership of land are seen to be something short of absolutes, binding upon all human beings under all conditions.

"But the ultrarelativist anthropologists don't seem to be aware of the positive lessons to be learned from Relativity. They should learn to seek the higher invariants, the invariants of human needs. If the Christian shows his respect for God by removing his hat in a place of worship, and the Orthodox Jew shows his respect by leaving it on in his place of worship, the relativity of rules governing hats is established, to be sure, but in this case there is a higher invariant revealed by the comparison, namely, the need of both Christian and Jew to symbolize a respect for God. Or you can go still further. If one group of people support their system of social order by postulating a God who commanded such a system and another group support theirs by not postulating a God at all but by postulating certain philosophical principles, the relativity of philosophical or theological principles is established, but the higher invariant, namely, the need of some systematic and thoughtful rationalization of social order is also established. What are the invariant human needs beyond the needs for food, shelter, and procreation?

"One of these is surely the need of all people for good maps of the territories of human nature and experience, so that they can solve the problems of food getting, shelter, child care, social order, or war and peace as they arise. Isolated groups are no doubt content with their maps; but few groups are isolated any longer, and even those groups which believe they are will soon find out they are not, in which case they will also find that their maps are not so adequate as they thought they were. In so far as people have a basic need to adjust somehow or other to the world as it is, they are trying, as they have done throughout history, to improve their maps. The alternative to improving their maps is non-survival.

239

"But how do people improve their maps? One of the most important ways since the beginning of time has been for people to compare their own maps with those of other groups. In other words, better mapbuilding gradually leads to a *culture-studying culture*. Here is where the ultrarelativists—those who have learned only the negative lesson of Relativity—make their mistake. They do not realize that a *culture that can emerge from the study of other cultures* is by no means the same as a plain, hand-me-down culture in which one simply continues to do what one's neighbors and forebears have always done. A culture$_1$-studying culture$_2$ is of a different order and cannot be placed on the same level with the existing cultures$_1$.

"A culture-studying culture! What a relief that would give us from the clamor of economic ideologies, for example! Here is one group shouting that taking a profit on the exchange of goods and services is utterly immoral. Another group shouts equally loudly that everything people hold dear—human character, scientific advancement, the sanctity of religion and the home—depend on the preservation of the profit system! Freed from moralistic shackles, a culture-studying society can study possible ways of organizing economy and *try* them. While the champions of 'ideologies' engage in lofty and ever self-righteous arguments about the superiority of capitalism to socialism or vice versa, the self-studying society would examine under what conditions what degree of control over what industries is required for optimum efficiency and adequate insurance both against scarcity of commodities and against the excessive concentration of economic might in irresponsible hands. It may well turn out that 'higher invariants' (abundance and decentralization of power) are best achieved if the production of transgalaxium is nationalized, the manufacture of parapetaculators is organized co-operatively, and the growing of nasturtiums is left to private individuals.

240

Epilogue

"What a relief it would be to discover that one does not owe loyalty to any one of the existing 'ideologies.' What a relief it would be to discuss the advantages or disadvantages of caprocity without having to listen to arguments whether or not it is 'evil.' In a culture-studying culture, we would work like mechanism-studying mechanics, evolving for each time and place and situation the best available arrangement of economic or social mechanisms, without worrying about 'succumbing to X-ism' or introducing 'un-Neptunian notions.' "

"But where is such a culture-studying culture being created?" I asked.

"All over," said Dr. N. "All people who disown shibboleths belong to it."

"Is it perhaps just another faith?" I asked.

"It is a faith," said Dr. N, "but of a second order—a faith-disavowing faith, if you will."

"Faiths too have order?"

"The basic notion embodied in the theory of types is a fruitful one. Faiths of 'higher order,' wills, sanities, cultures cannot be demonstrated with logical rigor as the existence of 'classes' can be demonstrated, because 'faith,' 'will,' and 'culture' are not logical categories like 'class.' Nevertheless, it is profitable to think of such hierarchies. $Hatred_2$ of $hatred_1$ is of a different order from the first-order hatred of Tom, or Mary, or Gaminos, or Plutonians. When Schopenhauer said 'Man can do what he will, but he cannot will what he will' he was aware of the hierarchy of types involving 'will.' Korzybski calls these hierarchies multi-ordinalities and conjectures the existence of neurological counterparts of the logical categories. If he is right, we should someday be able to demonstrate that the neural events involving, say, 'fear of fear' are of a different kind from those involving fear of tigers.

"But Schopenhauer in his pessimism was condemning man to

stay forever on the first rung or the 'will-ladder.' By learning the mechanisms of willing, man can perhaps learn to will$_2$ what he will$_1$. To take a homely example, the man who asks 'Why can't I make more money?' is operating on one level, but the man who asks 'Why should I *want* to make more money?' is operating on a higher level. He is 'freer'; and the man who asks 'Why am I concerned with what I want or do not want?' is probing still more deeply into his own nature and is potentially still freer. Self-study is the key to 'freedom' and sanity."

"You believe, then, in the ultimate victory of sanity?"

"That's a rather flamboyant way of putting it. Let us say instead that I hold a neurophysiological hypothesis—a hypothesis that fear and rage (which make self-study and hence sanity impossible) are not inherent invariants of human nature. Just as scurvy is due to a lack of vitamin C, so fear is due to lack of proper insight. But insight is a certain kind of functioning of the nervous system; human nerve cells are organized in such a way that the organism not only reacts to stimuli but can study its own reactions, and study its own reactions to its own reactions, and then ponder about them. Fear and rage, of course, block these neurological activities, so that the organism is limited to reactions of the first order and becomes incapable of those second- and third-order reactions which constitute self-study and hence insight.

"A forward direction for man is thus indicated. The full functioning of that complex and amazing machinery we know as the human nervous system means the acquisition of insight—self-insight, insight into the compulsions of one's culture, insight into what makes us do what we do. Once we know why we do what we do, we become free either to continue doing it or to stop. That is the goal of psychiatry—to learn why we do what we do, so that we may become free to stop doing it. That is the goal of the social sciences too, to learn why we as cultures do what we do, so that we may become free to do something else if necessary.

"That is why cultural anthropology is an important science— and so are psychiatry and semantics and neurophysiology, bio-chemistry, biophysics, mathematical biology, general ecology, etc. These sciences are all in the forward direction toward self-insight. Once this direction is taken, there is no going back."

Even three-quarters of a mile away, we could hear the campus clock chiming six. Dr. N and I adjourned and went our ways.

BIBLIOGRAPHY

The numbers in parentheses following each entry indicate the chapters in *this* book to which the entry is especially pertinent. The number o refers to the prologue and preface, and 22a to the epilogue.

1. AQUINAS, THOMAS. *Summa Theologica.* New York: Benziger Brothers, 1947 (19).
2. ARISTOTLE. *Organon,* Cambridge, Mass., Harvard Press, 1938 (7, 12).
3. ———— *Physica.* Oxford: The Clarendon Press, 1930 (4, 5, 11).
4. ARNOLD, THURMAN W. *The Folklore of Capitalism.* New Haven: Yale University Press, 1937 (10, 22a).
5. ———— *The Symbols of Government.* New Haven: Yale University Press, 1935 (2, 10).
6. AYER, A. J. *Language, Truth, and Logic.* Oxford University Press, 1936 (4, 5, 6, 7, 11, 15, 16, 17).
7. BACON, FRANCIS. *Novum Organum.* Oxford: The Clarendon Press, 1889 (4, 5, 11).
8. BARNETT, H. G. "On Science and Human Rights," *American Anthropologist,* Vol. 50, No. 2, 1948 (0).
9. BECKER, CARL. "Every Man His Own Historian," *American Historical Review,* Vol. 37, No. 2, January, 1932 (17, 18).
10. BELL, ERIC TEMPLE. *Men of Mathematics.* New York: Simon and Shuster, 1937 (19).
11. BERKELEY, GEORGE. *A Treatise Concerning the Principles of Human Knowledge.* Chicago and London: The Open Court Publishing Co., 1938 (17, 18).
12. BENEDICT, RUTH. *Patterns of Culture.* Boston and New York: Houghton Mifflin Co., 1934 (0, 22a).

245

13. —— *Chrysanthemum and the Sword*. Boston: Houghton Mifflin Co., 1946 (0, 22, 22a).

14. BENTLEY, ARTHUR F. *Linguistic Analysis of Mathematics*. Bloomington, Ind., The Principia Press, 1932 (15, 19).

15. The Bible (0, 4, 13).

16. BLIVEN, BRUCE. "What *Is* Anti-Semitism," *New Republic*, Dec. 22, 1947 (3, 10).

17. BLOOMFIELD, LEONARD. "Linguistic Aspects of Science," *International Encyclopedia of Unified Science*, Vol. 1, No. 4. Chicago: University of Chicago Press, 1939 (7, 8, 11, 15, 16).

18. BRIDGMAN, P. W. *The Logic of Modern Physics*. New York: The Macmillan Co., 1927 (4, 5, 7, 11, 15, 16, 17, 20).

19. BURROW, TRIGANT. *The Biology of Human Conflict*. New York: The Macmillan Co., 1937 (1, 2, 3, 7, 18).

20. —— "Phylobiology," *Psyche*, Vol. 11, 1930 (0, 1, 2).

21. BYKHOVSKY, B. "The Morass of Modern Bourgeois Philosophy," *ETC: A Review of General Semantics*, Vol. 6, No. 1, Autumn, 1948 (17, 18).

22. CARNAP, RUDOLF. *The Logical Syntax of Language*. New York: Harcourt, Brace and Co., 1937 (2, 4, 5, 7, 15, 16).

23. —— "Probability as a Guide to Life," *Journal of Philosophy*, Vol. 44, No. 6, March 13, 1947 (20).

24. —— *The Unity of Science*. London: Kegan Paul, Trench, Trubner & Co., 1934 (15, 16, 21, 22a).

25. —— *Scheinprobleme in der Philosophie*. Berlin-Schlachtensee: Weltkreis-Verlag, 1928 (2, 15, 16, 17).

26. CHASE, STUART. *The Tyranny of Words*. New York: Harcourt Brace and Co., 1938 (16, 18).

27. —— *The Proper Study of Mankind*. New York: Harper & Brothers, 1948 (0, 18, 22a).

28. CHISHOLM, G. B. "The Reëstablishment of Peacetime Society," *Psychiatry*, Vol. 9, No. 1, February, 1946 (0, 22, 22a).

29. CHISHOLM, FRANCIS P. *Introductory Lectures in General Semantics*. Lakeville, Conn.: Institute of General Semantics, 1945 (10, 12, 13, 14, 15, 16).

30. COHEN, MORRIS R., and NAGEL, ERNEST. *An Introduction to Logic and Scientific Method.* New York: Harcourt, Brace and Co., 1934 (15, 16).

31. COOPER, LANE. *Aristotle, Galileo, and the Tower of Pisa.* London: H. Milford, Oxford Press, 1935 (4, 5, 11, 12).

32. DANTZIG, TOBIAS. *Number, the Language of Science.* New York: The Macmillan Co., 1933 (15, 19).

33. DE MORGAN, AUGUSTUS. *Formal Logic.* London: The Open Court Publishing Co., 1926 (5, 7, 12).

34. DOUGHTY, CHARLES M. *Travels in Arabia Deserta.* New York: Random House (11).

35. DUNHAM, BARROWS. *Man Against Myth.* Boston: Little, Brown and Co., 1948 (17, 18).

36. ECKSTEIN, GUSTAV. "Concerning a Dog's Word Comprehension," *Science,* May 13, 1949 (8).

37. EINSTEIN, ALBERT, and LEOPOLD INFELD. *The Evolution of Physics.* New York: Simon and Shuster, 1938 (0, 11, 15, 16, 17, 22a).

38. ENGELS, F. *Dialectics of Nature.* New York: *International Publishers,* 1940 (16, 17, 18).

39. FRANK, PHILIPP. *Einstein, His Life and Times.* New York: Alfred A. Knopf, 1947 (11, 15, 16).

40. ———— "Science Teaching and the Humanities," *ETC: A Review of General Semantics,* Vol. 4, No. 1, Autumn, 1946 (7, 11).

41. FROMM, ERICH. *Man for Himself.* New York: Rinehart and Co., 1947 (0, 22, 22a).

42. GALILEI, GALILEO. *Dialogues Concerning Two New Sciences.* Evanston and Chicago: Northwestern University Press, 1939 (4, 5, 11).

43. GEORGE, WILLIAM H. *The Scientist in Action.* New York: Emerson Books, Inc., 1938 (15, 16, 22).

44. GONCHAROV, I. *Oblomov.* New York: The Macmillan Co., 1929 (11).

45. GORER, GEOFFREY. *The American People.* New York: W. W. Norton and Co., 1948 (0, 22, 22a).

247

46. HAYAKAWA, S. I. *Language in Action.* New York: Harcourt, Brace and Co., 1941 (6, 7, 8, 10, 12, 13, 14, 15, 16).
47. ——— *Language in Thought and Action.* New York: Harcourt, Brace and Co., 1949 (6, 7, 8, 10, 12, 13, 14, 15, 16, 22, 22a).
48. ——— "Anti-Semitism: A Study in Mistaken Map-Territory Relationships," *ETC: A Review of General Semantics,* Vol. 6, No. 3, Spring, 1949 (3, 10).
49. ——— "The Non-Aristotelian Revision of Morality," *ETC: A Review of General Semantics,* Vol. 3, No. 3, Spring, 1946 (o, 22, 22a).
50. JOHNSON, ALEXANDER BRYAN. *A Treatise on Language.* Berkeley and Los Angeles: University of California Press, 1947 (6, 7, 12, 13, 14).
51. JOHNSON, WENDELL. *People in Quandaries.* New York: Harper & Brothers, 1946 (5, 6, 7, 9, 10, 11, 12, 13, 14, 15, 16).
52. ——— "Speech and Personality," published in *Communication of Ideas,* Lyman Bryson, editor. New York: Harper & Brothers, 1948 (9, 10, 12, 13).
53. ——— "How to Ask a Question," *Journal of General Education,* Vol. 1, No. 2, April, 1947 (1, 5, 7, 11).
54. KEYSER, CASSIUS. *Mathematical Philosophy.* New York: E. P. Dutton and Co., 1922 (15, 19, 20).
55. ——— *Humanism and Science.* New York: Columbia University Press, 1931 (o, 22).
56. KLUCKHOHN, CLYDE. *Mirror for Man.* New York: Whittlesey House, 1949 (o, 22a).
57. KÖHLER, WOLFGANG. *Gestalt Psychology.* New York: Liveright Publishing Corporation, 1947 (10).
58. KORZYBSKI, ALFRED. *Manhood of Humanity.* New York: E. P. Dutton and Co., 1921 (9, 22, 22a).
59. ——— *Science and Sanity.* Lancaster, Pa.: Science Press, 1933 (5, 6, 7, 8, 9, 10, 11, 12, 13, 14, 15, 16, 19, 20, 21).
60. LANGER, SUSANNE K. *Philosophy in a New Key.* Cambridge, Mass.: Harvard University Press, 1942 (21).

61. LAPLACE, P. S. *Théorie Analytique des Probabilité*. Paris, Vᵉ Courcier, 1812 (20).

62. LEE, IRVING J. *Language Habits in Human Affairs*. New York: Harper & Brothers, 1941 (10, 12, 13).

63. —— ed., *The Language of Wisdom and Folly*. New York: Harper & Brothers, 1949 (4, 5, 6, 7, 8, 9, 12, 13, 15, 16, 17, 19, 20, 21, 22).

64. LENIN, V. I. *Materialism and Empirio-criticism*. New York: International Publishers, 1927 (17, 18).

65. LEWIN, KURT. *Resolving Social Conflicts*. New York: Harper & Brothers, 1948 (1, 2, 3, 7).

66. LIEBER, LILLIAN. *The Einstein Theory of Relativity*. New York and Toronto: Farrar and Rinehart, 1945 (0, 15, 22a).

67. —— *Non-Euclidean Geometry*. Lancaster, Pa.: Science Press, 1940 (19).

68. —— *Mits, Wits, and Logic*. New York: W. W. Norton & Co., 1947 (12, 22).

69. LOCKE, JOHN. *"Essay on the Human Understanding."* Oxford: The Clarendon Press, 1894 (16).

70. LUNDBERG, GEORGE A. *Can Science Save Us?* New York, London, Toronto: Longmans, Green and Co., 1947 (0, 2, 19, 22, 22a).

71. MACH, ERNST. *The Science of Mechanics*. London: The Open Court Publishing Co., 1942 (11, 16).

72. —— *Popular Scientific Lectures*. Chicago: The Open Court Publishing Co., 1895 (5, 11, 16, 17).

73. —— *Erkenntnis und Irrtum*. Leipzig: I. A. Barth, 1905 (5, 11).

74. MANN, THOMAS. *The Magic Mountain*. New York: Alfred A. Knopf, 1939 (3).

75. MARX, KARL. *The Poverty of Philosophy*. Chicago: C. H. Kerr and Co., 1910 (17, 18).

76. MCWILLIAMS, CAREY. *Prejudice*. Boston: Little, Brown & Co., 1944 (3, 10).

77. MEYERS, RUSSELL. *"The Nervous System and General Semantics,"* *ETC: A Review of General Semantics*, Vol. 5, No. 4, Summer,

1948, Vol. 6, No. 1, Autumn, 1948, Vol. 6, No. 3, Spring, 1949 (4, 8, 9, 10, 11, 14, 21).

78. MORRIS, CHARLES. *Foundations of the Theory of Signs.* Chicago: University of Chicago Press, 1938 (6, 7, 8, 9).

79. —— *Signs, Language, and Behavior.* New York: Prentice Hall, 1946 (6, 7, 8, 9, 10).

80. NORTH, R. "Semantics, the Science of Mutual Understanding," *Hilbert Journal,* Vol. 45, No. 3, April, 1947 (1, 2, 3, 7).

81. NORTHRUP, F. S. C. "The Neurological and Behavioristic Psychological Basis of the Ordering of Society by Means of Ideas," *Science,* April 23, 1948 (22a).

82. —— *The Meeting of East and West.* New York: The Macmillan Co., 1946 (4, 7, 18, 22a).

83. OGDEN, C. K., and RICHARDS, I. A. *The Meaning of Meaning.* New York: Harcourt, Brace and Co., 1936 (6, 7, 8, 9, 15, 16, 17, 21).

84. PAUL, SHERMAN. "Whitehead, Langer, and the Uniting of 'Fact' and 'Value,'" *ETC: A Review of General Semantics,* Vol. 6, No. 2, Winter, 1949 (21, 22).

85. PIAGET, J. *The Language and Thought of the Child.* New York: Harcourt, Brace and Co., 1926 (11, 13).

86. PLANCK, MAX. *Where Is Science Going?* New York: W. W. Norton and Co., 1932 (17, 20, 21).

87. POINCARÉ, HENRI. *The Foundations of Science.* New York: The Science Press, 1913 (11, 15, 16, 20, 21).

88. RAPOPORT, ANATOL. "The Criterion of Predictability," *ETC: A Review of General Semantics,* Vol. 2, No. 3, Spring, 1945 (1, 2, 3, 4, 5, 15, 16, 17 19).

89. —— "Semantic Aspects of Language and Mathematics," *ETC: A Review of General Semantics,* Vol. 3, No. 2, Winter, 1946 (7, 19, 20).

90. —— "Dialectical Materialism and General Semantics," *ETC: A Review of General Semantics,* Vol. 5, No. 2, Winter, 1948 (17, 18).

91. RAPOPORT, ANATOL, and ALFONSO SHIMBEL. "Mathematical

Biophysics, Cybernetics, and General Semantics," *ETC: A Review of General Semantics*, Vol. 6, No. 3, Spring, 1949 (22a).

92. RASHEVSKY, NICOLAS. *Mathematical Theory of Human Relations*, Bloomington, Ind.: The Principia Press, 1947 (22a).

93. RUSSELL, BERTRAND. "Les Paradoxes de la Logique," *Revue de Métaphysique et de Morale*, 1906 (22a).

94. —— "Mathematical Logic as Based on the Theory of Types," *American Journal of Mathematics*, Vol. 30, 1908 (22a).

95. SANTAYANA, GEORGE. "Some Meanings of the Word 'Is,'" *Journal of Philosophy*, Vol. 21, No. 14, July 3, 1924 (7, 12, 13).

96. SCHLAUCH, MARGARET. "Semantics as Social Evasion," *Science and Society*, Fall, 1942 (18).

97. SCHOPENHAUER, ARTHUR. *The World as Will and Idea.* London: Paul, Trench, Trubner & Co., 1907-09 (21, 22a).

98. SCHROEDINGER, ERWIN. *What Is Life?* New York: The Macmillan Co., 1945 (9, 21, 22a).

99. SPENGLER, OSWALD. *Decline of the West.* New York: Alfred A. Knopf, 1939 (0, 22, 22a).

100. "Statement on Human Rights," *American Anthropologist*, Vol. 49, No. 4, 1947 (0).

101. SWIFT, JONATHAN. *Gulliver's Travels.* New York: Harcourt, Brace and Co., 1920 (1, 7, 22a).

102. TARSKI, ALFRED. "The Semantic Conception of Truth and the Foundations of Semantics," *Philosophy and Phenomenological Research*, Vol. 4, No. 3, March, 1941 (2, 4, 5, 15, 16).

103.* THORNDIKE, EDWARD L. "Science and Values," *Science*, Jan. 3, 1936 (0, 22, 22a).

104. VAIHINGER, H. *The Philosophy of "As If."* New York: Harcourt, Brace and Co., 1935 (15, 16, 17, 19, 20, 21).

105. VOGT, WILLIAM. *The Road to Survival.* New York: William Sloane Associates, 1948 (13, 14, 15, 16).

106. WALPOLE, HUGH R. *Semantics.* New York: W. W. Norton, 1941 (6, 7, 8).

107. WEAVER, RICHARD M. *Ideas Have Consequences.* Chicago: University of Chicago Press, 1948 (3, 12, 13, 14, 19).

108. WELBY, VIOLA. *What Is Meaning?* New York: The Macmillan Co., 1903 (6, 7, 8, 9).

109. WHITEHEAD, ALFRED NORTH. *Science and the Modern World.* New York: The Macmillan Co., 1925 (21).

110. ——— *Symbolism, Its Meaning and Effect.* New York: The Macmillan Co., 1927 (6, 9).

111. WIENER, NORBERT. *Cybernetics.* New York: John Wiley & Sons, 1948 (22a).

112. WINTHROP, HENRY. "Two Concepts of Personality Disintegration," *Journal of General Psychology,* Vol. 40, 1949, pp. 177-218 (3).

113. WITTGENSTEIN, LUDWIG. *Tractatus Logico-Philosophicaus.* New York: Harcourt, Brace and Co., 1933 (15, 16).

114. ZIPF, GEORGE K. *Human Behavior and the Principle of Least Effort.* Cambridge, Mass.: Addison Wesley Press, 1949 (16).

CROSS REFERENCE TO BIBLIOGRAPHY

The numbers indicated for each chapter refer to the bibliography entries especially pertinent to the chapter.

Prologue and Preface: 8, 12, 13, 15, 27, 28, 37, 41, 45, 55, 56, 66, 70, 99, 100, 103.

Chapter 1: 19, 20, 53, 65, 80, 88, 101.

Chapter 2: 5, 19, 20, 22, 24, 25, 65, 70, 80, 88, 102.

Chapter 3: 16, 19, 20, 48, 65, 74, 76, 80, 88, 107, 112.

Chapter 4: 3, 6, 7, 15, 18, 22, 31, 42, 63, 77, 82, 88, 102.

Chapter 5: 3, 6, 7, 18, 22, 31, 33, 42, 51, 53, 59, 63, 72, 73, 88, 102.

Chapter 6: 6, 46, 47, 50, 51, 59, 63, 78, 79, 83, 106, 108, 110.

Chapter 7: 2, 6, 17, 18, 19, 22, 33, 40, 46, 47, 50, 51, 53, 59, 63, 65, 78, 80, 82, 83, 89, 95, 101, 106, 108.

Chapter 8: 17, 36, 46, 47, 59, 63, 77, 78, 79, 83, 106, 108.

Chapter 9: 51, 52, 58, 59, 63, 77, 78, 79, 83, 98, 108, 110.

Chapter 10: 4, 5, 16, 29, 46, 47, 48, 51, 52, 57, 59, 62, 76, 77.

Chapter 11: 3, 6, 7, 17, 18, 31, 34, 37, 39, 40, 42, 44, 51, 53, 59, 71, 72, 73, 77, 85, 87.

Chapter 12: 2, 29, 31, 33, 46, 47, 50, 51, 52, 59, 62, 63, 68, 95, 107.

Chapter 13: 15, 29, 46, 47, 50, 51, 52, 59, 62, 63, 85, 95, 105, 107.

Chapter 14: 29, 46, 47, 50, 51, 59, 77, 105, 107.

Chapter 15: 6, 14, 17, 18, 22, 24, 29, 30, 32, 37, 39, 43, 46, 47, 51, 54, 59, 63, 66, 83, 87, 88, 102, 104, 105, 113.

Chapter 16: 6, 15, 17, 18, 22, 24, 26, 29, 30, 37, 38, 39, 43, 46, 47, 51, 59, 63, 69, 71, 72, 83, 87, 88, 102, 104, 105, 113, 114.

Chapter 17: 6, 9, 11, 18, 21, 24, 25, 35, 37, 38, 64, 72, 75, 83, 86, 88, 90, 104.

Chapter 18: 9, 11, 19, 21, 27, 35, 38, 64, 75, 82, 90, 96.

Chapter 19: 1, 10, 14, 32, 54, 59, 63, 67, 70, 88, 89, 104, 107.

Chapter 20: 18, 23, 54, 59, 61, 63, 86, 87, 89, 104.

Chapter 21: 59, 60, 63, 77, 83, 84, 86, 87, 97, 98, 104, 109.

Chapter 22: 13, 28, 41, 43, 45, 47, 49, 55, 58, 63, 68, 70, 84, 99, 103.

Epilogue: 4, 12, 13, 27, 28, 37, 41, 45, 47, 56, 58, 66, 70, 81, 82, 91, 92, 93, 94, 97, 98, 99, 101, 103, 111.

INDEX

INDEX

257

INDEX

Learning, 70ff, 238
Lee, Irving J., xxvi, 166
Lenin, 24, 51, 182
Lermontov, 129
Lobachevski, 200
Lobbies, 36
Local morality (moral codes), xvi, 20, 229
    See also Values and culture, Values, relativity of
Locke, John, 162; cited, 163
Logic, xi, 4, 19, 20, 121, 122, 156, 202, 205
    Aristotelian, 115ff, 147, 208, 209
    of mathematics, 145
    See also Syllogism, Aristotelian laws of thought
Logic of Modern Physics, by P. W. Bridgman, cited, 178
Logical positivists, 165, 167ff
    See also Semantic current
Love, 228
Loyalty, xxiii, 232
Lundberg, George A., cited, xviii; xx; cited, 230, 231; 232
Lyceum, the, 112
Lying, 68

Macbeth, 220
Mach, Ernst, 109, 165
Magic Mountain, The, by Thomas Mann, cited, 17
Maimonides, Moses, 100
Man Against Myth, by Barrows Dunham, cited, 185
Mann, Thomas, cited, 17
Mapping, 42ff
    See also Experience mapped on language
Map-territory relations, 166
Maps, 82ff, 95 120, 201, 215, 224
    accuracy of, 85
    as symbol systems, 85
    distortions in, 86-87
    false, 98
    need for improvement of, 239-240
    obsolete, 85
    preoccupation with, 126
    scale of, 85
Marx, Karl, 24, 33, 182, 184, 190ff
Mass-energy (matter-energy), 133, 164
Materialism, 162, 170ff, 179
Mathematical Biology, 243

Mathematics, xi, xiii, 4, 122, 145, 156, 194ff, 237
McWilliams, Carey, cited, 93
Meaning, 61, 78, 156
    associated with experience, 53ff
Meanings of words, 52ff, 67
    See also Definition
Mechanist Revolution, 109-110
Mental disease, xvii
    See also Sanity
Metaphysics, xxiii, xxiv, 95ff, 131, 134
    Aristotelian, 147, 148, 164
    mechanistic, 99
    organismic, 99, 122
    pre-scientific, 232
Meyers, Russell, xxvi, 137, 166
Michelson-Morley experiment, xiv
"Morass of Modern Bourgeois Philosophy," by B. Bykhovsky, cited, 185-186
Morris, Charles, 166
Moses, 100
Motion, random, 210
    relativity of, xiv, xviii
Multi-ordinality, 155, 241
    See also Theory of types, Abstraction ladder, Levels of abstraction, Will ladder
Mystics, 164
Mythology, xvii

Naptha, 17
Napoleon, 100
National Association of Manufacturers, 232
National Geographic Magazine, 82
National honor, 12, 229
Nationalism, 232
Needs, xii, 239
Negative postulates, 146
Nervous system(s)
    abstracting function of, 82, 154
    analogous processes in, 64
    and structure of language, 166
    Aquinas' ignorance of, 203
    full functioning of, 242
    responding to stimuli, 15
Neurath, Otto, 165
Neuro-linguistic current, 165-166
Newton, Isaac, xiv, 45, 98, 105, 144, 218
Non-allness, principle of, 161
    See also Negative postulates

259

INDEX

Relativist
  attitude toward values, xvff, 238ff
  anthropologists, 238ff
  psychologists, xvii
  revolution, 165
  ultra, 238ff
Relativity, theory of, xiiiff, 212, 238ff
  of knowledge, 231
  of motion, xiv, xviii
  of values, xvff, 238ff
Religion(s), xii, 167, 179, 201, 216, 232
  compared by anthropologists, xvi
Repertoire of reactions, 75
Retribution, 230
Revenge, 229
Richards, I. A., 165
Richelieu, 110
Riemann, 200
Right and wrong, *see* Good and bad
Rochdale principles, 187
Russell, Bertrand, 165, 236, 237

Saint Joan, by G. B. Shaw, 23
Sanity, 224-225, 229, 242
  definition of, 228
Schopenhauer, 219, 222, 241
Schlauch, Margaret, cited, 185
Science and Sanity, by Alfred Korzybski, cited, 154; 165
"Science Teaching and the Humanities," by Philipp Frank, cited, 58
Scientific activity, 91
  behavior, x, 231-232
  inquiry, 35
  language, xix, 45, 110, 131, 142
  method, xi
  morality, 232
  outlook, xxii, 232
  social order, 232
Self-insight, 242
Self-reflexiveness, principle of, 155, 163, 166
  See also Theory of types
Semantic disturbance, 154, 177, 191
  current, 165
  environment, 216
  reaction, 130, 132, 165
Semanticists, 109, 179
Semantics, xxiii, 48, 49, 185, 205
"Semantics as Social Evasion," by Margaret Schlauch, cited, 185
Senses, the, 26, 31, 37
Servo-mechanisms, 236

Shakespeare, William, 45
Shaw, G. B., 23
Shibboleths, 241
Shimbel, Alfonso, xxvi
Shimbel, Connie, xxvi
Signal language(s), 67, 78
Signals, 76, 77, 81
Social order, 216, 232
  philosophies, 232
  responsibilities of the scientists, xxii
  science, xviii, 134, 242-243
  structure, xvii, 181, 224, 225, 226
Socialism, 130, 186, 240
Sociology, xix, 167
Solon, 100
Sophistry, 167, 237
Space, absolute framework of, 212
Space-time, 133, 148, 149, 164
"Speech and Personality," by W. Johnson, cited, 80
Spengler, 217
Stalin, 24, 160
Stalingrad, battle of, 221
State, 224
Status of the individual, 228
  of the scientist, 226
Stimuli, 15, 27, 138
  non-symbolic, 15, 29
  symbolic, 29ff
St. John, cited, 22; 25, 127
Structural differential, 155, 157
Structure, 207, 211
  of language, 111, 115, 122, 154, 165
  of symbolic maps, 215
  social, xvii, 181, 224, 225, 226
Subject-predicate form, 115
  relation, 9
Subliminal cues, 217
Superstition, xvi, 16, 231
Swift, Jonathan, cited, 1, 57
Syllogism, 117ff, 121, 209
  See also Logic
Symbolic sense, 28ff
Symbol(s), 28, 77, 81, 129, 130
  systems, 85, 197
Symbolization, 70ff, 80
Syntax, 8, 9

Taboo topics, 225
Tarski, Alfred, 165
Technology, xvii, 115, 181
Theology, 158
Théorie Analytique des Probabilités, by P. S. Laplace, cited, 213

261